D0866775

PEAK PERFORMERS

PEAK PERFORMERS

The New Heroes of American Business

Charles Garfield

William Morrow and Company, Inc. / New York

Library of Congress Cataloging-in-Publication Data

Garfield, Charles A.
Peak performers.

Includes index.
1. Success in business. 2. Employee motivation.
I. Title.
HF5386.G216 1986 658.3'14 85-21711
ISBN 0-688-04243-0

Printed in the United States of America

First Edition

1 2 3 4 5 6 7 8 9 10

BOOK DESIGN BY RICHARD ORIOLO

To my grandfather Harry Freedman,
a tailor with the spirit of a scholar

ACKNOWLEDGMENTS

During the years I spent developing and writing this book, I benefited from the support of special friends and associates. The first of these to be acknowledged is John Poppy, my close collaborator and friend through the numerous drafts in the book's evolution. John's varied skills and patient wisdom were invaluable assets.

To my colleagues at Performance Sciences, Inc., in Berkeley, California, who daily further our organization's mission: to help establish the study of peak performance as an area worthy of interest and support. Special mention must go to Maggie Dresbach, who coordinated my complex speaking schedule throughout the writing of the book. The calls we responded to and engagements we arranged allowed me hundreds of additional opportunities to study the skills and strategies of peak performers in corporations and associations across America. I especially appreciated working in the pragmatic business context. A researcher with theories is fine for academic settings. But my findings had to stand the test of action with people who demand results right away, in companies such as IBM, Merrill Lynch, Bank of America, AT&T, Arthur Andersen, and organizations such as the American Society of Association Executives and the American Hospital Association.

Recognition events for high achievers such as meetings of the Young Presidents Organization's International University, IBM's 100% Club and Leadership Forum, and Stanford University's Business School alumni, offer as rich and varied a selection of peak performers as any investigator could want. The generous and hard-nosed realists among them have helped immeasurably in our efforts to isolate common denominators of personal high achievement in business. Especially helpful in this ongoing effort were Roger Birk, chairman emeritus, Merrill Lynch & Company; Ben Weider, chief executive officer, Weider International; Beth Milwid, president, Lifeworks, and organizational psychologist; Robert Maynard, owner and publisher, the Oakland *Tribune;* Jim Gray, supervisor, Cable Maintenance, Pacific Bell; Lane Nemeth, chief executive officer, Discovery Toys; Joe Murray, senior vice-president, Security Pacific Leasing Corporation; Alvin Burger, chief executive officer, Bugs Burger Bug Killers; Karl Kamena, manager, Government and Public Relations, Dow Chemical Company.

To Brandon Hall, partner in our training company, and to Terry Bronson who both read and commented on the entire manuscript, giving me practical suggestions on key points. Thanks are also due to Gwynne Hooke for her superb typing and attending to the myriad details in the final push to complete the manuscript.

To Pat Golbitz, my editor and friend, whose intelligence, enthusiasm, and accessibility never flagged from day one to the finish line. I am also indebted to Al Marchioni, chief executive officer, and Sherry Arden, president, of William Morrow and Company; to Larry Hughes, president of Hearst Trade Book Group; and their colleagues, particularly Barbara Stevenson, Tom Consolino, Lela Rolontz, Jean Griffin, and Jennifer Williams, who, despite their direct responsibility for hundreds of books and authors, seemed only a phone call away.

I must also acknowledge the continuing assistance of Lloyd Conant and Earl Nightingale, co-founders of Nightingale-Conant Corporation. These gentlemen, along with David Nightingale, Vic Conant, and their colleagues, provided an opportunity to interview ten of the book's peak performers for an album, so that we might hear them discuss their successes and struggles in their own words. These ten men and women constitute a small segment of our sample of inspired and inspiring individuals working in America and throughout the world. This book is really their story and it is to them that I offer my deepest thanks and admiration.

And finally, to three individuals who constitute my personal bottom line:

My father, Ed Garfield, a retired sales engineer, and my mother, Sylvia Garfield, a retired schoolteacher, whose successful careers taught me invaluable lessons and whose love has been a sustaining force; and

Cindy Spring, America's premiere audio information producer, whose debut in the print medium was indeed an auspicious one. Her ideas and organizational skills were major contributions, and her uncommon devotion to this book an expression of the heartfelt love we share.

CONTENTS

INTRODUCTION

America is producing peak performers; peak performers are producing a renewed America.

There is a kind of everyday hero whom many of us admire: the man or woman who possesses the ability to achieve impressive and satisfying results, not just once or twice but repeatedly, consistently. These people have always been with us. They are superior managers, successful entrepreneurs, accomplished professionals, top salespeople, and innovative technical specialists. They have also seemed apart from us, seen in ways that identify them as somehow different. Peak performers were, by common agreement, exceptional.

Now they are surfacing in dramatically larger numbers. It appears that they may not be so different after all. Now we can see that the differences between peak performers and their less productive co-workers are much smaller than most people think—that extraordinary achievers are ordinary people who have found ways to make a major impact.

We are moving beyond the malaise of the recent past. America is recapturing the drive that founded the nation, explored its frontiers, assimilated its immigrant sons and daughters, and that now finds expression in the entrepreneurial spirit of its citizens. Our nation now offers many of us a renewed context for peak performance, for impressive achievement and substantial personal development. We have the opportunity to embark again, to leave the shore of the known and to gather strength from the restlessness of the human spirit.

A generation ago we were told we were not as smart as our parents. Today we are told we are not as smart as our children. Evolution, it seems, is now moving fast enough to be visible. Its new velocity is fueled by intense and opposing scenarios: major strides in technology and human development on the one hand, planetary extinction on the other. For the first time we have the capacity to participate in our own evolution, to function as cotrustees in the process.

What skills and strategies can we learn from the peak performers?

How do we achieve and maintain peak performance in ourselves?

This book is about people who translate mission into results, people who are the basic unit of excellence in every organization. Here you will meet individual peak performers and learn what they do and how they do it—not rare and remote individuals who miraculously achieve far beyond the norm, but people who are setting a new norm, a kind of person we all can be. These peak performers are developed by the process of engaging their primary work. They are always willing to evolve and grow, to learn from the work as well as to complete it, to be "better than I ever was."

Our findings about peak performers emerge from an eighteen-year investigation of high achievement in a number of fields. In gathering and analyzing information from some of the most productive people in our culture, we came to see that the heart of the peak performer's ability to function is neither a singular talent nor even a collection of behaviors, but an overall *pattern* of attributes. Possessing these attributes, a peak performer will very likely:

- Be motivated toward results by a personal mission.
- Possess the twin capacities of self-management and team mastery.
- Have the ability to correct course and manage change.

For the peak performer and would-be peak performer, these resources constitute a new meaning of "private enterprise." This is enterprise fueled by more than economic self-interest. It gains its power from the broader human values of innovation, worthy purpose, contribution, and love—values that reveal peak performers as more intent on creating than on collecting.

My grandfather, a tailor who arrived in 1909 from a small village in Lithuania, spent most of his adult life working in the garment district of New York. My father is now retired after thirty years as a sales engineer. Both of them accepted a load of grief in their working lives so that they could be proud of what they provided at home. They worked hard during the day, from Monday to Saturday, but they *lived* in the evenings and weekends. My grandfather and father settled for freedom, dignity, and pride off the job. My contemporaries and their children want those rewards on the job.

The current generation of working Americans lives in a privileged situation; the members of the so-called baby boom have not seen a depression. Yet all Americans have lived in a society undergoing radical transformation during the past twenty years. We have experienced changes that have forced many of us to grow beyond the expectations our parents had for us. Almost without noticing it, we have started living with heightened expectations: personal growth. Mastery. Achievement. The desire to do great work and in the process to make a recognizable contribution as part of an organization one can be proud of.

In studying high achievers I have concentrated on understanding why and how they perform at their best. During the past six years I have worked with American corporations and associations to communicate my findings. Collectively we are on the verge of even greater breakthroughs in our understanding of the psychology of the peak performer. The arena where the greatest investments in these discoveries are being made is business.

An increasingly competitive world marketplace is going to continue pushing Americans and American companies toward new approaches to every conceivable point of leverage in the productivity equation. One such point—in the minds of many, the point of greatest leverage—is the full utilization of people, the human resource. This does not mean what it meant during the height of the Industrial Age, using people as anonymous units for the sake of profitability and the primary benefit of the corporate organism and then discarding them. What the Organization Man as a model could not offer, with his boiler-plate job descriptions and normative expectations, was an appreciation of flesh-and-blood human beings, people with hopes and dreams, skills and strategies, who are members of families and larger communities. What the Organization Man could not expect, with his view of people as jobs-to-be-completed, was the power of peak performance.

Today, the emerging wisdom of the peak performing organization is that "it all boils down to people."

People make financial decisions.
People develop innovative products.
People conduct marketing campaigns.
People are the basic natural resource of business.

Throughout the United States, there appears a growing fascination with people functioning at their best. We hear peak performers talk of steadily developing their abilities as a natural part of "knowing what I want and what I'm about." Their internal strength suggests an approach entirely different from any perfunctory attempt to tack on skills to the same old person. Some speak of single powerful occasions or periods, "sweet spots in time," that offer them a glimpse of themselves as capable of "a great deal more than I previously thought possible." All maintain that the potential for major increases in achievement and self-development exists in everyone, and that the starting point is an internal decision to excel. Until that decision is made, nothing much will happen.

Thus we arrive at the key question: How do we get ourselves and others to commit, to make that internal decision to excel, and to develop ourselves in the process?

One peak performer speaks for most others when he replies, "I got jump-started by watching others, by learning from the people I most admire." The peak performers say repeatedly that stories of our most productive people provide them not only with strategies but also with values—values as leverage points for triggering that impulse to excel. Why do human beings care so much about some things that they will concentrate every resource on them? For answers, look to their values.

Why is it that Alvin Burger in Miami has an employee turnover rate of 2 percent in the pest-elimination industry, where 60 percent is the standard?

How did Lane Nemeth in Pleasant Hill, California, go from living on food stamps to running her own $35 million-a-year toy business?

Why was Jim Gray told suddenly that next Monday he would no longer be climbing telephone poles but instead be managing his own department at Pacific Bell?

The remarkable success of these individuals is not the result of luck. It is the predictable outcome of intense concentration on values and strategies, on cultivating what the German writer Goethe called "the genius, power and magic" in ourselves. The book contains no pat answers, no self-help panaceas. Why? Because the peak performers, to a person, assured us emphatically that none existed. Too often in our search for the proverbial "silver bullet" we have expected miracles from small investments. The skills presented in the book can best be understood as signposts. People who search incessantly for the quick fix will climb these signposts, while the peak performers are guided by them.

The people you will meet in this book will not be, with a few exceptions, those who attract frequent headlines. Of course some corporate superstars have stories too compelling to omit. Far more exciting, though, is the news that increasing evidence of superior performance is appearing at every level of the American business scene, from the middle manager in chemicals to the salesperson in computers, from the chief executive in financial services to the director of human resources in health care, from the home remodeler to the pipe fitter in aerospace.

I have chosen deliberately to focus on the similarities rather than the differences among the peak performers. The people I highlight were selected purposely from different industries, at different levels, from different ages and sexes. My reasoning is similar to that used by Joseph Campbell in *Hero with a Thousand Faces.* In any chart of anatomy, the variations of race are disregarded in the interest of a basic general understanding of the human physique. Of course there are differences between the numerous peak performers, but this is a description of the similarities. Once these are understood, the differences will be found to be much less than is popularly supposed.

The peak performers are realists who believe: "In the final analysis, I will make it." They focus on achievement, not only as "flat numbers on a page, an invisible piece of the bottom line," as a forty-two-year-old sales manager in insurance put it, "but as an indicator that I am getting better, making progress toward being the best I can be." And in their statements I heard again and again a sense of history—that we do not have the luxury of mediocrity, or pessimism, or apathy—that peak performance is demanded in this period when the question of survival is paramount. I have been consistently impressed with the willingness, bordering at times on urgency, with which the men and women I met communicated a single theme: "I have done well, and I am capable of achieving much more. I am not finished yet. There is much more to me than this."

To these people, going through the motions is anathema. From them you hear precious little talk of settling for a comfort zone where you try (but not with all your energy) and achieve (but not all your dreams). They face at least as many obstacles as other people, and go through at least as many rough times. So it will not be surprising if we learn in the months and years ahead that some of our peak performers have landed in situations that are not profitable and in ventures that do not pan out. It would be deeply surprising, however, to hear that any of them stopped at that point. No matter how rough it gets, no matter how great the assault on mind and body, peak performers always feel they can do something. Invariably, they move on.

We are speaking not of superhumans but of human beings like

you and me, whose working environment may be less than ideal, who struggle with personal shortcomings. These people focus on transforming the inevitable stumbling blocks into stepping-stones. As they progress, they improve their companies and themselves. They trust that in the end they will make it. More often than not, they do.

1

THE SEARCH FOR PEAK PERFORMANCE

"These people are doing the best work of their lives. And I have no idea why. None of us knows why."

George supervised a team of scientists and engineers at a company on the move from building fighter planes to inventing spacecraft. He was doing his best with my questions about the stories we all heard around the project, yet his reply only sharpened my curiosity. Something was happening in our office cubicles, conference rooms, and machine shops that people did not know how to talk about.

What had several thousand ordinary men and women done that turned them within a few months from competent workers into superachievers?

It was my first job—novice computer programmer—and I wanted with all my heart to do it well. The Grumman Aerospace Corporation plant at Bethpage, Long Island, looked stark enough to daunt a twenty-three-year-old mathematics graduate student, with its windswept array of anonymous buildings and the government-green paint in its office corridors. Yet in 1967 going to work there every morning was like signing up for one of the great adventures on Earth. We were to design and build the Lunar Excursion Module (LEM), the first manned craft that would land on the moon, for the Apollo 11 mission.

Nobody needed to tell me this was a technological challenge unlike any other the United States had ever taken on. The lives of the astronauts and the prestige of the country would depend on the LEM's success. Were the people planning and completing it, therefore, all winners, standouts, geniuses? No. The mission was far too complex for that. Its success depended not just on its bright stars with the right stuff, its astronauts and technical prodigies, but in equal or greater degree on its middle-range people—thousands of reasonably successful men and women who'd had rather predictable careers before joining the race to the moon. I found myself among many, older than I, who had also wanted to make their mark in the world when they were young and who had faded as they lost sight of the meaning in their work. Now they were waking up.

UNEXPECTED LEAPS

Every week, I heard stories about people who were lifting their performance to levels that none of them would have predicted a few months before.

"Well," you might say, "of course. There are always a few who rise to an occasion." But here, exceptional performances were coming not from a few but from many, not just from the top twenty but from the average man and woman.

Project managers, machine operators, secretaries, engineers, computer analysts, executives—wherever I turned there were people making leaps in performance that no one could have anticipated. The leaps were not necessarily major and unique; we did not see managers suddenly solving equations in planetary mechanics. They were, rather, major in impact, within the context of these people's jobs. My initial curiosity grew into a serious question: What is happening here?

In conversations with co-workers, I started asking informally: "Why are you doing so well? Exactly what do you do each day to make it happen? What is different now?"

George was one of them. The scuttlebutt said he had been there a long time, doing okay. Trained as an engineer, he went through the motions as a technical manager, leading a group of engineers who were not quite a team. His section's ratings (on measures such as productivity, turnover, and absenteeism) were in the bottom half of the company. His people tended to be loners. George himself preferred solitary problem-solving to the "gab" that giving and getting feedback would involve him in. His management style emphasized numbers and authority over human relationships and collaboration. George handed out assignments and invited few comments.

That was before the LEM project on Apollo 11. During it, George changed direction. He redefined himself as a coach with a team to motivate. He helped its members establish bridges between individual goals and team goals, all the way up to the goals of the overall LEM project. In eighteen months George's section moved its ratings from the bottom 50 percent to the top 15 percent.

So I asked him my questions. One evening as we strolled outside Grumman headquarters he answered: "I've been a piece of furniture in my job for years. Do you know what it's like, working forty to sixty hours a week and not knowing whether your work makes a damn bit of difference to anybody? Now, look at that." He pointed to the pale moon barely visible in the eastern sky. "People have been dreaming about going there for thousands of years. And *we're* going to do it. You want to know why we're doing so well? Want to know my secret? I've got a mission, something that matters to me, something that matters to all of us. We finally have something we can sink our teeth into and be proud of."

The Apollo project was offering me a powerful lesson in high achievement:

PEAK PERFORMANCE BEGINS WITH A COMMITMENT TO A MISSION.

We have all been in situations where the best of ourselves emerged at levels we previously thought impossible, and have seen such moments in our families, in sports, in projects that worked. Dozens of our colleagues in the space program echoed George's sentiments about the strong sense of purpose and enthusiasm that came from being part of the upcoming lunar landing. When I looked around, I couldn't miss it. Grumman did an excellent job of communicating the mission statement and goals of the whole enterprise—to push back the frontiers of space and put Americans on the moon—through all sorts of symbols. They circulated slogans and put up posters. There was even a model of the LEM in the cafeteria.

I was excited. All around me people were acting out exactly what I wanted for myself: to find ways of doing outstanding work. To learn how to be a star in a big, complex organization. To be somebody. People starting out in business often attach themselves to a mentor, and here I had dozens of examples to follow: a collective mentor. Their commitment to a mission showed me a beginning.

And only a beginning. George and the others could sense that something was different; but to a specific question—"What do you *do* to make these things happen?"—their answers were vague. They were men and women of action. They hadn't given it much thought. It remained for someone else to study what they did each day to liberate the motivation, and the ability to excel, that had been locked inside them for so long.

WHERE TO LOOK —OUTSIDE OR INSIDE?

Few of my co-workers in the LEM project had a history of peak performance. When I questioned them, most said they had had little in their past that matched the extraordinary levels at which they were now working.

For many the increase in performance was so dramatic, in fact, that it seemed the reasons for it might have less to do with the people than with their surroundings. Maybe, I remember thinking at the time, this powerful project was pulling its people into success, acting as an external locus of control—to use a technical term I learned later. Everyone thought so. They kept pointing at the moon.

I kept asking, "What's different now?" and people gave me images from before, during, and, eventually, after Apollo. "Before," one manager said, "I had essentially the same number of people reporting to me, only every day was business-as-usual. The bureaucracy bored us; we got tired easily; it didn't matter if one of us took an extra half hour for lunch. No challenge. I don't remember any feeling of doing what *we* wanted to do. When there was any initiative, it always came from someone else.

"Now," he continued, "this damned place is so exciting! You spot a way to de-bug a program faster, or put together an on-the-spot team to attack a problem, and you just *do* it."

They kept saying "this damned place" and pointing outside themselves. They had been provided by senior management and by fate with a compelling project in a fascinating context. Anyone who really appreciated those conditions had an ideal launch pad for peak performance.

Then it was over. On July 20, 1969, Neil Armstrong stepped off the porch of the LEM into the fine dust of the moon. "One small step for man," he said. "One giant leap for mankind." Except that within months, those of us here on the ground could see that *we* had taken a step backward. Performance reverted to business-as-usual. Since we had known how it felt to soar, business-as-usual was a crash landing. We felt underused, like big-league players in a minor-league game.

People discounted their own recent success as an aberration, just one more of those things that happen sometimes, you don't know why. They told themselves that wasn't what life really is. The good times were an accident. It wasn't me. It was luck; it was John Kennedy; it was Apollo; it was the time and place.

Attributing their performance to influences outside themselves, then finally labeling their best as a fluke, was a way for many of those men and women to cope. They had risen to a peak; then they had fallen back to earth. Brick, the withdrawn husband in

Tennessee Williams's *Cat on a Hot Tin Roof,* couldn't get over the fact that life was not like the day he scored his famous touchdown. Why, he asks on behalf of all of us, can't it always be that good?

If the moon lifted us, how could we have kept it from dropping us? Maybe success comes and goes, like the tide.

Yet . . . Yet, I had a nagging doubt. Success could not have come only from the challenge of the environment. When you look, you see something else at work. The people in the environment must supply something essential, perhaps even something that amplifies the power of the environment. What explanation is there, otherwise, for the high achievers in other settings who do not wait for the environment to jump-start them?

The improvements in performance we saw during the Apollo LEM project can occur in everyday life. From that beginning I could see, as if through a veil of smoke, the outline of something more than an accident, more than one isolated, unrepeatable experience. Not quite sure of what I would find, I set out to search for a clearer view.

COLLECTING EVIDENCE

I left behind my career in mathematics and completed a Ph.D. in clinical psychology, aiming to acquire research skills that would best serve an investigation of exceptional productivity and performance for individuals and teams. Among the first groups with whom I worked as a research psychologist were patients at the Cancer Research Institute at the University of California San Francisco Medical Center.

If Apollo 11 was an example of the most positive of compelling situations, I wanted to learn what happens in the most negative. Among people afflicted with cancer, I thought I would find the opposite of the grand, positive mission—its total absence. Could those who survived cancer be peak performers of another sort? If so, how did they achieve?

I found, of course, that although the conditions were excruciatingly difficult for the cancer patients, far more so than in any job, the long-term survivors among them did speak of a powerful mission that inspired them. Their mission was even more compelling than the one Apollo provided. It had the clarity that can come with a fight for your life. Samuel Johnson was brusque about it two hundred years ago: "When a man knows he is to be hanged in a fortnight, it concentrates his mind wonderfully."

Apollo people and cancer survivors were not opposites at all. As far as external circumstance was concerned, they did live at opposite poles, the one strongly positive and the other negative. But at both poles, some people used the circumstances to mobilize inner resources; they found a clear, compelling mission.

Anyone who works with seriously ill cancer patients frequently sees courage of the highest order in the face of a terrifying disease and the prospect of death. All my life I had heard, as we all do, of people overcoming adversity, of the occasional triumph of life in extremity. Adversity often draws out resources and capabilities one does not know one has. So it is that one sees certain low-probability cancer patients—some diagnosed as having less than a fifty-fifty chance of living more than a few months—who live longer and experience a higher quality of life than do others.

The first time I heard the term *peak performance* was from a cancer patient, a nationally known concert pianist.

"Why do I survive?" he replied when I asked him. "I've drawn on resources I didn't know I had. What I'm doing to stay alive is the toughest thing I've ever faced, physically, emotionally, mentally—much more difficult than playing Mozart or Chopin. Staying alive these days is my peak performance."

William James, arguably America's greatest psychologist, wrote eighty years ago:

> Most people live, whether physically, intellectually or morally, in a very restricted circle of their potential being. They *make use* of a very small portion of their possible consciousness, of their soul's resources in general, much like a man who, out of his whole bodily organism, should get into a habit of using and moving only his little finger. Great emergencies and crises show us how much greater our vital resources are than we had supposed.

We have all heard stories about access to those resources opening in a flash. Laura Schultz of Tallahassee was sixty-three years old in April 1977, when she told me she usually picked up nothing heavier than her Pepto-Bismol bottle; but three weeks before, she had run outside to the driveway and lifted the back end of a Buick off her grandson's arm.

I have never been comfortable with the assumption that great feats grow just from external surroundings—adrenaline pumping in response to an emergency and so forth. I knew from sports, in particular, that the drive to excel comes primarily from inside. In other arenas as well, we can see achievements that are neither genetically ordained nor environmentally determined. Even the Apollo environment was not sufficient to fire up everyone. There were people who, because of untenable job situations or problems of attitude, did not respond to that supercharged situation. The hypothesis was beginning to take shape:

THE PRIMARY "LOCUS OF CONTROL" FOR A PEAK PERFORMER IS NOT EXTERNAL, BUT INTERNAL.

If that was so, then it would be reasonable to look for ways to bring peak performance under voluntary control, to find ways to *initiate* action aimed at exceptional achievement, not just respond to challenges from outside. It was important to find basic characteristics that cut across all the fields, from the Apollo mission to the cancer wards. Were there qualities common to top performers in science, sports, the arts, and the business world too?

In the middle and late 1970s the issue of "productivity"—getting individuals to produce their best efforts—moved to center stage in business. As a researcher in the field of human achievement I was drawn to this arena, where intense concentration was being focused on issues of motivation and performance.

We were surrounded in those days by accounts of U.S. industries becoming demoralized by what they perceived as the challenge of superior Japanese productivity. The demand for researchers with practical insights into human performance was acute. My research had begun in a workplace—Grumman—and even during the years of research with cancer patients I was often asked to apply my findings to hospital administration. The fit was clear: Dedicated researcher looking for characteristics of peak performance meets companies looking for ways to explain and increase productivity. By 1979 my research into extraordinary achievers had shifted its focus almost entirely to the business world.

Since then I have met with senior managers, middle managers, salespeople, and technical personnel in more than thirty different industries across the spectrum of American enterprise. My research has been focused on, but not limited to, certain industries: health care, high technology, insurance, banking and financial services, broadcasting and publishing, aerospace, telecommunications, and pharmaceuticals. Our aim throughout has been to distill the characteristics of peak performers regardless of environment.

RESEARCH METHODS

During the eighteen years since I first met those peak performers in the Apollo 11 project, I have been interviewing people with similar accomplishments in business and other fields and studying secondary source material on high achievers.

Some people make an internal commitment to excel, and to follow through with self-development and training. Others do not. I wanted answers to one very simple question: How do we get ourselves and others to make that commitment?

An interview typically begins as a request for informal reminiscences about a peak performer's work and accomplishments. We meet people in their offices, in restaurants, at conferences in hotels around the world. Formal question-and-answer interviews too often lead to conditioned clichés, particularly when the topics are such loaded ones as personal success and performance on the job. Can we not all recite in unison the winning coach's locker-room answers about dedication, teamwork, and playing one game at a time? A more inviting and genuine way of eliciting information has been sharpened into a fine art by investigators such as Studs Terkel in oral histories like *Working,* and Robert and Jane Coles in *Women of Crisis.* These Pulitzer Prize winners ask the kind of questions you would ask while having a drink with someone, Terkel notes. And that leads to talk that is "idiomatic rather than academic."

We have collected responses from more than 300 top performers since 1967 in one-to-one sessions lasting at least an hour and in many cases much longer. We have had more limited discussions with 250 others. Although all were offered anonymity, most people were pleased to be identified by name and share their skills and strategies with us. My focus since 1979 on peak performers in business has expanded on useful insights gathered from earlier investigations of peak performers in science, the professions, sports, the arts, and several special groups including people facing life-threatening cancer.

The research concentrates on people with impressive career records, and on people who have performed extraordinarily well in specific situations. Money and fame are often attached to success, but in selecting and understanding individuals to study, we make an effort to keep such externals in perspective. What we are really looking for is a person's talents and strategies, as well as the impact and originality of his or her contributions.

In doing this research my own motivation reflected that of the people I was studying. As a researcher, I wanted to excel in increasing our understanding of human productivity at maximum levels. As an individual, I was using the arena of that work to provide elements of self-development that were important to me. Achievement and self-development are always intertwined. That is true for me and true for peak performers.

At the outset, my notes show that I was hoping as much for mentoring as for general principles. As time went on, I concluded that individual anecdotes, while interesting, were not as valuable as the pattern that emerged from the overall collection. High achievers most often gave me their best shot, yet their understanding of their own success and the ways in which they communicated it were hardly unbiased and, as one would expect, sometimes highly idiosyncratic. Analysis of their responses, though, discloses six attributes that they share:

- *Missions that motivate:* the call to action, the "click" that starts things moving

- *Results in real time:* purposeful activity directed at achieving goals that contribute to a mission
- *Self-management through self-mastery:* the capacity for self-observation and effective thinking
- *Team building/team playing:* the complement to self-management—empowering others to produce
- *Course correction:* mental agility, concentration, finding and navigating a "critical path"
- *Change management:* anticipating and adapting to major change while maintaining momentum and balance within an overall game plan

I do not contend that these are the only factors related to peak performance in business, merely that they are the ones stressed repeatedly by the peak performers themselves. An individual's genetic endowment, developmental history, education, and current surroundings can affect every performance. Over and over, peak performers demonstrated superior awareness of the full range of factors determining the difference between what they could change or adapt to and what they could not.

Secondary sources include some nine hundred articles describing and analyzing many of America's highest achievers in business. America's business community is currently conducting a vigorous investigation of these matters: not just about productivity, but about how and where people find the productive capacities in themselves. Business journals and general-interest periodicals feature high-performing individuals repeatedly. We draw on many of these examples.

I should point out that these individuals, despite their impressive achievement records, are hardly infallible. It is the rare business or person that never runs into difficulties. The odds are that in the future you will read of some high achievers having difficulty in career or personal life. The odds are also that they will come out of it learning from their setbacks and moving on. As a group these people risk more, and more often; setbacks are thus a part of the game. Their visibility and quasi-heroic status, within their organizations and sometimes nationally, make their exploits tempting morsels for discussion.

More to the point, these are people in process, not infallible heroes, and in many cases they are only a stride or two ahead of the rest of us.

Our research shows what common sense would suggest: These peak performers have no guaranteed strategies for winning, but rather an uncanny knack for increasing the odds in their favor through the use of the skills and attributes we will examine in this book. They give themselves a great chance of achieving peak performance in new areas, and maintaining it once they get there. This chance stems not from actions so drastically different from those of others, but frequently because they act with unusual consistency, with an iron determination and a basic sense of mission.

The intent of our current research is to provide a launch pad for future investigations and to raise additional questions about the top performers among us. Areas of interest include longitudinal studies of specific individuals, analyses of the childhood histories of peak-performing adults, and situational variations in performance among high achievers.

Compared to the decades of research on remedial efforts geared toward bringing people up to average, and the billions spent on training people for competence, there has been precious little systematic study of the upper levels of human achievement. In the years ahead I expect to see a variety of such studies, including research by academicians of differing orientations, in-depth journalistic analyses, and interdisciplinary investigations combining the perspectives of psychology, business, organizational development, and sociological field work.

WORKING "BECAUSE I LOVE IT"

The practices that lead to high achievement need no longer be a mystery. Like Edgar Allan Poe's purloined letter, they have been hidden in plain view.

The clues are right in front of us. Peak performers see themselves, and people in general, as the basic natural resource. They act with a confidence that human beings are capable of much more than defending the status quo, slightly upgrading skills, or adapting somewhat to changing conditions. Their confidence is based on experience, and as one result of it they find ways of making significant changes in their habits of mind and work, so that they progress from adequate to good to great.

They are not mere idealists. Our peak performers talk not of business utopias but of team productivity and exceeding sales quotas. Most have met basic survival and security needs and are pushing on to achievement that serves self-development and personal fulfillment, and by extension, the vitality and prosperity of their organizations.

Often they comment that they feel most alive when engaged full-throttle. Call it a positive addiction, a contributory obsession, a passion to create one's self through one's work. When asked, "Why are you so thoroughly involved in your work?" they most frequently answer, "Because I love it." To refuse the call, or to diminish the involvement, feels to them like taking a wrong turn, like "losing one's life in living it."

These people are not job addicts or workaholics. A peak performer expresses satisfaction and fulfillment; a job addict, numbness and depletion born of a psychological hunger that cannot be gratified. Rather than using himself fully, the job addict uses himself up. This depletion results from a grinding addiction to activity, which is quite different from a focus on activity with purpose and clear direction.

It would be an oversimplification, though, to regard peak performers and job addicts as two distinct groups of people. They overlap. Many of our peak performers noted, accurately, that it is easy to get pulled toward job addiction. It is there all the time, like the bottle for an alcoholic, as a challenge. Part of what makes them peak performers is that most possess a capacity to pull back from such "frenzied pursuits," as one put it, "and correct my course before too much damage is done to body and soul."

PROFILES OF PEOPLE AT THEIR BEST

What do the peak performers that America is producing look like? Here, in sketches of people in action, are the major characteristics that we will see more fully in Chapters 3 through 8.

MISSIONS THAT MOTIVATE

That young man who showed up for his first job at Grumman wanted to feel proud of himself. I was searching for a career in which to achieve impressive success and improve myself in the process. And I did not know where to start.

Then I was swept up by the powerful mission of Apollo 11. That was it! I could put my best efforts behind a mission that really mattered. At first it was enough for the mission to come at me from outside. The President said, "Do it." NASA and Grumman said, "Do it." George said, "Do it." So I wanted to do it. But there had to be more. Did all those people doing the best work of their lives, many of them twice my age and far ahead of me in experience, have to wait every time for orders from outside before they could reach their personal best?

I had to find out more about high-level achievement. As I devoted myself more and more consciously to deliberate study of peak performers, I gradually began to see a point around which to gather all my best efforts.

Moving on to work with cancer patients, I saw more evidence of the power that individuals can develop to influence the outcome of their efforts. Still, I was looking at missions imposed from outside. And still I did not know how—or if—peak performance could be brought within the reach of any person who desired it, in any environment. What I did know was that I did not just want to collect a lot of facts about extraordinary people. I wanted the facts to come together so that I could orchestrate peak performance for myself and assist others as well. I was looking for a bird's eye, not a worm's eye, view.

Then, in 1979, a chance meeting with a group of Soviet-bloc physiologists, physicians, and research psychologists in Milan, Italy, changed the whole nature of my study. Details are in Chapter 2; for now I'll just say that one night's work with the Soviets did more than confirm a conviction that genuine, sustainable high performance begins with an *internal* decision to excel. That encounter also underscored my belief and hope that an internal locus of control could be found and cultivated.

The search continued. The Soviet-bloc researchers had devised programs that proceed along the lines of human engineering, an approach that focuses not so much on what an individual is committed to as on general principles that can be applied to programs of behavior change. As my attention had turned by 1979 to some of the most extraordinarily productive people in American business, I knew there was a more person-centered view of achievement and self-development, one that in this country we would consider more valuable.

For example, a passionate sense of mission got Joseph and Benjamin Weider moving in the 1930s and 1940s—and gave them the staying power to overcome one obstacle after another and sustain their achievements over four decades. There was no health-and-fitness industry to speak of when the two brothers from Montreal founded a family of organizations that now reach into 128 countries and generate revenues of hundreds of millions of dollars a year. Few people had even seen a barbell, and exercise—particularly the vigorous kind we now take for granted—was commonly viewed as potentially dangerous. Events like marathons, and capabilities like great endurance and strength, were all considered the province of a few specialists. Joe Weider, whose passion for bodybuilding and high-level fitness initially sparked the mission, teamed up with his brother Ben and set out to get others to see the connection between health, productivity, and quality of life. Their magazines, *Muscle and Fitness, Shape, Flex,* and *Sports Fitness,* promote a vision of physical and mental health. The International Federation of Body Builders (IFBB) promotes their conviction that "bodybuilding is essential for nation building." Ben is founding president of the IFBB. Joe, recently named the Magazine Publishers' Association Publisher of the Year, is known worldwide as a consistent innovator in the development of exercise equipment and weight training for participants in a variety of sports.

The Weider brothers started with no money and little education (neither man graduated from high school), just a love and understanding of fitness—being not just moderately fit, not just without symptoms and medical problems, but fit at very high levels, mentally and physically. They campaigned for bodybuilding when traditional sportsmen warned against being "muscle-bound"; for advances in equipment and nutrition when the medical community scoffed; for exchanges of information between athletes and scientists when both camps balked. They supported the advance of women in bodybuilding and sport in general, even though sportsmen of their generation have a reputation for machismo. They have consistently supported fitness for senior citizens, for children, and the development of home exercise equipment for the family.

They have persuaded millions of others to see their vision. Partly through their influence, an estimated 35 million Americans by now have trained with weights, and gyms abound like Chinese restaurants.

As a sixteen-year-old, I was inspired by the Weiders' magazines to get stronger for football. I memorized training routines, studied pictures of weight-trained athletes, and dreamed of the glory they had achieved. Years later, Joe Weider read newspaper accounts of my meeting with the Soviets in Milan, saw that they had conducted a weight-training experiment with me, and wrote to ask for details on what had happened. A trainer of champions, a publisher of magazines, he was still an excited student looking for new information. The Weiders' mission is so clear that its message is contagious. Their powerful motivation to improve themselves and others came through the pages. The mission had staying power because of its clarity, and because it produced results.

As for me, the experience in Milan helped greatly to focus the search for a mission. Over time, I had sharpened an idea of what I was campaigning for: the principle that there must be ways to orchestrate the elements of high achievement. Now I began to understand what I was hearing and seeing, as one peak performer after another spoke of self-training, learning by experience, organizing that experience around a single theme, seeking and finding a purpose, a personal mission that represents something important. They were talking about what management theorist Warren Bennis calls "working near the heart of things." They want to feel proud of themselves, to achieve something, to leave a mark and a contribution, and they follow their plans for doing all that purposefully and tenaciously. That is what I—and many others I knew—wanted. So peak performers are not merely exceptions. They represent a kind of person any of us can be—once we find the capacity in ourselves.

RESULTS IN REAL TIME

Beth Milwid was Phi Beta Kappa at Stanford. She had a master's degree. She did public policy work for nine years in the San Francisco mayor's office and the California State Department of Education. In every organization, she saw talented women "hitting the cement ceiling"—moving up as far as middle-level responsibility and then being stopped as if there were a solid slab between them and senior positions in management, policy-making, and authority.

At that point, many people, men as well as women, fall prey to "learned helplessness." They quit pushing, exactly as if they had learned to know there was nothing more they could do. Milwid, less interested in anger or despair than in results, responded differently: with purposeful activity.

"I wasn't taken seriously and I couldn't tell if it was because I was a woman, or young, or relatively inexperienced. Whatever it was, for about eight years I was the only woman in the meetings." Milwid had a motivating mission; the problem was her inability to get results. Determined to expand her ability to make sense of what was happening, she earned a Ph.D., combining a systems approach to organizations with psychological studies of the individuals working in them. Her dissertation examined what happened in the 1970s to the wave of women in banking, law, and architecture—environments that have traditionally been run by men. Her motivations were similar to mine: wanting recognition in her career for contributions she would make, while using that career to gather data for personal development.

After a post-doctoral business program at the UCLA Graduate School of Management, she joined Crocker Bank in San Francisco. As manager of career development, she ran workshops, helped employees with career questions, and worked for senior managers who wanted to make sure that the aspirations of people they recruited were being met. She resolved to accomplish her mission by working *with* the surrounding forces, not against them. She set to work purposefully to de-bug the problems she saw. Her aim was results, now, in real time.

The cement ceiling has not dissolved, but when a results-oriented woman like Beth Milwid hits it, she keeps on going. "When people at the bank heard I had a Ph.D. in psychology, a lot of them were leery of me. A doctorate sounds scholarly, pie-in-the-sky, not bottom-line oriented—as a psychologist you're insight-oriented and that's it." She would tell them: "Look, I may have a Ph.D but I'm from the Midwest. I know insights don't equal results, but I appreciate both. I grew up in the suburbs, the first-generation daughter of the 1950s Organization Man. My grandfather had come from Lithuania, and Dad grew up in neighborhoods where people do things for those they care about; there was little money, so they may not give you any, but instead they'll plant your flower garden. I grew up with people who express their caring through concrete actions. We were all raised with an orientation toward results. So I'd tell the people at the bank: 'Let's roll up our sleeves and get down to it.' "

Beth Milwid moved on from Crocker to form a company, Life Works, and to research a book based on her doctoral dissertation—both steps that built on what she had done previously. Her mission has not changed: to understand the dynamics of organization and apply that understanding to helping women gain major corporate responsibilities. She has been refining her methods. "I really need to be sure I see the forest before I start in on the trees. When I think of my mission, I think of strong interests that continue over time. I pay attention up front to clarifying my goals. When I think about concrete goals, I think about a series of specific projects that build on one another. One of the goals I have right now is writing the book. That builds on the previous goal, which was to do the dissertation, so I am leveraging up to the next level. My next task will be finding the right company, where I can put my skills to work.

"The issue in most companies is no longer who will be the first woman senior vice-president or woman partner or whatever. The real issue is: How can organizations continue to afford to overlook all available leadership and talent? No company that considers itself peak-performing can afford to overlook the potential contributions of the fifty-two percent of the adult population that is female.

"What frustrated me, and fascinated me, and prompted me to investigate the issue, was not just the cement-ceiling phenomenon for women, but instead, the very *lack of results-oriented productivity* that seems to pervade most bureaucracies. When work is not challenging and exciting, people get bogged down in power plays." In looking at the cement-ceiling phenomenon, she noticed that men who put obstacles in the paths of women or members of minority groups are running not on insight but on memory, on old information—information that may not have been accurate in the first place—that women are not leaders, that they are not as mission-oriented as men, and therefore not as apt to be productive. She seeks to set the record straight.

"I continue to want to learn more about social systems and how individuals operate within organizations so that I can help organizations run more effectively. Too often we have a huge disparity between the vision of senior management and what actually occurs in the trenches and in the cubicles. I'd like to help close that gap."

SELF-MANAGEMENT THROUGH SELF-MASTERY

Employees who look for direction every time they have to make a move are a hindrance to their organizations and themselves. The rising stars are those individuals who can align their own missions with an organization's mission, keep their motivation refreshed by achievement, aim for results, and manage themselves.

Any specialist in corporate training programs can recall 1981. It was a bad year. A recession led most companies to cut back, and in major companies the hardest-hit department was often HRD, human resources development. And 1981 was the year psychologist Brandon Hall joined Wilson Learning Corporation of Minneapolis, a major supplier of training programs in management and sales, as an account executive in Silicon Valley. His job was to be a consultant to corporate clients and to recommend Wilson programs that would produce results for them.

His first nine months were a real struggle, giving little indication of successes to come. "Business was not happening as quickly as I or my boss had planned for it to happen. It wasn't just the recession. I had to learn a new company, new territory, new products. Moving up that learning curve was not comfortable at all."

Finally Hall began to find his own particular pattern of rapport with clients, and his results picked up. After eighteen months he was fully self-confident on the job.

When I asked him what got him through that difficult year and a half, he described a set of self-management skills:

- *Self-confidence:* being willing to go out, hear "no," and move on to focus on the next opportunity
- *Bimodal thinking:* combining *macro* and *micro* forms of attention. Analyzing problem situations within a company requires the overall macro view. Applying specific solutions requires its complement, the detailed micro view.
- *Mental rehearsal:* Hall calls it "self talk." He uses it to prepare himself for a meeting, to prepare in advance his approach, his presentation, and the results he wants. Depending on the stage of a negotiation, he envisions specific actions such as a handshake, or an agreement to proceed, or a signed contract.

Hall's belief in himself allowed him to keep on trying, not to let rejections waylay him, but instead to apply himself to the number of opportunities for sales that he could create. Another element of success was the company's support. Through the tough times, his boss trusted him to make decisions in the field, gave him autonomy, kept him free to concentrate on doing his job. "After all," Hall remarked, "Wilson teaches management and sales. Our managers know what it takes to succeed in our own business."

By 1983, Hall had decided to shoot for the first $1 million sales year in company history.

> For all of us it was kind of like the four-minute mile before Roger Bannister cracked it—a level we all wanted to achieve. At the beginning of the fiscal year I put a graph on the wall over my desk and tracked out twelve months, with dollar increments going up the side, to one million dollars. That picure of where I was going helped guide me in making day-to-day decisions. Every month I would plot out my results and where I was going on the graph, and it kept me focused on the overall goal.

Three months before the end of the 1983–1984 fiscal year, he got another challenge besides the quest for the million-dollar sales record. He and his wife, Vicky, had a son, Brian, born three and a half months prematurely. Brian weighed one pound fourteen ounces at birth, and spent his first few months in intensive care. His life hung in the balance as he overcame two different viruses. During that period, Brandon divided his time between sales calls and visits to the hospital. He told me later: "All I could do was be there. I could do nothing to help Brian. Sometimes I just cried from frustration. But there was something I could do with the energy I generated from the intense experience of pulling for Brian on the sidelines. I poured it into my work."

For most of that year he was Wilson's top account executive, the first in the company's history whose annual sales exceeded a million dollars.

Brian came home after four months in the hospital, temporarily needing an oxygen unit to ensure that he could breathe properly. Brandon had to be on hand to help Vicky give him the special care he needed. During the next twelve months, Brian came through as a completely healthy baby, and Brandon repeated his feat of the year before, again selling programs worth more than a million dollars. This time, however, he was not Wilson's top salesperson—and that pleased him as much, in a different way, as being number one the year before. Like Roger Bannister leading the way for other runners by breaking the barrier of the four-minute mile, Hall created the momentum at Wilson for other million-dollar salespeople.

TEAM BUILDING/TEAM PLAYING

The top performers in company after company demonstrate that peak performance is frequently a collective act. Individuals we studied show a high degree of self-mastery, plus the flip side of independent action—they manage collaborations with other people to leverage their results.

As marketing manager for a new product from the Dow Chemical Company, Karl Kamena marshaled the skills of an entrepreneur to help focus the resources of a large organization. In the early 1980s, Dow started looking into whether it should develop a polycarbonate resins business. These plastics are so hard to break that they make good drill housings, football helmets, even bulletproof shields. Competitors in this line include General Electric's Lexan, and a decision to go ahead would mean major investments such as building a new factory and committing significant resources to marketing. A decision on whether to "build it or bury it" would have to be interdisciplinary, emerging from an alignment of people with very different career backgrounds and responsibilities.

Four managers—from research and development, technical services, production, and Kamena from marketing—formed a team to coordinate the efforts and talents of a larger team that eventually expanded to include more than two hundred members. Such a situation can turn out to be a Tower of Babel with deadlines. Marketing promises delivery to customers before manufacturing even begins, and worries about whether production is on schedule; production wonders whether R&D has supplied them with the best formulas and components; R&D tries to do its job right and be scientifically sound, cost-effective, and on time. Over two years, Kamena's team produced a go-ahead for the product that would be called Calibre, and devoted the next two years to preparing a launch strategy.

Complex teams with high stakes do not work well when an autocrat decides to beat a bunch of followers into line. Kamena and his co-leaders were neither dictators nor jellyfish. They did not dominate; they led, communicating the mission clearly to people who would catch fire from it and generate their own motivations and drive for results.

Once Calibre was launched, Kamena's team saw stronger reasons than ever to maintain the camaraderie they had developed. When any new product hits the marketplace, in any business, things can turn out to be not so neat as they were on paper. If the going gets heavy, teams can fall apart or fall back into parochial squabbles ("It's not my fault, it's manufacturing's. . . .").

Kamena's teammates are confident of the strengths that emerged as they built the team. At a celebration for the success of the "Polycarbonate Launch Team" (I was there to help with the kick-off), I asked one of them: "If I come back in two or three years, what will I find?" He said, "You won't be telling us about peak performance. You'll be studying us as a case history of a peak-performing team that made it."

COURSE CORRECTION

Men and women who get things done are not people who never lose their way. They are people who know how to find it again. They take setbacks as information, and mistakes as signs that it is time to correct course. And they know how to act decisively when windows of opportunity present themselves.

Fran Tarkenton's switch from sports to chairmanship of a management consulting company, the Tarkenton Productivity Group, attests that the skills of a peak performer are transferable. Tarkenton went from being the equivalent of a senior technical person in a corporation—quarterback of the Minnesota Vikings—to being his own boss. Many do not make that switch easily, because they are unwilling or unable to see the flow of the action around them and alter their course to capitalize on it.

Tarkenton's professional football career from 1961 to 1978 not only set records that today's stars are shooting at: yards gained passing (47,003), completions (3,686), touchdown passes (342). It also changed the game's fundamental notion of how a quarterback was supposed to do his job. Before Tarkenton, a well-drilled quarterback would stand resolutely in the pocket of protection formed by his linemen, looking for a pass receiver. That did not show enough imagination for Tarkenton. "If the rush was on and the pocket collapsed, the play was over," he observed. He began to improvise, scrambling around the field until, as a writer described it, "his pursuers are exhausted and his receivers are somewhere in the next county." He was also one of the first quarterbacks who routinely changed plays at the line of scrimmage. Exactly, in other words, the type of behavior we see in successful entrepreneurs who leave the pocket of a corporation and venture out on their own, or managers whose mental agility allows them to make quick decisions while firefighting on the job.

As his playing days drew to a close, Tarkenton was sure that the quick reflexes required of football players would be valuable assets for an executive. Although he had majored in business administration and was on the dean's list at the University of Georgia, he told me his experience on the football field was more important to his business career than a formal education. He has new fans who think he was right. "Why Fran Tarkenton ever wasted his time in football, I'll never know," says John F. Bergin, president of the McCann-Erickson advertising agency. Bergin claims Tarkenton is "an intuitive genius in the art of motivation."

Translating that genius into results took some scrambling. Tarkenton went from quarterbacking to four years of television work as a football commentator and host of a show called *That's Incredible!* while he sorted out his entrepreneurial impulses. Once, on a trip, he got the idea that airline ticket envelopes would be a good place for advertisements. He formed a company and checked into the Waldorf-Astoria Hotel in New York for five weeks, selling $7.5 million in advertising. He sold the company because, he says, it was "too big a hassle." His energy ("More than God usually allows on Earth," a former colleague once said) and interest in what makes people perform led him to management consulting.

He had something more, three characteristics that we have observed in peak performers who check their bearings to stay on a "critical path," the boundaries of a course within which they can accomplish a mission:

- *Mental agility:* the flexibility to change perspective and do the creative thinking necessary to deal with challenges
- *Concentration:* consisting of the stamina to work long, adaptability to change, and the hardiness that could also be called resilience under stress
- *Learning from mistakes:* taking appropriate actions based on updated information

Starting with one employee, he attacked ways of reducing employee turnover at textile mills in North and South Carolina. After the annual turnover among twenty thousand workers at one company dropped from 50 percent to 20 percent, its president asked Tarkenton to put experts in sixty plants. Tarkenton suddenly had to start thinking bigger about his business. Recognizing the signs nudging him toward a critical path, he started learning to grow. Tarkenton & Co., the original firm, specializes in training and practical programs for productivity. In a football huddle, Tarkenton was an early exponent of participatory management. He would sometimes let linemen suggest plays because, he says, "They were closer to the action than the head coach pacing up and down the sidelines." Tarkenton consultants do what is appropriate to a company's situation, from establishing quality circles to revising compensation programs to speeding up the inspection process at a piston-ring plant. Meter readers at the Delmarva Power & Light Company used to make an expensive number of errors. The solution there was, according to Delmarva president Nevius Curtis, "maddeningly simple." The company gave the meter readers hand-held calculators on which they could immediately record their data.

"As a professional athlete," says Thomas Joiner, president and chief financial officer of the Tarkenton Productivity Group, "he's action-oriented." Combining mental agility, concentration, and learning from mistakes leads an action-oriented person such as Tarkenton to a sense of self-authorization, the confidence that he can always alter course to stay within his critical path.

Jenette Kahn pulled together her own strengths to guide a dramatic course correction in a field that was, until her arrival, dominated by men. Kahn was twenty-eight years old in 1976 when William Sarnoff, chairman of the publishing division of Warner Communications, Inc., asked her to come over and talk about an ailing subsidiary, DC Comics. Kahn was no newcomer to publishing—she had launched three children's magazines, one of them financially successful and all critically acclaimed—so when she arrived in Sarnoff's office the next day she was prepared.

The venerable comics company, home to such heroes as Superman and Batman, was demoralized. The superheroes were aging, the kids were not buying as they used to, and, as Sarnoff explained to Kahn, the parent company cared more about the licensing revenues that came from DC than about the comics. Kahn disagreed entirely. The real assets of a company like DC are its characters, she told the chairman. "If DC isn't going to rejuvenate them, they will live on for a while in a morbid half-life, but eventually the company will have no more assets."

The next day Sarnoff offered her the job of publisher. Being only twenty-eight in a conservative company, and unknown in the comics industry, Kahn was greeted with skepticism, if not outright shock. Nobody cared about the heroes anymore, she concluded, because "all the talent that created them had been driven away." She took action to attract the talent back to DC. The company owns rights to its characters (hence the lucrative licensing contracts from toy makers, movie studios, even food manufacturers), but the artists and writers who invented the heroes, such as Superman's creators Bud Shuster and Jerry Siegel, had never participated in the profits their characters generated. Enough of such inequity, Kahn decreed. She started the first royalty program in the comic-book industry. Artists and writers now receive a 20 percent creative share of all licensing revenues their characters bring in.

At the same time, she told the writers to breathe new life into the heroes, who had strayed from their original identities—pay attention to the motivations of characters, create plots that stay within the realm of fantasy but are relevant to modern times, and start thinking of new characters and story lines. The strength of the comic-book market was no longer little kids. It was young men from sixteen to twenty-four. Noticing that comic-book specialty stores were replacing traditional outlets such as mom-and-pop candy stores and the supermarkets who didn't like kids hanging around anyway, Kahn established a marketing department at DC, the first in the comics industry, and directed sales toward the specialty stores.

Still, in her first five years, most of the ways she could leverage DC's properties were not under her control as the publisher. That was what she calls her "Zen rock garden period; I sat and thought about all the things I'd like to do if I were the president of DC." When she was appointed president in 1981, she was able to get started right away, revitalizing and expanding DC's licensing program. Her ace in the hole was Superman. "Over ninety-eight percent of the population recognizes Superman," Kahn says. "That's a higher recognition factor than for either Ronald Reagan or Abraham Lincoln." In the first *DC Comics Super Healthy Cookbook,* published in 1981, he and other DC characters urged children to eat healthy foods. Superman peanut butter arrived in 1983. There are Superman raisins, Super Heroes cookies, and Super Heroes yogurt.

Kahn's plan of action worked. DC's 1984 revenues of approximately $70 million came about one third from comics and two thirds from licensing and other products. Kahn has turned DC into what she calls a "creative rights company," whose products provide licensing and movie revenues for other Warner divisions as well.

CHANGE MANAGEMENT

Jim Gray is not the man that twenty years ago he thought he would be. Changes he never expected came at him from every side, and he rode them out. More than that: To his own surprise, he thrived on them.

He started his career in 1969 in a blue-collar neighborhood of New York where "nobody ever moved. If you worked for the phone company, or the post office, or any secure organization, it was the best thing in the world and you never left." The telephone company craftsmen one level above him had been hired fifteen years before, and Jim figured a promotion was that far off. Besides, his foreman at the time despised the way he looked. Toughened by five years as a "gruntman" in the navy, Jim came to work with long hair, stars on his boots, American flags sewn on the back of his work jacket, and his Vietnam patches on his sleeve. "The foreman wouldn't even talk to me. He would talk to the mechanic I was with. That's just the way it was. Until you had been there five years, you didn't exist." Jim figured there was one way to say "here I am" to the company: to focus all his energy on doing extraordinarily excellent work. "My seniority was zero." He told me: "All I had to show them was that Jim Gray and doing good work were synonymous."

They saw. They knew that even if Jim was working in a manhole that nobody else would ever enter, one that was going to be sealed like a vault, the work would still be perfect because he did it. And that was his horizon: being the best craftsman on that crew.

What he hadn't counted on was that his reputation would lead to faster moves than the guys in his neighborhood ever imagined. From construction to maintenance: "Now you can go out and fix what other people messed up." Then, in 1978, a chance to move to Southern California, where a population and technology explosion put the phone company in need of Jim Gray types. The guys at the pool hall said he would never go. To himself he said, "I've got to do something." Maybe the cold in New York had become too much for him; maybe it was realizing that "wires are wires anywhere in the world." Anyway, he applied for the move, and got it.

Then began something really unexpected: He started having to change his view of who he was. He had had no idea of how expert he had become. In New York, "You worked on that, you worked on this, you were just a regular person." No feedback. In California, he found his foreman coming to him for advice. Then bosses higher up started calling: "We need Gray on this special project."

He knew more about the job than they did, and he never would have noticed it if he hadn't moved away. One of the two constants in his life—consistently high performance—had been invisible to him until then. Another, newer constant—learning the skills of managing change—soon got his attention too. He realized that he was developing a sense of the future, not merely reacting to the present.

Construction boomed in the San Fernando Valley in 1979, 1980, and the phone company needed people to train new technicians. They pulled Jim down off a pole and said, "You're a manager. You start on Monday." Twenty-four hours later he had seven people to supervise. He built his crew into a team, almost a family, that operated with the same pride in its work that he had as an individual. For a year or two he could not see himself as a manager. "In my mind I was still in the manhole, just training, telling them technically what to do." But changes continued to come at him, and he responded. He started to understand some key skills of change management:

- *Anticipate*
- *Adapt*
- *Act*

He could no longer be the same old Jim Gray. He had to look ahead, find ways to move with any changes he saw coming, and do what would work.

He got waves of new people to train. He was switched to control supervision and scheduling. Then—finally—back to maintenance, the area he had known so well in New York. But this time as a manager, and thinking as one. He recruited the best people for his crews. He got them the newest equipment. He protected them from company rules when a job would go better outside the rules. He devised ways of turning a temporary repair job into permanent construction, saving the company money by doing it all in one visit instead of two or three. "My dream. I had always wanted to become a maintenance supervisor, but I knew in my heart in New York that I could never make it. It just takes too long."

Then the biggest change of all: the divestiture of regional operating companies from AT&T. One day Jim Gray and his friends were working for a monopoly that provided service in its own lordly way, a ponderous bureaucracy that left you thinking it would take fifteen years to make a move. The next day they were working for a somewhat uncertain new company, one that had to learn to be aggressive and sell its services in a teeming marketplace. Some were caught short by the opportunity of the new company, frightened of the new world in which they found themselves. Not Jim Gray. He sees the entire company beginning to change in his direction, like a battleship changing course. Now that profits are a matter of local concern, now that efficiency means keeping each individual's motivation alive, now that incentive means showing people from the bottom up that they are valued, the company's management style begins to resemble Jim Gray's management style. In 1983, Pacific Bell made him supervisor of maintenance. "The company let me know that my thinking is all right."

Jim Gray did his change management within the structure of an organization. Robert Maynard did, too, and went on to change the direction of his company as a whole. Maynard emerged from a childhood in the Bedford-Stuyvesant area of Brooklyn to become the owner-publisher of the Oakland, California, *Tribune.* Maynard's father, an immigrant from Barbados, would ask at the dinner table every night: "Tell me what it is you know now that you didn't know when you got up this morning." Thus oriented to educate himself and plan for change, Maynard constructed a career based on the achievement of goals that other people told him were unreachable. He was one of the first black reporters to break the racial barriers in newspapers, the first black national correspondent and editorial writer for *The Washington Post,* and the first black editor and publisher of a metropolitan daily newspaper in the history of the United States. Like Jenette Kahn at DC Comics, by the time he took over he had made his plans.

He had the paper redesigned. He improved its news coverage. That particular course correction included recruiting young, ambitious reporters and editors, many of them from minorities, who shared Maynard's sense of mission. An aggressive marketing plan called out to readers who had been wooed by neighboring dailies.

He extended teamwork from the newsroom throughout the readership, aiming to increase community participation in the paper by creating neighborhood advisory boards made up of civic leaders who promised to keep him posted on local concerns. He wanted the challenge of turning around a venerable daily that had lost an estimated $3 million the year before he bought it. For the time being at least, Maynard and his team are meeting that challenge.

THE POWER OF THE PROFILE

Here we have managers and nonmanagers. Men. Women. Top executives. A laborer turned supervisor. Entrepreneurs. Researchers. People in marketing. Sales. Manufacturing. In such industries as health and fitness. Aerospace. Banking. Print communications. Telecommunications. Sports. Some people maintain peak performance over years; some rise to it in a particular situation. Some we see as they begin, others when they are well along.

Each is an individual approaching a mission and its challenges in his or her own way. Yet if science has taught us anything, it is that the exceptional case informs us about all the others. The similarities among peak performers—and what they tell us about ourselves—are more powerful than their differences.

As our research progressed, one point became increasingly clear. Peak performers are not people with something added; rather, they are people with very little of their potential taken away. They develop an ability to achieve what they set out to, and to cultivate within themselves the characteristics they value most. More than any other factor, the difference between them and ordinary performers is that they consciously, persistently, intelligently refine and develop those characteristics.

You might say that a peak performer is a person exploring the farther reaches of his or her abilities. Chapter 2 examines how far those abilities extend.

2

ACCELERATING ACHIEVEMENT: THE FARTHER REACHES

When Victor Kiam decided to buy the Remington electric shaver company from Sperry Corporation in 1979, the United States was in a recession and Remington had lost $30 million. The company's major competitor, the Dutch giant Norelco, had 50 percent of the U.S. market. Remington's share was 19 percent and sinking. Kiam, then fifty-two, had just finished turning an old watch company, Benrus, from a loser into a profit maker, but he didn't have the $25 million that Sperry was asking. In addition, Sperry was putting prospective buyers through a screen as fine as any they put on their shavers. They wanted to save the jobs of Remington employees, if possible; the average worker had been with the company for more than twenty years. They were not overly impressed to see that Kiam was primarily a marketer, not a manufacturer.

Here was another American company being beaten on its home field by foreign competitors, with little hope of even making it a close game.

Except that Kiam did not see it that way. Here, to his way of thinking, was another opportunity to turn a company around.

"Remington's business was declining," he remembers thinking, "but still they had nineteen percent of the market, and that's not to be sneezed at when you consider some of the costly battles companies wage for a one percent share of beer, toothpaste, and other markets. Remington, furthermore, was well thought of abroad."

Ellen Kiam bought her husband a Remington electric razor as the most direct way of finding out if the product was any good. If it wasn't, they could stop right there. "I really wanted to buy the company then," Victor says, "because the essential starting point is a good product, and this one was good. You can hype a questionable product for a little while, but you'll never build an enduring business, and that is what I was interested in building." That focus on quality, the confidence to change the course of a large corporation, the determination to save as many jobs as possible (and as a consequence build a loyal team), all were aspects of that enduring business—of his mission.

Kiam pushed past the first financial obstacle, borrowing most of the money he needed with a lot of leverage; Chase Manhattan Bank put up forty dollars for every one of his. The loan was secured by Remington's assets. Then Kiam went to work on cash flow. Within his first week he fired seventy executives, trimming $2 million from the payroll. No more company cars. Economy-class air travel ("The front of the plane arrives the same time as the rear"). He called a halt to the frequent model changes that, he was convinced, confused retailers, and did away with decorative chrome. He hit the road to reassure storekeepers, urging them to build up their inventories of Remingtons.

And he mounted the aggressive television advertising campaign that made him one of the most recognized American businessmen in the world. Standing in his bathrobe, holding up a Remington, he told viewers in thirty-eight countries: "I liked the shaver so much that I bought the company." (In English and French, which he speaks, he simply learned the scripts. In Italian, German, Spanish, Norwegian, Japanese, and a dozen other languages, he memorized them phonetically.) No fancy effects, just straight talk about a powerful motor, a shave as close as a blade or your money back, and a good price.

The commercial resulted from a chance inspiration. He was in London discussing commercials, and at one point his advertising people asked how he had gotten into the shaver business. He noticed their fascination with his explanation, and had an idea: Why not tell the story on television? And who could play the company president better than the company president?

Now, Kiam exults, "The only American-made electrical product in Mitsukoshi, Tokyo's oldest and largest department store, is the Remington microscreen shaver. Sure, you'll find American brand names, but flip them over and they'll say, 'Made in Taiwan,' 'Made in Hong Kong,' or someplace else. Ours are made in Bridgeport, Connecticut."

Kiam got results. He realized a profit in his first full year, and within four years had turned Remington around. He paid off $6 million in bank debts three months ahead of time, and in June 1983 he paid off Remington's whole debt eleven years ahead of schedule. Remington sold 1.6 million shavers worldwide for $50 million in 1979. In 1984 it sold nearly 5 million, tripling its income, bringing pretax profits since Kiam's arrival to $32 million, and pushing its share of the U.S. market above 40 percent. Its worldwide share also climbed, to more than 25 percent. Kiam not only saved the jobs of most of Remington's employees, but the domestic payroll has doubled to a total of eight hundred.

One basic motivation among his team members is a straight, no-nonsense goal to be achieved every day: 100 percent quality control. Every shaver, not just random samples, is inspected before it leaves the factory. "When you shave," Kiam explains, "you can tell whether it's close just by rubbing your hand over your face. Every morning, we have to deliver."

Kiam is clearly the point man for such motivations, as he is for the mission that turned the company around. When he is in Bridgeport he devotes some time almost every day to getting out of his office and walking around the factory floor, checking in with employees. Some people who work for years at other big companies and never meet the boss never feel the impact of that. Kiam shuts down the factory four times a year, at a cost of $10,000 each time, to deliver a quarterly report and answer questions. Remington team members are keenly interested, since they share in profits. During the year, every one of them also gets to come to the regular Friday morning coffees in the conference room, where they hear the latest news about the company, air any complaints, and put forth ideas. Not only is production up, so are morale and health: The average Remington team member runs up only 14 percent of the expected national workers' compensation rate.

Kiam trained himself to accelerate his achievements. After Yale, language study at the Sorbonne, and Harvard Business School, he sidestepped the usual middle-management openings and started selling cosmetics and toothpaste for Lever Brothers. He quickly observed that he had a capacity for self-management. Never mind what everyone else was doing. He gave selling on the road his own structure, including a seven-day workweek. "Saturdays were great, because even though the stores were busy, hardly any other salesmen were on the road, and I could talk to the drugstore owners more easily. I'd write up all my orders on Sunday." Just the extra effort alone generated so much more volume that he began to stand out.

To many Americans, the Victor Kiam they saw selling Remington shavers came to represent a heartening comeback spirit—a true example of keeping a mission alive and putting it to work, with each achievement building the motivation for the next. Soon after *60 Minutes* on CBS ran a story about him, more than six thousand people phoned and eleven thousand wrote letters, most congratulating him for helping to restore their pride.

"What's really important in life?" Kiam asks. "Sitting on the beach? Looking at television eight hours a day? I think we have to appreciate that we're alive for only a limited period of time, and we'll spend most of our lives working. That being the case, I believe one of the most important priorities is to do whatever we do as well as we can. We should take pride in that."

UNDERSTANDING GROWTH

Victor Kiam is not the only entrepreneur who wanted to turn a company around. Jim Gray at Pacific Bell is not the only supervisor learning how to manage big changes in his job. Karl Kamena at Dow is not the only marketing director whose team is launching a new product.

The differences between peak performers and ordinary performers do not stem primarily from the situations in which they operate. The differences appear in the attitude and skills a peak performer brings to a situation. Given similar work realities, a Beth Milwid, a Fran Tarkenton, a Jenette Kahn often make more of them than an ordinary performer does. The peak performers follow the impulse to use those "typical" situations as opportunities for achievement and self-development. They show—through their approach to the work, through perfecting technical skills, and through their commitment to results—that they understand growth.

Aldous Huxley, the scholar and writer whose best-known novel is *Brave New World,* remarked, "Experience is not what happens to you. It is what you do with what happens to you." We looked into some pretty uninspiring kinds of work—toll-taking on a bridge, plumbing maintenance. Even there we found high achievers in pockets of peak performance that they had sculpted for themselves. Sometimes they were staying because they were preparing themselves for a move up, or out, or across. Sometimes because they had made their jobs work for themselves and their companies.

The most intriguing quality of the peak performers is that no matter how rough "it" gets, how much of an assault on mind and body, they always feel they can do something about it. Victor Kiam's rescue of Remington, Brandon Hall's breaking the million-dollar barrier at Wilson Learning, the steady leadership of Ben and Joe Weider in health and fitness, of Robert Maynard in newspapers, all reflect confidence in growth and change.

Another intriguing quality is their constructive restlessness. A task may appear impossibly difficult. Everyone else may be moping around. The peak performers can be found exploring possible solutions, something that might work. Or something else that might work. Or something else. They always have another idea to test, an extra possibility to explore.

Whether they are organization leaders or lone-wolf researchers, their confidence is based on their productive human capacities rather than on brandishing personal power.

They are not like the ship captain who, the story goes, saw one night at sea what looked like the lights of another ship heading toward him. He had his signalman blink to the other ship: "Change your course 10 degrees south." The reply came back: "Change your course 10 degrees north." The captain answered, "I am captain. Change your course south." To which the reply was, "I am seaman first class. Change your course north." This infuriated the captain, so he signaled back: "I am a battleship. Change course south." The reply came back: "I am a lighthouse. Change course north."

Peak performers never stop searching and learning. Among them we see mostly high-initiative, energetic individuals. And more: The men and women among them who are leaders cultivate those qualities in others. They are attracted to people who are, in the words of psychologist Richard DeCharms, "Origins," not "Pawns." DeCharms wrote in a study of personal efficacy:

> An Origin is a person who feels that he is the director of his life. He feels that what he is doing is the result of his own free choice; he is doing it because he wants to do it, and the consequences of his activity will be valuable to him. He thinks carefully about what he wants in the world, now and in the future, and chooses the most important goals, ruling out those that are for him too easy or too risky.
>
> A Pawn is a person who feels that . . . what he is doing has been imposed on him by others, that he is doing it because he is forced to, and the consequences of his activity will not be a source of pride to him. Since he feels that external factors determine his fate, the Pawn does not consider carefully his goals in life, nor does he concern himself about what he himself can do to further his cause.

INVESTING IN HUMAN CAPITAL

Reality is not what it used to be. If the controlling reality in the Agricultural Age was land, and in the Industrial Age financial capital, the controlling reality of the Information Age we have now entered is *human* capital—the ability to use human intelligence and the demonstrated open-endedness of human capacities.

This goes beyond the platitude some senior executives deliver when they say, "Our people are our greatest resource." That sentiment fills corporate meetings. Of course it is true that any enterprise grows from its people. But only an outstanding enterprise treats intelligence and human capacity as resources to be actively, consciously cultivated with as much attention as land and financial capital were given in the past. Property and money can be manipulated as passive articles. Human capital, however, is a resource that is best invested in and developed with the full, conscious participation of motivated human beings. It is human capital that is building bridges from the Industrial Age to the Information Age.

What you do to identify and activate this human capital depends on your assumptions about management. In his book *The Competent Manager,* Richard Boyatzis of McBer and Company gathers the broad range of assumptions into two opposing traditions of management which he calls "scientific" and "humanistic."

Are you interested in the kind of human engineering that Boyatzis describes as "scientific management"? Then you might define characteristics of peak performers as "specifications for the human machinery desired to provide maximum organizational productivity." You will set about training the characteristics as skills, without much allowance for individual variations in mission and values deeper inside. An internal decision to excel, or its absence, is not quantifiable enough for human engineering.

Or are you part of the "humanistic management" tradition, working with ways of harnessing the sometimes unpredictable call to action that, once it clicks for an individual, shows up as a mission? Then, as Boyatzis points out, you will be interested not in just tacking on skills to otherwise unchanged subjects, but in addressing "these same characteristics as the key that unlocks the door to realizing maximum human potential, developing ethical organizations and providing maximum growth opportunities for personnel."

Almost all the peak performers in our study used some form of "unlocking the door" metaphor when they talked about human resources. Few showed much interest in growth without achievement. As pragmatists, they had discovered a payoff, for both business and personal life, in developing their potential to increasingly higher levels.

They have a strikingly sharp view of *how* they develop that potential into tangible accomplishment. They do it not by merely adding skills, but by activating capacities. They value any skills they can acquire. As one put it, "The unskilled are handicapped." Yet technical skills training, no matter how useful and necessary, is ultimately not what keeps them moving. The key is something internal. Some referred to it as a set of values. Abraham Maslow, the psychologist whose studies of "self-actualization" began to influence management theory well before his death in 1970, referred to "capacities clamoring to be used which cease their clamor only when they are used sufficiently."

In other words, an internal impulse to growth. Training in career and technical skills is a $10-billion-a-year industry in the United States. Many trainers, and the skills they teach, can be highly effective. Yet when the context in which the skills are taught is merely mechanical, it leaves people feeling manipulated, momentarily pumped up, and wondering a few months later why their learning has faded.

Peak performers see their potential emerging not only when *something is added,* but especially when *nothing is taken away.* A fifty-five-year-old vice-president of operations for an aerospace company summed up the characteristics presented in this book as "not additional capabilities tacked on to plain old me, but strategies to prevent the taking away of parts of my potential, my essential ability to achieve and improve."

MOBILIZING HUMAN RESOURCES

The most productive people tend to be students all their lives. Discovering and developing new facets of their potential excite them the way mastery of a sport excites an athlete, particularly when mastery increases the speed at which improvements occur. In our studies, peak performers often commented that regardless of past accomplishments—which in many cases were formidable—they knew they were using but a small fraction of their capacities: "I am still developing and have a long way to go." "I'm starting to hit my stride now."

From their observations we distilled four main ingredients of the potential they have managed to mobilize:

- *Inherent talent*
- *Acquired information*
- *Restlessness*
- *Passion and preference*

Inherent talent, an inborn predisposition, whether handed down from prior generations or not, is the wiring in one's system that is unique to each individual. One can either identify and develop the specific talents and capacities he or she has, or leave them buried. Peak performers in business find compelling reasons to cultivate relevant inherent talents. Matching a mission to such gifts greatly enhances the possibilities of peak performance. What often happens is that a vast reservoir of hidden resources becomes available for use.

Acquired information, the complex mass of skills and data about the world learned since the original wiring was set, may or may not be of much use. That depends on how much of it a person can recall and use appropriately. Teachings we don't apply are not going to produce much—witness innumerable company training programs from the old "human engineering" days that came and went without changing a thing in the company's or individual's performance. Insight, as Beth Milwid noted when she worked at

Crocker Bank, is not equivalent to results, and people often do not act in their own best interests even when they possess the knowledge they need. Acquired information—like inherent talent—may lie dormant until a peak performer develops an action plan and a compelling reason for using it.

Restlessness, an inner urge to apply one's talent and information, is not a learned skill. It is part of the "hard-wiring," the fixed circuitry that a human being comes with. Science writer Morton Hunt refers to "a capacity to find things interesting." What makes us want to know about something, even something of no practical value, such as the age of the universe or when human beings first appeared on earth? In *The Universe Within,* Hunt suggests it may be "an intrinsic characteristic of our nervous system . . . an inherent neurological restlessness, a need to do something with the thoughts in our minds and with the world they represent."

A baby in action—curious, energetic, reaching out to explore—embodies the inborn urge to grow, to achieve, to excel. This motivation need not be taught. It can be untaught, as suffocating organizations and limiting jobs demonstrate in squelching people's motivation. Peak performers taught me that human beings are goal-seeking—and, more importantly, meaning-seeking—organisms. That is, we are not only born in a state of arousal, of excitation or motivation. We not only grow. We also seek to grow in a particular direction. What determines that direction?

Preference with a passion—intense commitment to what they do—is one of the single most dramatic differences between peak performers and their less productive colleagues. High achievers differ in what they call it: passion, preference, deep feeling, commitment. They agree, though, that it determines their direction. Many told me they can trace their performance more clearly to preference than to aptitude, more to how they feel about what they are doing than what they know. One forty-four-year-old sales vice-president in the automobile industry remarked, "So many of us are top-heavy with skills, information, and talent—mostly unused—and light on commitment. I can't help thinking of Oliver Wendell Holmes saying, 'Every calling is great when greatly pursued.' "

That is what Charles House, head of corporate engineering at Hewlett-Packard, must have felt when he ignored an order from co-founder David Packard to stop working on a type of high-quality, large-screen video monitor; he pressed ahead anyway. The monitor has been used in heart transplant operations and manned moon landings. Hewlett-Packard sold more than seventeen thousand units instead of the thirty initially estimated, and the company gave House a medal in 1982 for "extraordinary contempt and defiance beyond the normal call of engineering duty."

HEART AND HEAD

This is not to say that surroundings don't count. If two people attempt to swim a river, one carrying lead and the other carrying cork, the challenge is hardly the same for both. It is to say that peak performers see themselves differently from other people. Having a calling greatly pursued—and, often enough, greatly achieved—does much to enhance one's self-esteem and self-confidence.

Nor is it to say that passionate commitment is just a matter of doing what you please and damn the others. At dinner one night, Dave Meggysey, West Coast director of the National Football League Players' Association, told me a story of how one man's passion—what he loved to do—developed into a high-performing organization that supported the missions and goals of many individuals.

In 1933, when the Depression had destroyed one of every four jobs in the United States, Pennsylvania lifted its antientertainment Blue Laws. With the thought that at last he and his friends could play ball on weekends, Art Rooney bought the Pittsburgh franchise for $2,500. It was not an investment. It was a pleasure. "I loved playing ball and managing teams," he said much later, "and just kept on doing it." More than fifty years later, the Pittsburgh Steelers weren't for sale, but if they had been, the price tag (judging by the $80 million paid for the Dallas Cowboys) might be thirty thousand times the original investment.

Two other men at the top, Lee Iacocca (who would go on to

Chrysler Corporation and one of history's most dramatic corporate rescues) and Vince Lombardi, the legendary coach of the Green Bay Packers, once had a conversation about keeping your dreams in sight. Iacocca remembers Lombardi saying:

> Every time a football player goes out to ply his trade, he's got to play from the ground up—from the soles of his feet right up to his head. Every inch of him has to play. Some guys play with their heads, and sure, you need to be smart to be number one in anything you try. But most important, you've got to play with your heart. If you're lucky enough to find a guy with a lot of head and a lot of heart, he's never going to come off the field second.

WHERE DO WE GO FROM HERE?

LINKS: INHERENT TALENT AND ACQUIRED INFORMATION

Peak performers start with potential. We all do. Yet history is littered with the bones of people who never converted potential into achievement. Inherent talents turn useful only when you examine what yours are and cultivate them.

Linus Pauling told me in 1977 that he never thought he was born to be a Nobel Prize winner, but he certainly loved chemistry. Donna de Varona, who won an Olympic gold medal as a swimmer in the 400-meter medley in 1964, discussed with me her role as an ABC broadcaster prior to the 1984 Olympics. It was clear that she had to learn a set of skills as complex as those she used in the water to be a peak performer on the air. Luciano Pavarotti told a number of us that he hardly showed the promise of things to come as a singer in a boys' choir in Italy. Harvard M.B.A. Victor Kiam had to sell a lot of toothpaste on Saturdays before he had the skills he used to sell shavers to the Japanese.

Training can be dull, tedious, and onerous when it is simply tacked on to a manager's everyday routine. But when it serves a passion and follows a mission, it becomes a practice as pleasurable and full of promise as refining a golf swing or making a successful investment. Top performers do not leave training to chance.

A rule of thumb I have noticed in working with organizations is that when times get tough and companies look for ways to reduce budgets, the marginal ones—which have seen training all along as a fringe benefit—often cut their training programs. By contrast, peak-performing companies most often increase theirs, exactly like an individual who pulls in resources to deal with a threat or an opportunity. Organizations such as Arthur Andersen, Merrill Lynch, Abbott Laboratories, Hewlett-Packard, and the Young Presidents' Organization do not throw money at their training budgets. They focus carefully on what they need in order not just to survive but to excel—which is the surest way to survive.

Joseph Murray is executive vice-president for marketing of Security Pacific Leasing, the most profitable bank-related leasing operation in the United States. His San Francisco-based company took in $600 million in 1984 leasing "large assets" such as 747 jetliners, oil tankers, drilling rigs, and satellites. "When times are tough," Murray emphasized during a workshop we were doing for his salespeople, "it's not the time to huddle in the dark, using the same old solutions to the same old problems. It's time to identify new solutions to old problems. The key is to investigate top-flight training in the same way that we investigate any other top-flight investment. In the long run, training our people may be as important as anything we do."

Joe Murray's team members at Security Pacific Leasing have developed an intense loyalty to one another, which has its roots in Murray's loyalty to the people who work with him. "We're in this for the sake of one another, to help each other achieve our personal financial goals and day-to-day satisfactions. That includes legal, operations, credit. All the departments that usually fight with one another in other companies are really peaceful here. Competitors who do less business than we do often need more people to do it."

MAKING SENSE OF RESTLESSNESS: THE "ACTUALIZERS"

Real training is obviously based on the premise that people can grow—often dramatically. We see that people with a mission to direct what they do, and an action plan to focus it, are motivated to seek training. Beth Milwid undertook an extraordinary amount of training, including a Ph.D., to equip herself for a career in helping bureaucracies overcome inertia and, as she put it, their "lack of results-oriented productivity."

Change, growth, mission as a vehicle for releasing tremendous potential: These indicators of "neurological restlessness" are familiar topics in organizations today mainly because Abraham Maslow and others turned their careers toward the study of healthy people. Maslow did not invent the concept of "self-actualization"; another psychologist, Kurt Goldstein, did. But Maslow developed self-actualization as a fertile area for research and practice. Mainstream psychology had always concentrated on neuroses and deficiencies. The normal personality attracted little interest. And *positive* psychological health was completely uncharted territory. Several of Maslow's mentors, including the anthropologist Ruth Benedict and the psychologist Max Wertheimer, not only stood atop their fields; he saw them also as exceptionally responsive, active, warm, fine people. In 1942, puzzling over his notes on Benedict and Wertheimer, Maslow spotted something that opened a new tributary for research, an alternative to the old mainstream psychology.

> I realized in one wonderful moment that their patterns could be generalized. I was talking about a kind of person, not about two noncomparable individuals . . . I tried to see whether this pattern could be found elsewhere, and I did find it elsewhere, in one person after another.

Maslow resolved to study "the farther reaches of human nature," which is what he called his last book. Through twenty-eight subsequent years he charted the makeup of exceptionally healthy individuals, working as (in his words) "a reconnaissance man."

Self-actualization is neatly summed up by writer George Leonard in his assessment of Maslow's work. Every human being has certain "deficiency-needs" such as oxygen, water, food, up through safety, belongingness, love, and esteem. Each lower one is "prepotent" to those above it. For example, a hungry person will quickly forget about food if deprived of oxygen. Once these needs are fairly well satisfied, then a need for "self-actualization" emerges, as much a part of human nature as the deficiency needs. Self-actualization is, in short,

> the tendency of every human being . . . to *make real* his or her full potential, to become everything that he or she can be. The self-actualizing person is the true human species-type . . . not a normal person with something added, but a normal person with nothing taken away.

True to his explorer's nature, Maslow refused to stop with one discovery. Toward the end of his life in 1970 he was pushing on toward the study of a stage beyond self-actualization: the individual's contribution to the whole.

Maslow noted also that the tendency to self-actualization is just that: a tendency, not a certainty. It does not automatically kick in every time a person fulfills the basic needs. Throughout my studies of peak performers I have been fascinated by people who were well past any worries about security but were still stuck—millionaires who continued to talk as if they were fighting for survival, managers with a string of successes who still grabbed for attention and could not give credit to colleagues.

What kept those people stuck in an excessive need for security? Why were they afraid to venture, as Fran Tarkenton did when he scrambled for touchdowns, outside a comfort zone where things were familiar, unchallenging, not at all exceptional, and therefore less productive?

Part of the fear stemmed from an uncertainty about what peak performance is and how it fits into life, career, and society. Average levels of performance became acceptable. They represented long-ingrained habits and compliance with the way it was supposed to be: "The way we've always done things around here." People were being held back by their perception—rather, a lack of perception—"fixated," as Maslow put it, "at lower levels."

They had no powerful image of peak performance, no role

model—not even the language to give the image an outline—drawing them into the future. Who was the peak performer? Not me. Someone else. All the evidence people had in those days were stories about great men and great women, and most of those stories made us see the differences between them and us, not the similarities.

THE FACT IS, THE DIFFERENCES BETWEEN PEAK PERFORMERS AND EVERYBODY ELSE ARE MUCH SMALLER THAN "EVERYBODY ELSE" THINKS.

The expanding and increasingly effective training industry in the United States presents a clue: Millions of people suspect, and every one of the peak performers we studied confirms, that the gap can be spanned. People can learn to be peak performers. Those we studied confirm, too, that the difference between them and ordinary performers is, in the memorable phrase of anthropologist Gregory Bateson, "the difference that makes a difference." Living and working at our best makes a difference not only to ourselves but also to the world around us—the company, the community, the family.

Yet in seeking ways to "actualize" that nature, we often settle for small potatoes. Even since Maslow, the concept of becoming all you can be is often trivialized into a limited notion of self-improvement: We tack on skills to "plain old me"—some strategic planning here, a bit of time management there—while neglecting to exploit the talents, information, restlessness, and preferences already present. Yes, we see clues to what we want to achieve. No, we do not often know how to use the clues to do it.

Why have the characteristics of "unusual" people, the top performers whom we admire so much, escaped systematic study until recently? We vicariously enjoy their celebrity, always from afar, wondering what their mysterious extra ingredient is. We take them to be aberrant, accidental, lucky. "This damn place" did it for the Apollo mission engineers, not the engineers themselves. John Kennedy started it. It was the astronauts and geniuses. Not me. Somebody else. When the excitement collapsed—at least among my colleagues—after the first manned moon landing and performances reverted to business-as-usual, that was proof: The real me doesn't perform the way I have been performing. It's still the same old jungle out there.

One trait that makes the United States so great is our inclusiveness. Everything gets taken in, including an interesting state of tension between a yearning for achievement on the one hand and the principles of equality on the other. We gear our lives to success—and when you make it, you discover sometimes that you intimidate people who do not yet see themselves as peak performers (and in most cases are not). On Monday morning your boss promotes you to sales manager. As soon as word gets around, you can bet that at least one friend whom you'll now be supervising will suddenly turn a little cold, for you are "no longer one of us; you're working for *them.*"

The climate of ambivalence is changing. Studies of peak performers are helping to make it clear that the nation's most noble principle—all men and women are created equal—is not a formula for shaving the peaks down to some dusty plateau. It is a call to see that the *normal* person has an opportunity, and the ability, to stand out.

So it becomes clear that the internal restlessness has at least as much power as external circumstances to set up a success. What about the power to sustain it? When I asked Linus Pauling what one does to keep going after one wins a Nobel Prize, he laughed and said, "You change fields, of course!" You look around for another mission, something else to sink your teeth into. Does that imply that the power resides outside you, in the mission? Not at all. Pauling did not say you wait until the field changes. He said *you* make the change. *You* look at the environment. You know *you* supply something essential to it, something that amplifies whatever power there is in it.

Athletes regularly accomplish great feats in surroundings that are not just indifferent but downright negative. Roger Bannister of England is a classic example. Until 1954, no one had ever run the mile in less than four minutes. During the year before Bannister, a young premed student, did it in 3:59.4, a number of scholarly papers were published arguing that the four-minute mile was physiologically impossible. The lungs, circulation, muscle fibers, autonomic nervous system of a human being were not designed to function at that level. That should have been environment enough to slow him down. Would any rational person feel he could do something that all of history said was not within human capability?

But Bannister had internal resources that kept him from tripping over the so-called evidence; he was determined to see for himself. And he pulled in some external resources for support, getting his friends Brasher and Chataway to act as "rabbits." One paced him through the first half mile; then the other gave him an extra challenge in the third quarter.

Bannister broke more than a world record. He broke through a self-limiting attitude. After his feat, runners throughout the world—including several high school students—started recording sub-four-minute miles regularly. The barrier had been more mental than physical, more internal than external, more self-set than biologically set.

PUTTING PASSION AND PREFERENCE TO WORK

In 1979, I got a firsthand demonstration of a challenge to old belief systems and a move beyond self-set limitations. A separate body of evidence not only helped support my findings; it took me a step further and showed how what we found could be put into practice in everyday life.

Our work with peak performers in health care and other fields had attracted some attention, including an invitation for me to keynote an international symposium in Milan. There I met a group of scientists from East Germany, Bulgaria, and the Soviet Union who had been studying optimal achievement for more than thirty years. They indicated that their research had contributed to the Communist bloc's successes in international sports competitions, including the Olympic Games. Since 1956, the USSR and East Germany had pushed aside, summer and winter, the once-traditional United States dominance of the Olympics. In the 1976 summer games the Russians had even won two of the three gold medals in judo that ordinarily went to the Japanese, and East German women won eleven of the possible thirteen medals in swimming. The United States placed third that year in the unofficial national medal count.

The Soviet Union, East Germany, and other Eastern European nations recognize the study of human maximums as a distinct scientific discipline, and as an instrument of national policy. While Americans at the time regarded such study basically as psychology, it was, to the Soviet-bloc scientists' way of thinking, more like physiology and physics. Hence their tendency to characterize themselves as specialists in "psychophysics" and "psychophysiology." The name they had coined for their new discipline is almost impossible to translate adequately. The most literal approximation is "anthropomaximology," a tongue twister for which I will gladly substitute "the study and practice of peak performance."

Their research held implications beyond sports—for education, therapy (they had films of cures for stuttering, for example), and a constellation of other uses. They had even studied survivors of the Nazi death camps. They had been so intrigued by the phenomenon they called "hidden reserves" that they set up rigorous investigations of both physical and psychological capacities of a wide array of high achievers, including athletes, artists, and scientists, as well as Zen masters and yogis. No matter what field they investigated, they found that top achievers could perform beyond the capabilities of average men and women because they had mastered ways to access their hidden reserves. We might say they had found ways to "actualize their human potential."

The Soviet-bloc researchers claimed, quite matter-of-factly, that high performance can be trained—deliberately, systematically, predictably. My heart started to pound. After several days with them I had heard enough theory. I wanted to see some action. They knew of my long-term interest in weight training, that in times past I had developed my strength to world-class levels, and that I still worked out occasionally. So we decided to apply some of their techniques to the nearest and most interested subject: me.

A formal reception sponsored by the mayor of Milan ended

around midnight, and we started searching for a gym with a good set of weights. With no public gym open at that hour, we returned to the hotel, where we got on the telephone and prodded a conference organizer out of bed and asked for his help. He proved most generous and effective. A round of calls produced the desired result. He announced that he had arranged to put the gym in our hotel at our disposal.

It was well past 2:00 A.M. when we assembled around the weight-training equipment in our rumpled formal attire. The Soviets opened several cases they had fetched from their rooms, hooked me up to various measuring devices—EEG for my brain waves, ECG for cardiac activity, EMG for muscular tension—and started doing calculations.

They asked if I was currently in competition or working out regularly. No, I said. I hadn't been in a gym for several months and it had been more than seven years since my last serious training. At that time I had bench-pressed 365 pounds. When I had weighed thirty pounds more, my best lift in the gym was 435. Now I seldom lifted more than 280.

"How long," they asked, "would it take you to get into shape to lift 365 pounds again?" Oh, I said, nine to twelve months of serious training. They talked among themselves for a few minutes, then asked, "What is the absolute maximum you could lift right now?" Well, I was willing to try for 300 pounds, but I hadn't made such a lift in years. "Try it," they said. "This is essential to our demonstration."

To my own surprise, after several warmups I managed to lift the 300 pounds. It was difficult—so difficult that I doubt I could have done it without the mounting excitement in the room. The Soviets then really went to work on another round of measurements and calculations.

Eventually we went on to the next step. They asked me to lie down on my back. Then they guided me into a deep state of relaxation. "Imagine your arms and legs becoming increasingly heavy and warm. . . ." Fully awake and alert, I began to feel more at ease.

When nearly an hour had passed, they asked me to get up slowly and gently. They had added 65 pounds to the 300 I had barely pushed off my chest earlier. Any weight lifter knows that you go up in smaller increments; you just don't make a 21 percent increase all at once. That didn't bother them. Firmly, thoroughly, they talked me through a series of mental preparations. In my mind's eye I saw myself approaching the bench. I visualized myself lying down. I visualized myself, with total confidence, lifting the 365 pounds. I imagined the sounds I would hear, the clink of metal as I tipped the bar and the weights shifted, my own breathing. . . .

Suddenly I became apprehensive. They actually thought I was going to try lifting 365 pounds! I "knew" I could not do it. I knew my limits. The needles on the monitors jerked back and forth, reflecting my anxiety. Patiently, they talked me through more relaxation, more visualization. They asked me to zoom mentally in and out of the images now becoming familiar imprints in my mind: approaching the bar, grasping, lifting smoothly and confidently. All the while, they checked my responses on their monitors and gauges.

At length, everything began to come together for me, just as it does an instant before you know you are going to succeed in some task for which you have been preparing. One more time they talked me through the lift. In my mind I became convinced I could do it. The world around me seemed to fade, giving way to self-confidence, belief in myself, and then to deliberate action.

I lifted the weight.

Astounded, exhilarated by the triumph, I wanted to go on. I felt ready to challenge the world record. But more rational minds prevailed.

"We calculate your present capabilities at somewhere between 345 and 395," the Russians said. "We chose 365 as a midway point. No doubt you could do more, maybe 395, but there are current physical limits that should be respected. You could tear a muscle or tendon. It makes no sense to chance it."

The sun was rising as I returned to my hotel room. I went to bed but I could not sleep. It was so overwhelmingly exciting to make a lift that should have been impossible. What excited me more than my lift was that night's irrefutable evidence of a system for tapping hidden reserves in a dependable manner.

I had seen, not in theory but in practice, that you do not have to wait for external missions and motivation. You can determine a mission for yourself, and you can create the capacity to achieve it. In the process you can greatly exceed your previous levels of performance.

The Soviet-bloc scientists had supplied the one piece of information that had eluded me up to then: There were techniques available to effect major leaps in performance. It is no secret that a person can practice to become a better ballerina or shortstop, even a better decision-maker. This is different. We are not talking here about improvement alone. We are talking about an entirely different order of performance.

The work of the Soviets, East Germans, and Bulgarians dovetailed with my work up to that point. It told me that one can achieve astounding results, not through one approach alone but through intelligent combinations. Passion alone had never been enough. Nor had mindless hard work. A belief in the human potential was not enough by itself. Nor was laboratory science. The human engineering of the Russian "psychophysicists" and "psychophysiologists" worked well enough in athletic contests and demonstrations of technical skill—language learning, some aspects of cosmonaut training, and the like. But would it, alone, make much of a difference in other situations where the crucial skills included initiative, vision, and the capacity for independent action? I think not.

What really works is a marriage of scientific technique and human passion—the engineering approach of the Soviets linked to the mission-oriented characteristics I had studied in Apollo 11, in health care, among athletes and high achievers in business.

WHAT THE SOVIETS PROVIDED WAS A NEW PERSPECTIVE: PRACTICAL, RESEARCH-BASED STRATEGIES AIMED AT ALLOWING ALL OF US TO MAKE MAJOR—NOT MODEST—INCREASES IN PERFORMANCE.

Their research as well as ours revealed that preference is a more accurate predictor of success than aptitude. You don't have to be born specially endowed to deliver superior performance. Certainly there are geniuses like Mozart and Einstein who may have had extraordinary genetic endowments. But the key is not to try to be a Mozart or an Einstein. Rather, it is to be a far more productive version of yourself. Once you have identified a mission that calls you to action, you can train yourself in the skills to succeed in it. Those skills are contained in the six characteristics detailed in the chapters that follow.

The encounter in Milan provided one of those moments of consolidation that Abraham Maslow described when he exclaimed, "I was talking about a *kind* of person, not about non-comparable individuals." As Maslow did, I saw a pattern in one person after another.

Like many breakthroughs, these seem obvious in retrospect. Also obvious are their consequences: the tremendous opportunities for peak performance at all levels—personal, organizational, national—in the increasing complexity of working and living in this century and the next.

A NEW MEASURE OF WORTH: THE PEAK PERFORMER'S TIME HAS COME

The attitudes of people at work have changed drastically since most of us were born. In the 1950s the usual goals were upward mobility and material success. Traditional values showed the way: Work hard now; save for later; delay your pleasures until you can afford them. The 1960s and 1970s saw a desire emerge for more immediate gratification—"I want it now." Much has been said about narcissism and people's turn of attention toward the self. There is, however, a more potent side to the change in the 1980s.

Many people act with more self-reliance than would have been common a decade or two ago. Many, too, are looking for something that motivates, in addition to material gain. Achievement and self-development are now the prime motivators for America's peak performers in business.

In lectures and workshops, I always ask, "If not money, what do you imagine is now the number one reward?" In corporate audiences the answer comes back: "Recognition."

We all know it. People want meaning. We want to know that our work matters, that we are not just "furniture," the word my supervisor George at Grumman used to describe what he felt like before the Apollo program arrived in his life. Going to the moon was mission enough, he and our other colleagues on the Lunar Excursion Module team said, to put meaning in your life, to provide challenge worthy of your best efforts.

Clearly, success on the Apollo team was sanctioned from above, by a President of the United States, by an entire nation's enthusiasm and financial commitment to the technological achievement. John F. Kennedy had said that no project would be so difficult or expensive to accomplish, and that "it will not be one man going to the moon . . . it will be an entire nation."

Back then, no matter what George and the others told me about the power of their environment—"this damn place"—I had suspected that they were also doing something on their own. Now I could see more clearly what it was. They might indeed have been waiting for a mission to come along from outside. Once it did, though, they took advantage of it. They acted, not in opposition to the environment or independent of it, but aligned with it. Once they made the mission their own, they could issue their own call to action. From there, it all began to take shape: results in real time, self-management, teamwork, course correction, change management.

Now, what about the rest of us in everyday life? Do we have to wait for an Apollo mission to come along? No. The high achievers in American business are identifying their own missions, and are charting their critical paths to peak performance.

3

MISSIONS THAT MOTIVATE

Life in the organizations that surround us can look like combat. In fact, Jack Tramiel, who drove other companies out of the home computer market when he ran Commodore and set out to do the same when he moved to archrival Atari, said as much: "Business is war." Maneuvers for promotion, battles for a market, mergers and takeovers, campaigns to upgrade productivity and customer service are conducted by men and women whose energy comes in part from a strong desire to win. Yet it would be a mistake to see competing individuals and companies only as adversaries. Their similarities tell us more about them than their differences.

Many of those similarities stem from the one characteristic that appears in every peak performer I have studied: A sense of mission. Mission is the source of peak performance.

Mission—an image of a desired state of affairs that inspires action—determines behavior and fuels motivation. When you pay attention to someone who is clearly going somewhere, you can soon see at least an approximate statement of that person's mission. We can discern mission statements for people we have met in Chapters 1 and 2. My own is: to discover the principles of high achievement and communicate them to top performers and would-be top performers. Those of others are:

- To bring the satisfactions and benefits of physical and mental fitness to an initially unreceptive public
- To understand the dynamics of organization and use that knowledge to help individuals in organizations gain their objectives
- To develop a loyal team that guides a new product from research to commercial launch, and then sustains the effort
- To transfer the ability to motivate from a career in pro football to a new career in management consulting
- To turn around a failing American company and make it a world leader in its product line

The specific wording of a mission statement helps individuals focus on achievements they most desire. And of course, action expresses it even more clearly. Chester Barnard, a towering management theorist who retired from New Jersey Bell to write and teach at Harvard in the late 1930s, set more store by what executives do than by what they say: "Strictly speaking, purpose is defined more nearly by the aggregate of action taken than by any formulation in words."

Actions express priorities. So among peak performers it is easy to see an underlying passion, not only to achieve but to achieve at progressively higher levels while continually developing their abilities in the process. More than their less-productive peers, the peak performers understand that people can change dramatically, and train themselves for impressive increases in performance. Their method is simple to understand: It consists of sustained effort and commitment to a personally compelling mission.

The challenge of fulfilling a mission can strengthen a wide array of personal characteristics: leadership, collaboration, communication skills, logical problem solving, intuitive pattern recognition, and concentration. Yet studying peak performers compels me to conclude that there is an underlying consistency to all their missions. All have a basic drive:

To *stand out,* to excel in achieving something uniquely one's own that one cares about deeply, and simultaneously to *stand in,* to excel in achieving something important to others (one's organization, team, or family). These are the dual needs of autonomy and affiliation, the twin aspects of mission. With them a peak performer lives a dual life, wanting both the rewards of uniqueness and the pride of belonging (to a good family, a winning team, a strong country, a successful planet).

The anthropologist Ernest Becker traced much of human activity to a burning desire to matter. In examining the dark side of that desire he wrote, "What man really fears is not so much extinction, but extinction with *insignificance.*"

There is more to that desire than fear, however. There is also love—of one's work, of doing well, of expressing essential values, such as "I will be all that I can be. I am going to do my best work." Almost without exception, the peak performers I know conceive their missions as practical expressions of intrinsic values. They say things like:

"I am attracted to unsolved problems, to the unknown."

"Nothing makes me feel better than good workmanship."

"I'm fighting not because I'm hostile but because I want to see this thing turn out right."

"It is a pity for talent to be wasted."

More often than not, they are practical, even shrewd, about the ways in which they put their values to work:

"I like being effective; what gets me really irritated is spinning my wheels and not doing what I'm good at."

They love most the tasks that embody their deepest values. From those values come missions. And from missions come the tasks that call for the most creative, productive efforts.

THE CALL TO ACTION: FROM VISION TO REALITY

The competitive world is full of dramas such as that of Apple Computer and IBM, apparently a David squaring off against a Goliath—an upstart $1.5 billion company and a mammoth $43 billion institution vying to increase their share of the personal computer market. Go back to the beginnings, though, and you see that both organizations exist in their present form not so much because of world economic fluctuations, or the "invisible hand" of the marketplace, but because of three individual human beings. The Apple founders, Steven Jobs and Stephen Wozniak, were in their twenties when they made their move. The IBM founder, Thomas Watson, Sr., was in his fifties before he started making his impact. Regardless of age, each had a mission, and each knew how to translate mission into reality.

They did what others can learn to do. They saw beyond the probable by envisioning the possible: a state of affairs that they desired to bring about, and believed in. Then they found their place, took a stand. By acting on their view of the possible with a clear sense of purpose, they created a work environment in which other people could share their commitment, and in which commitment was the norm, not the exception.

Peak performers take the time to assess their actions and their motives, setting aside the nonessential, until they isolate the mission, the essence of their commitment, that will sustain them through the roughest times. Their sense of mission is the beacon that keeps them on the critical path to where they are going.

But what got Jobs and Wozniak and Watson going? What sustained the energy and perseverance that we associate with *mission* and often experience as *motivation*? The three computer company founders clearly belong to that class of self-starters who manage to motivate themselves without waiting for someone else to push or pull them into action. John Gardner, the social theorist and activist who founded Common Cause, writes:

> Everyone has noted the astonishing sources of energy that seem available to those who enjoy what they are doing or find meaning in what they are doing. The self-renewing man knows that if he has no great conviction about what he is doing he had better find something that he can have great conviction about. Obviously all of us cannot spend all of our time pursuing our deepest convictions. But everyone, either in his career or as a part-time activity, should be doing *something* about which he

cares deeply. And if he is to escape the prison of the self, it must be something not essentially egocentric in nature.

At IBM, Thomas Watson, Sr., imagined the specifics of what we now call a computer fifteen years before the term was coined. His vision was not that of an inventor; the significance of the early computers he sponsored was not in their hardware or engineering. He saw instead the role of *data processing* and *information,* terms that had much different meanings to him than they did to other people of his time, in pulling an entire culture from the farms and small towns of the nineteenth century to the technological sophistication of the urban world we now inhabit. The company Watson joined as general manager in 1914, when he was forty, made meat slicers, grocery store scales, time clocks, and primitive tabulators known as punch card machines. Ten years later he gave his little Computing-Tabulating-Recording Company the grand new name of International Business Machines Corporation, a name to match his mission.

The mission was actually not to build computers. It was to build a philosophy of management and service: Hard work pays off. Company loyalty makes a difference. Precepts such as those go right along with the mottoes Watson promoted in laying the foundation for IBM: *Think. Be better than average. Serve and sell.* The great management theorist and adviser Peter Drucker asserts:

> Watson . . . was a uniquely American type and one the Establishment has never understood throughout our history. He was possessed of a towering intellect but was totally non-intellectual. . . . Typically the men of this type have a gift for words—and Watson fully shared it. But they are not men of ideas. They are men of vision. What makes them important is that, like Watson, they act on their vision.

Fifty years after Watson started re-shaping IBM, Steven Jobs and Stephen Wozniak set out on their mission: to build a computer so advanced that it would actually be simple to use. Theirs was not the first computer you could take home and plug in. As far back as 1962, Digital Equipment Corporation had built a relatively small computer, but it could hardly be considered a home item; it cost $43,600. Engineers at other companies, including IBM, designed machines that never got to market. By 1975, though, any hobbyist with a soldering iron and $397 could get the Altair 8800 from a company called MITS in Albuquerque. The Altair had no keyboard or monitor, no software, and one had to be technically inclined, or at least industrious, to get anything out of it. You programmed it by flipping switches on its front panel. The Altair started the rush. In 1977, Radio Shack—a well-established company with a bigger network of outlets than McDonald's—produced the TRS-80, complete with keyboard, monitor, and software. And in the same year, two kids—raising money by selling a VW bus (Jobs's) and a few calculators (Wozniak's), working in a garage—produced the Apple II.

Wozniak and Jobs were convinced that their computer—"personal" and friendly as its name, by contrast to the equipment that preceded it—could become as familiar an object as a telephone or an apple, and would then transform the nature of work and creativity. Wozniak designed it. Jobs sold it. Six years after they founded their company, Jobs persuaded the president of domestic operations of PepsiCo Inc. to leave an established career in soft drinks and fast foods for the presidency of Apple. Part of the enticement for the new Apple president, John Sculley, was Jobs's challenge, putting the original vision into words: "If you come to Apple, you can change the world." Jobs may not have realized at that moment that in choosing a peak performer committed to results, he was also choosing a man who would change Apple.

SEEING WHERE TO GO, SAYING HOW YOU'LL GET THERE

There is nothing especially logical about what Jobs said to Sculley. (One person change the world? Rational arithmetic says one out of 4.5 billion is too small a fraction to matter. Even if you tone down the hyperbole to one person playing a significant role with several thousand others, the fraction still appears insignificant.)

But the statement reflects precisely the first move one makes in constructing a powerful mission: exercising *vision.* You see something you want so passionately that it calls forth your wholehearted commitment. And with the statement to Sculley, Jobs demonstrated a second essential move: phrasing a *mission statement,* translating the vision into language that inspired him and others.

Great accomplishments are always the result of imagination translated through words and action plans. The interplay between vision and the action steps that follow it can constitute a peak performer's working life. A marketing strategy, new sales prospects, product designs, often come as "flashes." Then the challenge is to analyze the flash and devise the steps that will make use of it.

Developing a mission, therefore, means seeing a pattern in the things and thoughts that get you moving; assessing your resources; then formulating your feelings into words. It means bringing together two major components: visual and verbal.

Excellent companies and outstanding individuals always keep the visual element alive in the ways they state their mission, often conveying it to great effect through images and metaphors. A leader is photographed in the company of other leaders in national politics and business. People on the job get production awards and other reminders that they are engaged in important matters. The Arthur Andersen accounting firm recently produced a seventieth-anniversary brochure that placed key events in company history side by side with key events in the nation's history: The first Arthur Andersen training school opened in the decade that the United Nations charter was signed; the Mexico City office opened in 1955, and in that decade Sputnik precipitated the space race.

Such individuals and companies look back for a sense of where they have been that will influence where they are going. They also look forward. By definition, of course, mission moves toward the future. On the Apollo project, a number of us worked for some time in a building as large as an airplane hangar. On its walls were enormous pictures of the moon. Those posters summed up in one direct hit what we were doing there. More recently, since the AT&T divestiture, people at the new communications companies have been searching for missions under new pressures to sell and deliver services that were once taken for granted. Ted Vodde, a supervisor in marketing, is in his mid-thirties and sees an exciting career ahead of him at Bellsouth Services. During a meeting of the company's top marketing people in Sandestin, Florida, he told me of a mission he found worth believing in:

> I really get excited when I realize we will be implementing a data plug system in the not too distant future—plugs in everyone's home that connect to a home computer, appliances, stores, banks. . . . I can see having a robot at home so that if I am tired at the end of the day I can call my home system from the office and say, "Hello, Homer, it's Ted. Look, I'm beat. Please have my favorite chicken dinner ready in forty-five minutes, with chocolate chip ice cream for dessert. Oh, and remind me to watch the Celtics-Hawks basketball game this evening; I don't want to forget. Thanks, Homer, I'll be home soon."

Warren Bennis, one of the nation's leading management theorists, says of the images that often give missions their motivational power:

> It's the imagery that creates the understanding, the compelling moral necessity that the new way is right. . . . It was the beautiful writing of Darwin about his travels on the *Beagle,* rather than the content of his writing, that made the difference . . . the evolutionary idea had really been in the air for a while.

MISSION LEADS TO ACTION

Whether they are focusing on family, developing talents, or getting to the top of a particular field, peak performers refine their capacity to see clearly what they want and to state it in terms that motivate. The mission statement provides the *why* that inspires every *how.* It points the way. Then comes action, and in peak performance it is action based on a long view. Peak performers want more than merely to win the next game. They see all the way to the championship.

Lane Nemeth recently issued herself a challenge, saying that she wants to head a billion-dollar corporation before she dies. The thought probably had not occurred to her when she started a toy distribution company in her garage near San Francisco in 1977. At the time, she was reacting to a personal need; as she discovered that thousands of other people had that same need, the mission took on its present dimensions.

While directing a state-funded day care center south of San Francisco, Nemeth found it easy to obtain educational toys from catalogues. But as the mother of a baby girl, she found that retail stores did not carry the quality toys she used at her job. How to get those well-designed learning toys into the hands of people who wanted them? That became her mission. She put together a line of fifty toys and borrowed an idea from Tupperware and Avon: Go to people's homes and have display parties. This was more than just a selling strategy. The home demonstration allowed the parents to learn how to use the toys with their children. That did not happen in retail stores.

Nemeth started with three salespeople. With no advertising except word of mouth, gross sales of Discovery Toys went from $273,600 the first year to more than $35 million in 1984. Nemeth turned her mission to distribute toys that "develop a child's curiosity, creativity, and intellect" into a success for herself and her associates. Nemeth told me that initially her goal was to affect the way parents bring up their children. But as the company grew, she saw how it began to affect the lives of women as well. In 1985 the Discovery Toys sales force consisted of ten thousand "educational consultants"—independent businesspeople, primarily women, some of whom earned more than $200,000 a year.

In every organization that does things unusually well, I see people all the way up and down the line operating with a strong sense of mission. Long-range missions guide shorter-range objectives. Both in turn lead to high-quality action.

A senior vice-president of an aerospace company in Southern California piqued my curiosity one afternoon as we talked about a series of workshops I had just conducted for his managers and technical people. Developing a sense of mission makes sense at the middle and higher levels of a company, he said. But he suggested that there must be levels at which peak performance is just impossible because people have so little control of their circumstances.

"For instance," he said, "there's a group here that puzzles me. They maintain the pipes in our thermodynamics plant, checking temperatures and pressures. The situation makes me nervous. On the one hand, the enormous cost of the parts we test and the delicacy of the equipment means the pipes have to work within strict tolerances or there will be expensive damage. On the other hand, the work is mechanical and repetitive; essentially it's plumbing, and it seems impossible to me that anybody would find it even interesting, much less an occasion for peak performance. But here is the surprise: This group's attendance record is terrific; they have the lowest turnover in the entire company; their motivation is obviously high; their productivity and performance are excellent. How come?"

I went to visit the department. Sam Harrison, the foreman, gave me a tour. At one point I asked why all his people wore green surgical smocks. "Oh, you noticed," Harrison said. "I got them from my son. He's a cardiovascular surgeon, and he got them so I could give them to the gang." "Ah," I said, "you wear them for comfort."

"No, no!" Harrison said. "It's because we are surgeons. Just like my son. He takes care of pipes in the body—you're worried about a heart attack, my son works on your arteries. We take care of pipes in this plant. It isn't going to have any breakdowns as long as we're working on its arteries. We take care of these pipes the way a doctor takes care of your heart."

Sure enough, the stencils on their locker doors said DR., and Sam used the title—with a grin—as he introduced his colleagues. Their statement of their mission—"take care of these pipes the way a doctor takes care of your heart"—matched its importance. The way they spoke to one another, the mixed humor and pride with which they used surgery as their metaphor, helped them to share the special value that their work had for them.

The meaning they constructed was not illusion. They had devised a way to keep themselves at a peak of performance in a job that offered little glamour or daily stimulation, and their entire company shared the benefits.

ALIGNING MISSIONS: INDIVIDUAL AND ORGANIZATION

In recent decades America developed a folklore of heroes from sports, science, the performing arts and the military, with very few from business. Organizations, so central to the way we conduct the business that shapes our lives, became known as quicksand for the individual spirit. Sloan Wilson's *The Man in the Gray Flannel Suit* in 1955 made Madison Avenue a symbol of the rat race, and William H. Whyte's *The Organization Man* in 1956 showed the organization—corporation, economy, community—pressing its members to show their loyalty through self-denial.

Now, however, entrepreneurs and intrapreneurs (the internal entrepreneurs who pull together diverse strengths within their organizations to promote innovation) are the new stars. These are people who refuse to be cowed by the old image of the organization crushing the life out of its employees. Instead, they see the organization and its members creating life together. Rather than subjugate whatever personal mission they may have to the mission of the organization, or sabotage the organization's mission by substituting their personal one for it, they find ways to align the two. Sam Harrison's "surgeons" sculpted for themselves a personal mission that supported their company's mission.

ALIGNMENT IS THE KEY TO STANDING OUT WHILE STANDING IN.

People who were once supposed to be engulfed and depleted by organizations are now using those organizations to extend individual, distinctive missions toward peak performance. Alignment occurs when individuals perceive that contributing to an organization produces direct contributions to their personal mission. The more opportunities an organization gives its people to align their missions with its own, the more likely it is to survive and succeed.

Minnesota Mining and Manufacturing, which ranks high on

Fortune magazine's surveys of the most admired firms among America's largest, regularly comes up with more than its share of profitable new products. It is company policy to measure the results of innovation, and actually to *require* it. At least 25 percent of sales in every 3M division each year must come from products introduced within the last five years. Toward that end, employees can spend 15 percent of their office time on independent projects.

This is a story often told, but like a legend it bears retelling: Arthur Fry, a 3M chemical engineer, knew that Spencer Silver, a scientist there, had accidentally discovered an adhesive with very low sticking power. Normally that would be bad. For Fry, musing about it on company time, it was good. Pieces of paper he used to mark his place in his church hymnal always fell out when he stood up to sing, and that annoyed him. He figured that markers with a strip of the adhesive on the back would stick lightly to something and would come off easily. He made some samples, gave them to secretaries to try out, and 3M eventually began selling his little yellow pads under the name Post-it. Sales in 1984 topped $100 million.

Peak performers are not William Whyte's Organization Men. As Charles Kiefer and Peter Stroh of the management training firm Innovation Associates observe, "They do not give up their personal identity for an organizational one. They transcend it. Who they are becomes inextricably linked to a higher purpose to which they and their organization are committed."

MISSIONS FROM THE INDIVIDUAL

An individual with a mission can help make a larger company mission come to life. In first-rate factories, lively product development groups, superb accounting departments, we are likely to find that the source of excellence is peak performers who never assume that they are powerless. Even in organizations that others perceive as hopelessly complex and unresponsive, the peak performers retain a sense that they control their own actions. Jim Gray at Pacific Bell: "I give a businessman my card, telling him I would take care of his problem. When I go and talk to an engineer or one of my peers on the business side, sometimes they don't understand that I really am going to get back to that person when I said I would. . . . Sometimes I have to become almost animalistic in the way I speak to the phone company guy to let him know I'm serious: 'You'd better call him back! I gave this guy my *word*! He's been talking to clerks in a twenty-five-story building on Ventura Boulevard and getting jerked around. I just told the man, "Hey, I'm the last one. Call me up and I'll help you. If I don't know the answer, I'll direct you to the person who will get your job done." ' I walk out of the guy's office and say to myself. 'You're not going to mess it up.' "

The plumber "surgeons" at the aerospace company had none of the misgivings about their work that plagued their more detached senior VP. He worried about what they could possibly see in their environment that would provide a mission, while all along they were finding the source of their mission not in the outside environment but inside themselves—in their own sense of values and sense of humor and commitment to doing their job right.

An easy way to understand this kind of alignment is to look at an athlete's effort and contribution to a team. For both individual and organization, the mission may be the same: to be the best. The individual wants the team to succeed because it provides the context for his or her own personal achievement. Obviously, the presence of such committed individuals improves the odds that the organization will succeed. An individual whose mission is aligned with an organization's mission, keeps tabs on whether that organization is staying on track. That is especially true when the individual happens to be the founding entrepreneur.

Lars-Eric Lindblad's innovations have influenced the shape of the modern travel industry. He organized Lindblad Travel, the company he now runs from Westport, Connecticut, in 1958. Deciding that adventurous trips to offbeat destinations—the Gobi Desert, Antarctica, Patagonia, the Galapagos Islands—might be the wave of the future, he decided "to make adventure travel available to the general public. The age of discovery may be over in the larger sense. But for the average person it has hardly begun. I believe in freedom, creativity, and conversation. And further I believe that tourism is the handmaiden of them all." Lindblad followed his beliefs, and more than 170,000 clients have followed him to many parts of the world which, until he came, had been visited only rarely by outsiders.

Lindblad's success stems directly from his excitement about his life and his work, which to him are synonymous—not because he is a workaholic and cannot stop working but because he is aware of what he enjoys doing and has tailored from it a mission for himself. "People do not want merely to be tourists," he says. "They want to *know;* they want to *do.* Looking is passive. It's action that counts."

On one trip through the Indonesian Islands west of Bali, Lindblad's *Explorer* was the first cruise ship ever to enter the area, and as it pulled up to a smallish island, the captain became almost ecstatic. "This is not on my chart," he told the passengers. "We have discovered a new island." He sketched the coastline, sent a boat ashore to ask the inhabitants what they called their home, and sent the information to London. The tourists knew that when the next charts were published, this place would appear on them for the first time. "Now," asks Neil Morgan, editor of the San Diego *Tribune* and a longtime Lindblad friend who was there, "how many tour operators offer their clients that kind of experience?"

MISSIONS FROM THE ORGANIZATION

We do see numerous companies whose missions distinctly empower the individuals who work there.

Cray Research is such an organization. At the Minneapolis headquarters of his company, which builds the world's biggest and fastest computers, chairman and CEO John Rollwagen says, "We have always found that people are most productive in small teams with tight budgets, time deadlines, and the freedom to solve their own problems." Cray is, however, a place that most of its 2,500 employees find exciting, partly because of the challenge of building supercomputers used for immensely complex tasks in astrophysics, simulating nuclear power generation, and global weather forecasting—and partly because management promotes the practical side of mission.

At Cray, teams of people depend on one another for ideas, problem-solving, and follow-through. The process forms a perfect circle from individual to team and back to individual: The most productive team is the one in which every individual is important, and in which every individual is at the same time committed to the common mission of the team.

Within a Cray X-MP-I computer is a cylindrical mat about a foot thick, four feet in diameter, and five feet high, made of some seventy miles of handwoven copper wire. It takes three shifts of four people working three months to wire the more than 100,000 connections in a Cray. Many of the computers have been completed without a single mistake. Rollwagen points out that this is not only a source of deep pride for the wiring teams; it also has a direct impact on the company as a whole. A Cray X-MP-I rents for $200,000 a month, and a computer that passes inspection rapidly and is ready for early delivery saves costs and boosts revenues. With profit sharing, everyone in the company benefits from excellence that is, at its heart, a matter of personal satisfaction for members of the wiring team.

We have observed many times that an effective mission statement of a company bears a striking resemblance to the mission statement of a peak-performing individual.

Dayton Hudson, a large department-store chain headquartered in Minneapolis, tells its 88,000 employees that the company is, simply and concretely, "purchasing agent for its customers." The mission statement of such a company reflects its distinctive view of its commitments. Behind Dayton Hudson's apparently humble statement is a profitable reordering of the usual corporate priorities, which generally put making money for shareholders at the top of the list. Dayton Hudson sees its constituencies, in order, as:

customers
employees
shareholders
community

Attention to customers puts the company above $5 billion in annual sales. With a corporate staff of only 250, the company emphasizes employee participation in running its local operations. The shareholders benefit from the first two priorities, as they do from the fourth; Dayton Hudson is a founder of the Minnesota 5% Club, composed of corporations that give at least 5 percent of their pretax earnings to local social programs, investing in the proposition that its long-term profitability is linked to the well-being of communities in which it operates.

Similarly, at Cray Research, explicit statements of the company mission help keep individuals humming with a spirit of people engaged in a significant and daring undertaking. John Rollwagen sees the setting of "audacious tasks" as central to this spirit. Further, he believes that the audacious can be *easier* for an organization to achieve than the more mundane:

> Such a vision creates an environment that takes people beyond day-to-day problems. It creates enormous excitement. While this seems very risky, it's not really, because people are focused on a single purpose, and they know that there's no backup. . . . If we lost track of our overriding purpose, all the other things we do would not be enough to guarantee our success.

Cray's board of directors states their company's goal very simply: "Developing the world's most advanced computing systems." They expand on how they intend to reach it in a one-page mission statement that says in part:

> The company knows achievement of its mission is dependent on its employees. . . . We want to make Cray Research an exciting and rewarding place to work, a place where employees can experience achievement as individuals *and* as productive teams.

After spending a day with a team of corporate staff people, managers and engineers from their western regional office in California, I saw that Cray presents, both on paper and in actual behavior, one of the clearest and most motivating examples of mission I had ever encountered. The clarity of the written statements, and the way the men and women there incorporated them into the exciting spirit of the group, made me almost want to join the team myself. They gave me a copy of the Cray Style Statement which managers, employees, and directors had composed together as a statement of philosophy to back up the company mission statement:

> We . . . have a strong sense of quality—quality in our product and services, of course, but also quality in our working environment, in the people we work with, in the tools that we use to do our work, and in the components we choose to make what we make.
>
> . . . Cray Research is many things to many people. The consistency comes in providing those diverse people with the opportunity to fulfill themselves and experience achievement. The creativity, then, that emerges from the company comes from the many ideas of the individuals who are here.

FORMULATING A MISSION

Peak performers create their own missions. They do it by first determining what they truly care about, then devoting themselves to that pursuit.

In creating workable missions, there are guideposts. Among those with whom I have worked, half a dozen predictors of success appear repeatedly:

- Putting preference before expertise
- Drawing on the past
- Trusting intuition
- Having no preconceived limitations
- Combining profit with contribution
- Being pulled by values

These predictors have multiple uses. First, of course, is to help a person construct his or her own mission statement. They serve as a way to monitor motivation. They provide a checklist for decisions about career paths. And they can provide guidelines for other practical situations, such as staffing and hiring. When you ask job candidates what they want to accomplish, you can hear the strength of their sense of mission in the fit between their responses and the predictors.

Putting Preference Before Expertise. One of my favorite statements is Goethe's:

> Whatever you can do, or dream you can, begin it.
> Boldness has genius, power, and magic in it.

Donald Burr was thirty-eight when he and two colleagues made a bold and, some said at the time, outlandish move on April 7, 1980. Those were tough times for airlines. An abandoned terminal in Newark, New Jersey, was hardly a prestige address. But, figuring, "If you respect people and give them a good deal, they'll use the hell out of it," Burr and his associates started a no-frills airline. Burr had already been president of two companies—National Aviation Corp., an investment firm in New York, and Texas International Airlines in Houston—before founding People Express, a new commercial carrier whose name, in his opinion, put first things first. People Express was soon the fastest-growing airline in aviation history.

Burr based his strategy on keeping expenses low and pricing tickets far below those of major competitors. An extraordinary esprit de corps among the airline's "team members" (known in other companies as employees) grew in part from his insistence on each one's owning stock, with the company's help if necessary, and on the leanest possible management structure: Every team member does several jobs. When pilots are not flying, they come in and work in scheduling and recruiting. People Express grew from 250 employees to more than 3,000 in its first two and a half years; from three Boeing 737's making 24 flights a day to thirty-two big jets, including a 747, making 264 flights daily; from a start-up loss of $9.2 million on $38.4 million in revenues in 1981 to a net of $12 million on revenues of $236 million in 1983; to running the largest single airport operation in the New York metropolitan area.

Revenues hit a snag in 1984 and early 1985, as expansion and awakened competition from older airlines produced quarterly losses. Peak performers seldom have it easy. What they do have is an ability to correct course when they hit a snag, and to keep in sight the pattern that connects all their actions: their mission.

As a child in South Windsor, Connecticut, Burr discovered that whenever he did something he liked, he did it well. He liked airplanes so much that he would talk his parents into taking him to the nearby airport on Sundays so he could spend hours in wide-eyed admiration. There was one more thing he liked: business. "I used to go into the candy store," he once said. "I thought I could never do that—run a store, order all those things. Kids would talk about Mickey Mantle hitting home runs. . . . I've always wanted to know how you put [a store] together."

Through Harvard Business School and a career in which he did, in fact, pick up expertise in what it takes to start and run a commercial airline, Burr never lost the enthusiasm that comes from staying with his preferences. His friends often say he could have been a preacher—because of the energy and fervor with which he speaks, implores, jokes, and persuades in his business conversations. In all three of the companies he has headed, he has never strayed far from his feeling about airplanes and candy stores.

There are signs that the healthy airlines of the future will resemble People Express. Employees at Eastern have appeared in television commercials as "owners" of their company. Flight attendants at United used to have supervisors who scheduled their trips; now they schedule themselves. The trucking and rail industries are copying many of the airlines' innovations.

On the other side of the world, Maryles Casto knew she wanted to travel. When she moved from the Philippines to the United States in 1965, she promised her father she would visit once a year. "So I had to get a job with an airline or a travel agency," she recalls. First she worked for Philippine Airlines, supervising two hundred flight attendants. Settling in San Jose, California, with her husband, she then worked at a series of travel agencies. After rising to the level of office manager at a large British-owned firm, Casto asked that her husband be allowed to travel with her. Request denied.

In 1974, Casto and a friend put together $3,000, bought some desks, rented a small office in nearby Los Altos, and set up their own company to go after the jet-hopping executives of Silicon Valley, "Because I knew that's where the business would be. I wanted to be the biggest and the best." By 1981 Casto Travel was located in a luxurious new office complex. According to a spokesperson, the company grossed $30 million in 1984.

Clearly, we do not see in the Donald Burrs and Maryles Castos a demonstration of self-indulgence or merely following whims. We see a much-neglected form of discipline: determining what one truly cares about *and following through.* Malcolm Forbes, Sr., of *Forbes* magazine has said, "Part of growing up is realizing that you don't need expertise—you just need to want to, and then do it. Enthusiasm, not expertise, is the requisite."

"Then doing it" takes discipline. Peak performers hardly stumble into success unwittingly. Nolan Bushnell, founder of Atari and a host of other electronics-based businesses, points out: "Everyone who's ever taken a shower has an idea. It's the person who gets out of the shower, dries off and does something about it who makes a difference."

As Warren Bennis and other students of management confirm, putting preference before expertise in business has nothing to do with "humanizing the workplace," with Theory X or Theory Y or "participative management." It has to do with concentrating on what you hold to be serious acts, on seeing a connection between your mission and the ideas and institutions that make up your society, on being, as Bennis puts it, "near the heart of things."

The mission that allows its creator to work near the heart of things—in launching a new line of polycarbonate products, in providing superb service to business travelers, in bringing to market a highly successful pad of adhesive papers—is what motivates and empowers peak performers.

Mission starts with determining what you really care about and want to accomplish, and committing yourself to it. You can always develop expertise. First, discover your preference.

Drawing on the Past. Peak performers are adept in the art of replay. They mentally review their past successes and analyze what worked in times past to overcome obstacles, both personal and organizational. They ask and answer questions for themselves such as:

- When did I experience intense concentration and awareness? Feelings of joy and celebration?
- Where did it happen? Where was I?
- Was I working alone or on a team? As a leader or a team member?
- Was I performing some service? To whom?
- Was I an innovator? Of what?
- Did I champion an idea? A product? A service?
- Who was there to witness my success?
- What activities have given me a powerful sense of purpose? When have I felt deeply committed to:
  Another person?
  An idea, product, team?
  Developing a particular skill?
  Why?
- What did I learn from each experience?
- What benefits remain with me?
- How did it feel while it was happening?

The composite of answers distilled from these past successes yields clues to a mission.

When Victor Kiam took an ordinary product, an electric shaver, and parlayed it into worldwide prominence for Remington and himself, he was not starting from scratch. After his successful stint selling toothpaste for Lever Brothers, he went to Playtex, where he sold girdles. As marketing director there, he was asked to help the company enter a market new for it: brassieres. Borrowing an idea that had worked well for his former employer, Kiam decided to offer a free bra to anyone who mailed in a coupon, plus a dollar for handling. Thousands of women figured the "living bra" was worth trying, and Playtex had a winner.

It was also Kiam who boldly took bra advertising into television. His cross-your-heart commercials helped push sales to $400 million by the time he left Playtex in 1968. Drawing on such past successes gave Kiam not only a set of positive expectations for himself but also specific strategies and tactics that allowed him to speak with confidence in convincing Sperry that he could turn around its floundering Remington division. He did, and now his clean-shaven face appears on television screens in dozens of countries.

Another innovator who drew his mission from past successes is Earl Nightingale. Together with businessman Lloyd Conant, this radio broadcaster founded a company that has become the world's leading distributor of self-improvement information on audio cassettes. Nightingale was the voice of Sky King, a flying cowboy hero on early radio serials; by the 1950s he had moved on to establish himself as a "worldly philosopher" with his commentary of daily radio broadcasts in the Midwest. He kept a 40 percent commission from all advertising he sold for his shows. With the proceeds he bought an insurance agency; his talent for inspiring and motivating his sales force made it, too, a lucrative business.

In 1956, Nightingale announced that he was going on vacation and would be unavailable for several weeks. The agency manager asked him to record a message to the staff that could be used as a pep talk while he was gone. Nightingale thought about it for a couple of weeks, then one morning about four o'clock he jumped up and typed out "The Strangest Secret," a talk in which he defined success as "the progressive realization of a worthy ideal." He recorded it and gave it to the manager. By the time he returned from his fishing trip, dozens of requests for copies had piled up. No one then had cassette tape recorders, so he put the talk on a 33⅓ rpm record. Within a year, he was selling two thousand of the records a week.

Nightingale recognized his talents as a motivator and teacher and amplified them through his radio broadcasts and records. When audio cassettes and handy players became common in the late 1960s, he and entrepreneur Lloyd Conant realized they had the technology to send their motivational message worldwide. Drawing on the success of his own past, Nightingale decided to put other motivational speakers on audio cassette to reach that market. Today the Chicago-based Nightingale-Conant Corporation is recognized as the leader in the field of audio information by direct mail.

Peak performers draw on times in the past when they felt truly committed and ask themselves what it was about those situations that drew the best out of them.

Trusting Intuition. Six chief executive officers of major companies interviewed by researchers Harry Levinson and Stuart Rosenthal all expressed the same regret. Walter Wriston of First National City Bank; Thomas J. Watson, Jr., of IBM; Reginald Jones of General Electric; Arthur Sulzberger, Jr., of *The New York Times;* John Hanley of Monsanto; and Ian K. MacGregor of AMAX each said that he had not followed his intuition as frequently as he could have.

The "gut feeling" that every peak performer learns to recognize is not the opposite or the adversary of logical thought. It is, rather, a powerful complement to it. From their studies of skills acquisition, Hubert Dreyfus, a philosopher, and Stuart Dreyfus, a computer scientist, brothers who teach at the University of California, Berkeley, describe "everyday, nonmystical intuition" as a learned response based on past experience—the kind of experience that comes from being an expert in any field, from playing chess to playing golf, from conducting a meeting to flying an airplane. After interviewing fighter pilots and studying chess masters, they concluded that only novices feel bound by formal rules. As they gain proficiency, people act with increasing flexibility on the basis of context and experience. Expert pilots, for example, do not think of themselves as making an airplane go up, down, right, left: they think of it simply as flying. Chess masters do not analyze hundreds of memorized board positions; they sense the right move in what is spread out before them. They are guided both by analytic thought and by the intangible, which few can describe and nobody can diagram, called intuition.

A context for all you will do—a mission—emerges from wholes, not from parts. You link intuition with analysis to choose between competing options; you progressively refine the choices. There comes a moment at which you move beyond analyzing the pieces to seeing a pattern.

The philosopher Bertrand Russell wrote, "The sense of certainty and revelation comes before any definite belief." That is, a kind of knowing on the level of deep feeling comes before the concepts and words that you can comfortably use to describe what you know. The writer Colin Wilson cites Plotinus in observing:

> Vision needs no special gift or effort, but only the use of a faculty which all possess but few employ. That is to say, this "other mode" of consciousness is not in any way remote from everyday consciousness; it lies right at the side of it, only a fraction of a millimetre away. It is seen, like a lightning flash, in all moments of joy and relief, as our deliberately limited left-brain perception is replaced by a wider pattern.

The point is not just philosophical. It is practical. Martin Allen and his family were going through the Smithsonian Institution in 1964 when they stopped at a display of George Washington's tools. Allen was struck by the impression that drafting equipment had not changed much in two hundred years. In one of those flashes of inspiration from which entire industries can spring, he wondered, "Why not link the computer to product design? Now it's a long and excruciatingly costly process that can eat up 40 percent of the R&D dollar. Letting designers make modifications on visual displays instead of a drawing board or a model could drastically shorten the cycles for developing and manufacturing new products. It could be an enormous breakthrough." It was. Allen founded Computervision Corporation, the nation's largest producer of CAD/CAM (computer aided design, computer aided manufacturing) technology.

The ingredients were there. Somebody had to see a pattern, and see the connections in it. Often such connections depend as much on poetic sense as on logic. Francis Crick and James Watson, codiscoverers of the structure of DNA, told each other at lunch on the day they knew they had the answer: "A structure this pretty just has to exist."

An intuitive feel for the way something fits, for its natural "rightness," accelerates the creation of a mission that has power and workability.

Having No Preconceived Limitations. Before Ted Turner became the "Captain Outrageous" who successfully defended the America's Cup, bought the Atlanta Braves and Hawks, and created the first twenty-four-hour television news network on his way to building a communications empire, he was a young man whose course of study at college appalled his hard-driving father.

"I am a practical man," Ed Turner wrote to his son at Brown University, "and for the life of me I cannot understand why you should wish to speak Greek." It was not so much to speak it that Ted chose to study the Greek classics. It was to make closer contact with the mythical heroes who had inspired him as a teenager. Turner left college before completing that particular course of study, but the impulse that took him there is clear: Heroes have a mission and they expect to overcome all obstacles in fulfilling it.

Turner is a colorful figure in the worlds of television and sports—a maverick, some say—yet for hard work and faith in his own vision, he has few peers. He declared in an interview in 1984: "I just love it when people say I can't do something . . . because all my life people have said I wasn't going to make it."

Peak performers consistently maintain their conviction of their mission's value and their ability. In even the darkest moments they remain optimistic. They persevere.

When the great running back Herschel Walker played football at Georgia, sportscasters took to expressing admiration for his maneuverability and power with remarks about his "tremendous natural ability." The 6 foot 1, 225-pound Walker, then and when he joined the New Jersey Generals, was an imposing athlete—but always a natural? When he was in junior high school, hoping to play football, he was told by a kindly coach: "Herschel, you're too small. Go try out for track." Walker's response was to undertake a training program—calisthenics, running, stretching, eating carefully—to build himself into an All-American football player and Heisman Trophy winner. He said of his success: "My God-given talent is my ability to stick with it longer than anyone else."

Limitations are often set by fears of failure, and peak performers grant those fears very little power. Our study of peak performers turns up qualities similar to those found by other investigators—for instance, Warren Bennis in a study of ninety leaders in business, politics, sports, and the arts, including sixty board chairmen and CEOs of major corporations. These people often see their abilities and capacities as essentially unlimited because they are confident, not arrogant or reckless. With their attention on achieving their mission, the word *failure* seldom enters a conversation unless someone else brings it in. The scores of synonyms for it—glitch, bug, hitch, miss, bungle, false start, to name just a few—convey their view that what someone else might call a failure is something from which they intend to learn. As one of them said, "A mistake is simply another way of doing things."

Mission is bound by no preconceived limitations. It inspires people to reach for what could be, and to rise above their fears and preoccupations with what is.

Combining Profit with Contribution. "Doing well by doing good" is a way to say that you cannot separate a company from its context. Returning value to the community that supports you, whether you are an individual or an organization, is good business.

William C. Norris, who founded Control Data Corporation in 1957 and built it into a $4.3 billion international computer and software manufacturer, makes the point repeatedly to his 56,000 employees: "You can't be effective if you're just giving money away. But if you focus on [your connections with the community] as business opportunities, then you're really making the capitalist system work."

Control Data opened a plant in Shelby, a depressed suburb of St. Paul, in 1970. The abandoned bowling alley turned packaging plant became a model facility. Norris's strategy was to take advantage of the fact that many of Shelby's residents were female heads of household who could not leave home for full-time jobs, but would do well in part-time jobs that required unique kinds of concentration. The investment was sound. Control Data tapped an abundant pool of eager, available workers who became loyal to and protective of the company. In return, the effect was to inject hope and vitality into depressed neighborhoods. Other businesses opened near the packaging plant. During the next fifteen years Control Data moved five other plants to inner cities and provided basic skills and training for more than five thousand people. Other social programs include computer-based education offered in twenty prisons; one hundred small-business centers; and complete economic packages for depressed neighborhoods, both urban and rural. Norris is quick to point out that "companies have to assume social responsibility . . . because it has been demonstrated that the government is unable to. Things have gotten worse, taxes have gone up, and as a result, business gets it in the neck."

So business can save its own neck by looking out for other people's. Several studies have been done to test the correlation of social responsiveness and financial growth. In 1983, Dr. Ritchie Lowry at Boston College checked the performance of thirty companies he judged to be "socially conscious" over an eight-year period. He found that the companies on his list performed 106 percent better in capital gains on Dow Jones listings than did other, older blue chips. Lowry found no simple cause-and-effect relationship, but it seems clear that a company which makes it a corporate mission to combine profit with social contribution also provides incentive to individual employees to share in the mission. Individual missions succeed most often when they contribute to and enhance larger missions.

You cannot separate the mission from the context—social, financial, cultural, corporate—within which it intends to succeed. Individuals in a "company with a conscience" see values besides the bottom line that are basic to the company, and can believe senior managers who say, "People are our greatest resource." From there, it is a short step to alignment between individual and organizational missions.

Being Pulled by Values. Basic measures of worth differ from person to person—good workmanship, being effective, putting talents to use, leaving a positive mark on the world. No matter which predominates in any given person, when all else is said and done, the force with the strongest pull toward high achievement concerns quality, principle, intrinsic value. This is not the same as working to please a boss or to feed one's family, no matter how valid those motives are for many of the jobs available to many of us. This is, rather, a matter of knowing that one's work has a meaning beyond one's immediate survival.

"Will follows from caring," the psychologist and writer Rollo May wrote. The persistence, consistency, even obsessiveness that we see more in top performers than in also-rans follow from what they really care about—their basic values. What we see is a creative loop: Values influence one's choice of mission. Accomplishing the mission will test those values in the cauldron of the workplace. Will they hold up? A craftsperson who values making quality violins can maintain that value fairly easily when he or she is making one a month. But what happens when, with a decision to start a business, the demand increases to one a week? The quality of performance emerging from the mission ties back into the values from which the mission emerged. When I am standing in the Atlanta Airport between business trips on Thanksgiving Day, far from family and friends, I have to be consciously aware of my mission and its underlying values in order to keep going.

Crowley Foods had a long and honorable history as a supplier of dairy products. But the mid-1970s, though, the company was struggling with fierce competition and an old, entrenched management. That was the situation when Norman Roberts arrived as CEO. Seven years later, Crowley Foods was restored to health. Roberts reviewed the turnaround during a management retreat in the Pocono Mountains of Pennsylvania. In a discussion over lunch, I asked him not to dwell on the details—how many executives fired, how many visits he made to the factory floor—but rather, to give me the essence of what had happened.

He said, "We reminded ourselves that we're selling *food,* nourishment for people, not 'product.' Being in the people-nourishing business, we see quality not as desirable but as mandatory. If you skimp on quality in what you give people to eat, you hurt them. How do you suppose the people who work for us, from the newest handyman through senior managers, might feel if they knew we were shortchanging our customers on so basic and urgent an aspect of life? How can we possibly tell our own people that they matter to us if we encourage them to cut corners on food that our customers buy for nourishment?"

In another city, Boston, James Rouse looked at a drab, run-down neighborhood and envisioned it coming to life. He imagined couples strolling hand in hand, looking at shop windows, touching displays of brightly colored fruits and vegetables on sidewalk carts, listening to a band concert in a green park; children tugging at balloons; the scents of seafood, spices, and hot concoctions enticing people into restaurants; people coming to buy, to eat, just to be there at the center of their community. In 1976 his vision became reality when the Rouse Company completed building the Quincy Market. It continues as one of the centers of a city that is regaining much of its old luster. At the time he said, "It just seemed obvious that there was a human yearning for something like that in the heart of the city."

On retiring as CEO of his company in 1979, Rouse began devoting much of his time to helping poor people acquire and renovate decrepit housing—an activity consistent with the values that had always moved him: "Man is God's instrument for carrying out the ongoing creation. That means everything we do in the environment, what we build or fail to build, places a tremendous responsibility on us . . . and a tremendous opportunity."

Who knows whether James Rouse, Jim Gray with his work in telephone company manholes setting a standard of excellence "because I did it," the plumber surgeons in their aerospace plant, Thomas Watson and his business machines company, will be remembered in decades to come? For now, the point is that they have acted as people with the vision to see that the value they add will outlive them.

The peak performers in our study exhibit an impressive depth of commitment intimately related to a contributory and ethical "systems sense" of what they are engaged in. For them, producing value as well as goods and services—and combining those elements in practical, revenue-generating ventures—is the bottom line in business and in life. Saints? Hardly. Just human beings whose performance records reflect the values that sustain their deepest reserves of energy and motivation, even when the going gets roughest.

The sustaining source of mission is what you care about most.

MISSION AND THE REAL WORLD

Putting preference before expertise. Drawing on the past. Trusting intuition. Having no preconceived limitations. Combining profit with contribution. Being pulled by values.

These six principles are evident in the peak performers' ability to formulate missions with real power. I am often asked: "Do peak performers always have a mission?" No. But when they don't, they make finding a mission their mission.

And as they progress, they realize that even the most deeply felt mission ineffectually expressed is a mission jeopardized. For an example, look at the contrasting leadership styles of Presidents John Kennedy and Jimmy Carter. No matter what his personal weaknesses and strengths were, Kennedy inspired millions of people by articulating a vision of a prosperous, vigorous nation in a peaceful world. His use of symbols and imagery—he was the first President to grasp the power of television—carried that vision into the marketplace of ideas and action. Though in fact most of the problems he addressed have outlived him, the vision he projected still evokes respect.

Carter's impulses were at least as genuine as Kennedy's. He probably knew more facts than any President the United States has ever had. Yet no clear statement of what he stood for emerged from all the facts. He seemed to approach presidential politics as a series of problems to be solved, and thus came across more as an engineer than as a mission leader. People were not inspired by talks about the nation's limitations, and said so as they voted for Carter's opponent in 1980.

To produce great results, vision must exist and be communicated. In regard to Jimmy Carter, it may be that he never formulated a vision on the national scale equal to the vision he brought to state and local government in Georgia. He practically said so, without intending to, at a Young Presidents' Organization meeting in Australia where we both gave talks. Carter was dously well informed, obviously highly intelligent. He br the meeting a one-page résumé with "President of the Unit for four years" as a line item among other items such as "school board," "church elder," and "Governor of Georgia." One might see this as an example of superb one-upmanship. If one were to search for another explanation, however, it might have been a case of carrying modesty to an extreme, or of a vision that somehow stops short of the larger-than-life issues that compose the life of an American President.

Mission establishes the territory and sets a direction in which one can be impassioned, committed, and empowered for the long haul. Mission opens a direction for growth as well as for achievement. Mission sets up an individual to act in his or her own behalf, and to do it in the direction of progress. Abraham Maslow:

> Let us think of life as a process of choices, one after another. At each point there is a progression choice and a regression choice. There may be a movement toward defense, toward safety, toward being afraid, but over on the other side there is the growth choice. To make the growth choice instead of the fear choice a dozen times a day . . . making each of the many single choices about whether to lie or be honest, etc. . . . is a movement toward self-actualization. . . . A person who does each of these little things each time the choice point comes up will find that they add up to better choices about what is constitutionally right for him. He comes to know what his destiny is . . . what his mission in life will be.

As adults, we have much to work with. Most of us have a sense of our job (and life), of our preferences, of directions that suggest potential peak performance, of times in which we have glimpsed (or functioned at) our best—times and preferences that suggest a mission. The task is to move with increasing confidence and frequency in the direction suggested by those times; to grasp more firmly what is already there; to move toward achieving consistency at a level one has already attained.

Our best efforts represent a level of achievement at which we could function each day. Peak performers do not rely on being "pumped up" from some state of undermotivation. They are drawn to the peak of their abilities by the best of motivators, that internal decision to excel in the service of a compelling mission.

Once launched, compelling missions lead to results.

4

RESULTS IN REAL TIME

Reaching a goal once in a while is no special trick. What is special, then, about the results peak performers produce? Their *consistency*. Peak performers are people who approach any set of circumstances with the attitude that they can get it to turn out the way they want it to. Not once in a while. Regularly. They can count on themselves.

We notice that they keep goal-setting in its place. The number of courses, books, and tapes on goal-setting would fill a sizable library, and from the peak performer's point of view, that is where many of them should stay—because, as useful as goals are, they have an insidious way of impersonating missions. Short-range objectives, so useful as means to an end, can become ends in themselves. Some people get reverent about their to-do lists, checking off items every evening as if they had reached some destination, forgetting where the items were originally intended to take them. Peak performers achieve results in real time, measurable goals within time frames long and short, which move them closer to completing their mission.

On examination, we see peak performers organizing their actions around results:

- As *individuals,*
  envisioning and communicating a clear mission, following up with a plan of action that includes specific goals, complete with benchmarks necessary for assessing timing, quality, and quantity of results
- As *collaborators,*
  using a "magnet mentality" to draw in what they need from other people
- As *innovators,*
  understanding that there is no guaranteed linear path from A to Z, prepared to make new paths in the service of results

In Chapter 3, we examined two components of mission, the visual and the verbal. Goal-setting uses both. Goal-setting also frequently comes with oversimplified advice: See it in your mind's eye and it will occur; write it down and you'll make it happen. Of course you can envision outcomes. Jack Nicklaus explained in his book, *Golf My Way:*

> First I "see" the ball where I want it to finish, nice and white and sitting up high on the bright green grass. Then the scene quickly changes, and I "see" the ball going there: its path, trajectory, and shape, even its behavior on landing. Then there's a sort of fade-out, and the next scene shows me making the kind of swing that will turn the previous images into reality.

And you can commit goals to words—New Year's resolutions, diet cards, fitness routines, management objectives, all are familiar exercises. But as Nicklaus makes clear, peak performers strip away the oversimplification and do a thorough job of integrating visual and verbal, destination and process. The motivation, the drive that keeps you on track and ultimately produces results, comes from focusing on the destination (an end point which you keep in sight) and from seeing yourself move through the process (various stages of setting and attaining goals).

INDIVIDUAL: SEEING, PLANNING, EXECUTING

Margaret Chesney is director of the Department of Behavioral Medicine at the giant California-based research organization called SRI International. She knows what "going the distance" meant to the hero of the *Rocky* movies. Chesney has been setting goals and stretching for them since her early school days. Her mother once remarked of a trophy that her older sister received as high school class valedictorian: "Two of these would make a nice pair of bookends." Margaret, too, graduated as valedictorian. In college she drew up a grid of all the hours in a week, filled in the times occupied by eating, sleeping, and classes, then filled almost all the other spaces with studying. While looking for a summer job, she had a chance to observe a group therapy session at the University of Oregon in Portland. "It was just ten minutes of watching a counselor helping people," she recalls. Ten minutes was enough for someone who had been preparing herself all along. When she left she told herself: "That's it! That's what I want to do when I grow up."

She approached her mission as a series of goals and picked them off one after another. After making all A's except for two B's from high school on, she was a twenty-seven-year-old psychology Ph.D. in 1977 when her interest in "Type A" behavior—the tense, impatient, often aggressive personality that Drs. Meyer Friedman and Ray Rosenman see as a major setup for heart attacks—led to an invitation to join an SRI research team. Profiling her for *Esquire* in 1984, George Leonard characterized her as "a major force among scientists currently seeking to solve the mysteries of [the heart] . . . an ingenious researcher, a skilled administrator, and a master of scientific networking and fund raising."

Every step of the way, Margaret Chesney has enrolled others in her enthusiasms. Faculty members helped her with special courses. Academic mentors recommended her for graduate programs. A former teacher brought her to SRI. Much of her impact is achieved by making sure that other people perceive her goals as worthy.

Margaret Chesney leaves the high-powered surroundings of SRI once a week and drives thirty miles to San Francisco to counsel individual clients. Something about that commitment, along with all her scientific meetings and professional honors, restates the point: Her mission is to help people prevent or cure potentially debilitating disease. A well-stated mission can serve as an umbrella for a seemingly diverse set of activities. Chesney sees her mission as a progression of goals: first, studies and laboratory work to investigate causes of a disease. Then treatment: clinical application of the findings. Finally, prevention: involving the community at large. The goals get results. Therefore she attracts support. Therefore she positions herself for greater results.

MENTAL ENVIRONMENT

The skill of getting results contains no mysteries. As peak performers demonstrate, it is accessible. It begins with a basic attitude, one that each person creates, toward goals. The peak-performing attitude is the *mental environment* in which one sorts out and evaluates goals, sets result-producing goals, and implements innovative tactics for achieving goals.

Tom Landry, head coach of the Dallas Cowboys, may epitomize the get-it-done, goal-oriented spirit in America. What result is more clear than the score at the end of a football game? In twenty-three years Landry turned the Cowboys from an expansion club into a team that won 202, lost 115, and tied 6 while reaching the playoffs sixteen times in seventeen years, winning twelve divisional championships, playing in the Super Bowl five times, and winning there twice. Landry and I spoke at the same Young Presidents' Organization meeting in Australia in 1984. He is often portrayed as emotionless and authoritarian in his determination to win. That is not the way he looked in Melbourne as he spoke about the value of having results-oriented leadership come from assistants and players as well as from the head coach.

The "Cowboy philosophy," he said, developed as he asked his coaches to work with him on their versions of it. Together the coaches refined the team management strategies that Landry communicated to the players. A sign went up in the Dallas locker room: THE VALUE OF A MAN'S LIFE IS IN DIRECT PROPORTION TO HIS COMMITMENT TO EXCELLENCE. The Cowboy mission of winning through excellence expanded into an understanding that any man who plays for the team must commit himself to the team effort, not to individual glory. You can call that a synonym for "fit in or ship out," or you can hear in it a call to peak-performing organization.

To be effective, Landry emphasized, any strategy emerging from the overall mission has to be explicit. He draws a triangle to illustrate his approach to carrying out the Cowboys' mission:

Team Goals establish what you want to accomplish—say, improving the passing game.

Methods establish how each individual can contribute. Coaches come up with plays and training programs. Players work on them, setting individual goals aligned with the team goals. All of them look for leverage points that will provide the biggest gain per unit of training time.

Yardsticks show how the individuals, and the team, did. More yards gained through the air? Higher percentage of pass completions? More average yards per pass? More touchdowns scored through the air?

Say a *team goal* is to improve the Dallas passing game. The first decisions always have to do with available resources. On a football team, that means people: Who is available? How should they be used? In this organization and any other, the steps are clear: Staff key positions, help individuals set goals, and support them with expert coaching. In 1984 the Cowboy coaches had to make a difficult choice between quarterbacks Danny White and Gary Hogeboom, both excellent leaders in action, both capable of producing results. The team had to look to one of them, not both, for leadership on the field. Uncertainty about who is in charge at crucial moments on the field or in a conference room can undermine the results of all team members. With one quarterback identified as leader, the other (if he remains part of the team) acts as a leader, in reserve.

The principles are the same in every organization, whether the business is football or manufacturing. Robert Campion, chairman of Lear Siegler, told me: "We won't promote anyone until he has trained a capable replacement. Otherwise, the promotion would leave us too vulnerable."

In 1985, Landry took the risk of making a major change in personnel policy. The Cowboy tradition had been to draft young players and free agents and train them as they came up through the Dallas organization. For years, that provided all the depth Landry needed. If somebody got hurt, another capable player was ready to step in. As everybody else's scouting caught up to the Cowboys' sophisticated, computerized systems, and available top young players were spread thin because of the increase in the number of teams, the Cowboys lost their advantage in depth. Landry watched the San Francisco 49ers win the Super Bowl in 1985 after combining trades for key personnel and the development of young talent, and decided it was time to deal. The coaches already knew their needs: wide receivers. Linebackers. Maybe one of the quarterbacks would have to go. Like many organizations, they no longer have the time to bring people along from scratch at all points.

Many of the *methods* for improving a passing game are as well known as the usual management methods. What is needed at first is the initiative to set them in motion. Coaches develop specific plays, including new ones, and a training regimen. They increase practice time for passing; increase their reviews of key pass plays on game films; step up their emphasis on mental preparation and physical conditioning throughout the season.

Quarterbacks and receivers work on timing, deception, mastering the variety of options that can develop during a play. Running backs practice to increase the quarterback's options, both as potential receivers and blockers and as constant ground-gain threats. The offensive line works as the key to the whole operation, protecting the quarterback to give him more time to see receivers, who in turn have more time to break free. Like managers in any corporation, the linemen act as buffers to keep outside pressures away from skilled employees on whom they count to produce results.

Together, coaches and players developed the measurable results that Landry calls *yardsticks:* Two wide receivers who each catch 10 to 15 percent more passes than last year. A tight end who gains four hundred yards with thirty catches. Running backs who increase their yardage, controlling the running game more to set up the pass. A quarterback completing 62 percent of his passes for thirty touchdowns and fewer than eighteen interceptions. Offensive linemen allowing fewer than one sack per game for the entire season.

This is not some new religion Tom Landry just caught. After a 1966 playoff loss to the Green Bay Packers, Landry surveyed his players on what had gone wrong and how to improve ("We didn't like being bridesmaids"), and maintains that he is still open for comments—as long as they come as a contribution to results and remain within the Cowboy philosophy. That dent in the popular image of Landry as the impassive, computerized boss serves as a reminder of what we find frequently among peak performers on every rung of the ladder: They are leaders not because they care so much for the trappings of dominance, but because they care so much for results.

An organization's bottom line can take many forms: a Super Bowl trophy, profit, staying within budget, producing to deadline, winning new customers. An individual peak performer's bottom line, however, takes just one form: Make things happen toward goals, consistent with a mission, while developing oneself in the process.

To get there, the peak performer cultivates a mental environment in which he or she retains a clear image of the desired outcome; assumes the necessary risks; and judges when and how to take initiative. As our study progressed, we developed an increasingly clear view of the individual who most effectively makes things happen.

CULTIVATING NECESSARY SKILLS

Individual or team player, everyone who moves from mission and goal-setting to getting results in real time cultivates specific, necessary skills.

Peak performers:

- Acquire new skills that will serve a mission. An upstart entrepreneur might read marketing books; a salesperson moving to management might take a management skills course.
- Get more out of the skills they already have—they use leverage.

Stewart Brand, founder and publisher of *The Whole Earth Catalog, The Whole Earth Review,* and *The Whole Earth Software Catalog,* proposes "The formula for an interesting life: Acquire skills and use them—the more skills, the more interesting. Skills unpreventably give pride and confidence. . . . A wealth of skills doesn't insure freedom any more than any other wealth, but it surely can expand choice, which may lead out of some corners."

For the peak performers, skills translate as competence, pride, confidence, and personal power, *because they are motiviated to use the skills to accomplish personally meaningful results.* Without such meaning, all the skills training in the world will not eliminate the feeling that the steering wheel of one's ship is disconnected from the rudder. One can outline ninety-nine MBO goals, but it is the excitement of knowing that these goals matter deeply to you that cuts through the old "why bother?" attitude.

Among peak performers, leveraging old skills is a practice at least equal in power to acquiring new ones. Richard Byrne, a professor at the University of Southern California's Annenberg School of Communications, uses the expression *leveraging your skills* to mean getting more productivity out of the ones you have. Dr. Byrne advises many executives on how to incorporate the computer into their work. He asks, "What are you good at?" Writing sales reports? Managing people? Forecasting? Organizing production? Find the software program that helps you do that, learn it, and you'll amplify your skill in work you already do well. Do not expect the computer to do something completely new for you.

The same principle applies in noncomputer situations. People who are tops in their fields are always looking out for new information *in their field* to maintain their competitive edge.

Putting serious emphasis on leveraging what they have, peak performers distinguish between *deficiency training* and *growth training.* The impulse to acquire new skills comes most often from a desire to remedy a deficiency (the entrepreneur who feels ignorant about marketing, the new executive worried about accounting.) There is nothing wrong with the remedial aspect of deficiency training—unless it also comes with an illusion that "if only I can get this one under my belt, I'll be okay." That is not how peak performers operate.

Peak performers also identify lacks and fill them. But they have dropped the illusion of an "end state" of development for the skills they use. They invest in growth training—cultivating the aspects of their performance that they identify as likely to provide the most leverage.

I see that kind of leverage at People Express. When Donald Burr and his partners were establishing themselves as the fastest-growing airline in aviation history, they raised productivity in the company so high that competing airlines realized that matching People's fares would lead most to lose money even if they filled every seat of every flight. The leaders at People Express decided what the company was good at—imagination, personal commitment, service built on people more than on things—and pushed it as hard as they knew how.

One area in which Burr and his three thousand team members show extraordinary success is cost control. At the start, People Express opted for a "hub and spoke" operation in which every flight was a round trip between the single terminal at Newark (the hub) and a single destination (the end of that spoke). "A good hub-and-spoke operation is like a fortress," Burr points out, "because you can control the traffic at that terminal and shut out competition." They kept their planes in the air 10.4 hours per day instead of the industry average of 7.12 hours. They eliminated formerly free services such as magazines; passengers pay for baggage checking and drinks and snacks. Important though such tactics may be, they come second to Burr's view of the real source of good results: "The wholehearted personal commitment of everyone involved. You could do all of those things all day and still fall on your face. That's why we thought longer and harder about building our people structure here than we did anything else."

As Burr sees it, you build an enterprise by assuming that the heart of it is not plans, schedules, policies, or balance sheets, but *people.* A company that organizes itself around structures and policies in the traditional pyramid shape, with layer after ascending layer of authority, often leaves employees feeling they are, as Burr puts it, "guilty until proven innocent." The result, we have seen innumerable times, can be hopeless complexity, confusion about missions, resentment or indifference toward "the job." The experiment at People Express is to create an environment in which the usual distinctions between the company and the employees disappear. Burr wanted his company organized to let individual people work at their full capacity.

Managers at People Express offer direction and make sure their team members have the information and the tools they need to do their jobs. They do not dictate or police methods. This operating style, however, is based on a presumption of shared goals and aligned missions. Burr and other top executives direct it with a firm hand. "If you don't agree with that direction," Burr says, "you shouldn't be here." Going for results in his company means empowering people, involving them, giving them running room (at one point Burr let his top managers elect someone from their own ranks to be president rather than simply appointing the president himself), and still setting tough standards. (A manager at Honeywell confirms that approach in a comment on his own operation: "Participative management is not permissive management.")

Eight months after the airline's first flights, Burr became concerned that the daily distractions of a rapidly spreading business might be blurring the company's objectives. Since he is not inclined to think fine principles and good intentions alone will get results, he took action. He called a meeting of the company's start-up team to commit the overall objectives of the new business to writing—in effect, to compose a mission statement.

During an intense and argumentative day Burr asked each person there for his or her idea of what People Express was out to accomplish. He wrote the answers on large sheets of paper and taped them to the walls. "They put their blood on those walls," he recalls. The team produced a list of six "precepts" for the company:

- service, growth, and development of people
- becoming the best provider of air transportation
- highest quality of management
- becoming a role model
- simplicity
- maximization of profits

To stand the rough-and-tumble test of daily business, each precept has to produce visible results. For example, Burr points to the first two as practical guides for even the most harried manager: "If it's good for a customer or good for a peer, you're probably making a good choice."

One result of all this is that Burr can say, "People are getting rich here." Part of the feeling of identification with the company comes from a requirement that every employee own stock in it. The company helps them with interest-free loans and bargain prices. By early 1984 the average People Express employee owned about 2,500 shares worth about $46,000 at then-current prices. "We're not sitting around counting roses," Burr likes to say. "There are millionaires walking around here and tons of twenty-four- and twenty-five-year-olds worth seventy-five thousand dollars, a hundred thousand, two hundred thousand. The only way I know to wealth in the long term is to own a piece of something and build it."

LEARNED EFFECTIVENESS

Purposefully active people—the peak performers—separate action that produces useful results in real time from mere activity or busy work.

Their less purposeful colleagues put in time and wait for the day, the week, the work, to be over. They see the surrounding forces—co-workers, company, corporate culture—as too big for them to affect, so they live with what a number of researchers, notably psychologist Martin Seligman of the University of Pennsylvania, term "learned helplessness."

PEOPLE ARE NOT BORN TO INACTION. THEY LEARN IT.

By contrast, most of the purposefully active people we have studied over the past twenty years operate with what I call "learned effectiveness." These peak performers are comfortable with being distinctly action-oriented, focused on tangible results in real time, not very interested in activity for its own sake or abstractions that do not seem to lead anywhere. None call themselves peak performers—that is our term—and few would say they have mastered all the skills they would like to have. Yet that acknowledgment of skills still to be learned does not stop them from acting purposefully and effectively.

Peak performers operating with learned effectiveness know they don't know all the answers, and thus develop a most important trait: flexibility. While they are serious about achieving the outcomes they set out to achieve, the men and women in our study can vary their methods and adapt to changing circumstances. They maintain high standards for their work while staying free from the paralyzing compulsion to be perfect. Peak performers have little patience with what one might call "people of advocacy," those busy types who argue passionately for various "intriguing possibilities" that turn out to be mainly word games and idle theories, more talk than action toward results.

In looking to the bottom line—whether it's return on investment, staying within budget, producing on time, or keeping quality and service up to standard—purposefully active people think primarily in terms of progress. They move themselves; they move their projects; they move their organizations.

Learned effectiveness in the service of results allows you to enter areas you have not mastered with the attitude that you will acquire the skills you need to succeed. It supports a mental environment in which an individual knows *any* worthwhile challenge, familiar or unfamiliar, will mobilize the best of himself or herself.

Investment banker Felix Rohatyn once gave the idea a touch of affectionate humor while introducing his friend William Paley, founder of CBS, at an awards dinner. Recalling an Easter egg hunt in the Rohatyns' garden which had as its prize a golden egg, Rohatyn noted that not only did Paley find it and hold it up as if he had just triumphed in a marathon, "he was going to find that golden egg if my whole property was defoliated."

Maybe. But Rohatyn also made sure his listeners would remember Paley as the man who shaped the practices of objectivity and balance in early news broadcasting (partly on principle and partly from a shrewd desire to keep government interference at bay); who persuaded CBS Radio technicians on March 11, 1938, that even though they thought it impossible, the network could assemble live commentary from Vienna, Berlin, Paris, London, and Rome on the German invasion of Austria, and thereby pulled radio into a new dimension; who said, "A perfect strike in this business is getting something that is really high quality and popular at the same time"; and could point to *Playhouse 90, M*A*S*H, 60 Minutes,* and *All in the Family* on CBS Television as a few examples of what he meant.

COLLABORATOR: THE MAGNET MENTALITY

James E. Buerger, publisher of *Travelhost National* magazine, knows how to attract other people and their resources to his projects. To that end, he makes full use of goals that are *clear* and *clearly communicated.*

As a young publisher of several weekly newspapers, he outgrew his printer and decided to set up his own printing plant. "That was my goal." He ordered a press and then had forty-five days to raise $100,000, find trained operators, set up peripheral equipment, and get a building to house it all. A daunting prospect, but at the end of the forty-five days everything was in place. As Buerger recalls:

> First, I believed it could be done. Second, I believed it could be done within the time period that had been set. Third, I was consumed with accomplishing the task. Fourth, I told all with whom I came in contact of my goal and asked for their help.
>
> What happened was phenomenal! It seemed that everyone I told about my goal could recognize my sincerity and enthusiasm, and they seemed to become enthusiastic themselves. Their minds would go to work immediately . . . to help see that the goal was achieved. With each new person I approached, my enthusiasm grew and he also became consumed with enthusiasm. . . .
>
> A secret goal cannot benefit from the participation and force of others. A well-defined goal, shared with others and sparked with enthusiasm, will draw energy and forces that cannot be measured or suppressed.
>
> Define your goal. Place a time on achieving it. Be enthusiastic about its accomplishment. Share it with all with whom you come into contact. And feel "the force" working for you.

Buerger's poetic description of "the force" working for him is an eminently practical notion, like bringing a binocular lens into focus or aligning the strokes of a crew of rowers. Concentrating the energies of others on a project you care about is one of the most useful skills a peak performer can develop.

It is no mere country-boy pose when T George Harris, whose string of magazine editing accomplishments extends from *Time* through *Look* and the original *Psychology Today* to his most successful of all, *American Health,* goes around saying, "I need all the help I can get." He gets a lot. And he goes on asking.

COMMITMENT

The peak performer expects, prepares for, and works toward having the necessary elements—including the right people—fall into place. This is not to say that he or she expects the preparation or the work to be easy. Spectacular corporate turnarounds like those at Remington and Chrysler have many moments in them when the team knows, as Lee Iacocca said of his team at Chrysler: "You're playing with live ammunition."

More than once, a man or woman in a private office, surrounded by the furnishings of success, has asked, "Have you read this?" and handed me a neatly printed quotation from the Scottish mountaineer William Hutchison Murray:

> Until one is committed there is hesitancy, the chance to draw back, always ineffectiveness. Concerning all acts of initiative (and creation), there is one elementary truth, the ignorance of which kills countless ideas and splendid plans: that the moment one definitely commits oneself, then Providence moves too. All sorts of things occur to help one that would never otherwise have occurred. A whole stream of events issues from the decision, raising in one's favour all manner of unforeseen incidents and meetings and material assistance, which no man could have dreamt would have come his way.

The growth of companies like People Express and Discovery Toys would not have happened without the "magnet mentality" of founders Donald Burr and Lane Nemeth. That includes the extraordinary persistence and hard work that such peak performers devote to sharing their commitment with others. This is inspiration at its best: inspiration that makes it unlikely that Burr and Nemeth will merely command subordinates to produce while ignoring critics in the process.

Even though Steven Jobs was co-founder of Apple Computer, he went to great lengths to build and sustain the team that produced the company's potent Macintosh. Jobs had to maneuver himself into position as head of the development team over objections from some other company executives. Once there, he went to considerable lengths to keep the creative current flowing. He set his team apart from the rest of the company, at one point flying a pirate flag over its building to signify their determination to blow a rival team out of the water; he staged frequent parties, sushi dinners, and seaside retreats; he presented medals, and sometimes stock options in thin gray envelopes, to star performers; he had the development team's names embossed, "for posterity," on the inside of the mold for the machine's case; he bullied, threatened, and adopted slogans like "The journey is the reward"; he surrounded the entire project with his conviction that "the Macintosh is the future of Apple Computer."

Pointing to entrepreneurs such as Burr, Nemeth, and Jobs might leave the impression that "magnet mentality" is a synonym for the charisma of some senior managers. It is not. It is a quality we see in less visible people, many of them deep inside big organizations. The magnetism comes not from personal pizzazz, but from unswerving purpose.

TIMING

Almost every peak performer I studied could recall a moment when he or she was ready, after long preparation, to move quickly toward results. In every instance, the move came at a time when preparation and events converged in ways that made it possible for the person to construct or accept a job situation in which he or she could achieve results in real time and develop additional skills. A personal bottom-line attitude was to seek situations in which "my dream has room to grow," and avoid situations that threatened that dream.

Amey Shaw did not start out to be a chef. When she moved from Toledo, Ohio, to Monterey, California, she wanted to work at a newspaper but took the first available job, at a Pizza Hut, and discovered that she loved waiting on tables and preparing food. She enrolled at Contra Costa College in northern California for formal study with a classically trained chef. When she was ready, he steered her to an assistant's job at a small French restaurant. Eventually she moved to another, where she refined her skill in another style of cooking, mesquite grilling. She did some catering, began developing a name in the San Francisco Bay area culinary community, and in 1982 was hired as a dinner cook at the Claremont Resort Hotel in the Berkeley-Oakland hills. She was ready to make her impact.

The Claremont is a huge white castle on twenty-two acres of tennis courts, palms, and carefully tended gardens. New management wanted a kitchen as fine as the rest of the place. Their executive chef, Daniel Strongin, had their support. And Amey Shaw's accomplishments attracted Strongin's support. She immediately set about reworking the menus, buying her own ingredients, going to the markets herself, growing fresh herbs in the hotel's neatly clipped gardens. Her style combined her classical training with California regional cooking to produce an American cuisine emphasizing freshness and flavor.

"For years, hotel food was an inside joke," Strongin says, "but not anymore. I've watched Amey write a different menu every day for over a year and a half. It's an incredible creative effort, and she's been able to do it consistently and do it well."

I live three minutes from the Claremont and have been going there for business meals for years. The difference in the quality of the food, and in the overall ambience, is striking. Shirley Sarvis, a food and wine expert who works with Shaw occasionally on large Claremont dinners, admires her integrity. "She's phenomenal for her unending enthusiasm, her openness, and her eagerness to do it the best possible way," Sarvis says of Shaw. "She has an almost unbelievable understanding of grilling over mesquite. . . ."

And, in a conversation with my research associate, Shaw exhibited a fine understanding of how to draw staff members to her ideals of excellence. She reformed the cooking in her kitchen while keeping most of the staff. Shaw motivated her assistants by showing them how to do things, demonstrating why this worked better than that. Threats—a time-honored way of maintaining control in the frantic, authoritarian clamor of every big commercial kitchen—were out. Humor, she found, worked better. And so did patience. If she had to show someone a second time, she did. The person would learn, not least of all because the chef obviously cared so deeply about what she was teaching him to do. Leaving her imprint at the Claremont, Amey Shaw has once again moved on.

Amey reminds me of my Apollo 11 engineering colleagues, of Joe and Ben Weider, of all the peak performers absorbed in the technical challenges of an immediate task and committed to the highest level of quality in their work. Like Jenette Kahn at DC Comics, Robert Maynard at the Oakland *Tribune,* Jim Gray at Pacific Bell, and many others, Amey Shaw became the magnet for a team that vastly improved products and services. She came into her full powers the moment she saw it was time to bring everything she had—training, technique, artistry, enthusiasm, commitment—into action.

Peak performers tend to be stereotyped as people who start or turn around businesses. Yet most of the people doing impressive work are balancing innovation and consolidation, like Amey Shaw, *improving* businesses they did not start. They create new products, update old service strategies, try out ways to make the work climate more productive, stimulating, and responsive to the human beings doing the work. As Common Cause founder John Gardner sees it, they make possible "the system by which able people are nurtured and moved into positions where they can make their contribution."

WORK STYLE

People drawn to magnetic peak performers share an investment in seeing their work succeed. Rosabeth Moss Kanter, professor of sociology and of organization and management at Yale, calls the people with these magnetic skills "change masters." She puts it precisely when she writes that their results emerge from a working style that emphasizes:

- Persuading more than ordering, though managers sometimes use threats, direct orders, or pressure from a bigger boss as a last resort
- Building a team, which includes creating formal task forces or committees, frequent staff meetings, vigorous sharing of information, regular brainstorming sessions
- Seeking input from others, including needs of users, suggestions from subordinates, peer review

- Showing political sensitivity to the interests of others, their stake or potential stake in the project
- Sharing rewards and recognition willingly

THE RESULTS-ORIENTED INNOVATOR

In *The Lessons of History,* Will and Ariel Durant observe, "The future never just happened. It was created." If that is true for societies and organizations, it is true as well for individuals.

We see that some of the most impressive innovators in organizations today are those who seek ways to combine their work and its momentum with the work of others. But on what scale do they do it? Do they survey everything from atop and afar, seeing the world spread out below them, or do they go at every detail from beneath the surface, handling each one meticulously before going on to the next? Which view makes them what they are—bird's-eye or worm's-eye?

Thomas Peters and Robert Waterman's *In Search of Excellence* provides some support for the view that daily actions, more than big major strategies, make the difference: "The essence of excellence is the thousand concrete, minute-to-minute actions performed by everyone in an organization to keep a company on its course."

Corporate strategist Michael Kami, former director of planning for both Xerox and IBM, sees it a bit differently. We were looking out over Port Phillip Bay in Melbourne during a recess in the Young Presidents' Organization seminars that had brought us to Australia as faculty members. Given the YPO audience—people who had before turning forty become heads of companies with more than fifty employees and gross sales over $25 million—it was natural for us to indulge in shoptalk about "results orientation." Dr. Kami remarked, "Individuals are successful not because of the hundred and one good little actions they take to save money on paper clips and telephone calls, but because of one or two major strategies that are brilliant."

John Gardner would agree with Peters and Waterman that innovative results occur in every area where people work, large or small:

> Many of the major changes in history have come about through successive small innovations, most of them anonymous. Our dramatic sense (or our superficiality) leads us to seek out "the man who started it all" and to heap on his shoulders the whole credit for a prolonged, diffuse and infinitely complex process. It is essential that we outgrow this immature conception. Some of our most difficult problems today . . . defy correction by any single dramatic solution. They will yield, if at all, only to a whole series of innovations.

Of course all these observers know the secret: Results in innovation come from both views, bird's-eye and worm's-eye. Positions that appear to be opposite are actually parts of a greater whole.

PEAK PERFORMERS HANDLE BOTH *MACRO* AND *MICRO,* OVERVIEW AND DETAIL.

The brilliant strategy of the innovative planner and the hundred and one (or thousand) details of the innovative doer are inextricably linked—when the one is aligned with the other.

It took a brilliant strategist, Rene McPherson, to issue a statement on detail so potent that it is quoted in practically every recent book about organizations. McPherson came into the Toledo-based Dana Corporation, a $3 billion maker of automobile and truck parts, as chairman in 1973 and tripled its sales per employee during the 1970s. He did it without huge capital spending, although the United Auto Workers have Dana highly unionized, while productivity in similar companies was hardly increasing at all. Later, as dean of the Stanford Graduate School of Business, he wrote about the power in keeping planning and doing firmly linked:

> Until we believe that the expert in any particular job is most often the person performing it, we shall forever limit the potential of that person. . . . Consider a manufacturing setting: within their 25-square-foot area, nobody knows more about how

to operate a machine, maximize its output, improve its quality, optimize the material flow and keep it operating efficiently than do the machine operators, material handlers, and maintenance people responsible for it. Nobody.

. . . When I am in your 25 square feet of space, I'd better listen to you!

Again and again, we see results emerging from the many jobs that take meaning from—and give form to—a few strategies. Lawrence Gilson, a former vice-president of Amtrak, is one of a group that worked to build a high-speed "bullet train" railroad in the United States. The odds, as it turned out, proved too great even for peak performers. But it was a near thing: The Japanese government cooperated; Wall Street gave it a serious look; builders invested $1 million of their own money. Investors were not putting their money into a fuzzy R&D project. Gilson knew that "you have to know what the three or four steps out in front of you are. You have to set out milestones that are achievable. You can't expect someone to come in on the basis of being sold the big picture. You have to sell each incremental step. What you bring to them at each phase is not just conceptual, it is work completed."

Visionaries who were less than peak performers in handling incremental steps might have failed to get the project out of the dream stage, or might have deluded themselves that they could continue when the fact was that they could not. Gilson and his partners raised $10 million toward a $3.1 billion project. They knew they would need another $50 million in risk capital to keep operating until the planned beginning of construction in 1985. They had done their detail work. When they saw that the $50 million was not going to come in by the time they projected they had to have it, they knew it was time to quit, and sold their engineering plans to Amtrak. The peak performer's perspective not only lets you know when to continue. It also lets you know when to stop.

Results-oriented innovators get results in areas that less-productive people may not regard as areas of innovation:

Personnel. Small companies often find it a burden to pay the fees of executive search firms as they look for top talent. Ken Kingery, personnel manager of OCTel Communications in San Jose, California, spotted a piece of computer software that would help his company build its own executive search file, and learned to use it. Now, as résumés come in, he can enter pertinent facts such as job title, salary, specific skills, and special comments into an easily recalled information bank.

Sales. As a way to build her travel business, Maryles Casto started calling every client *after* the trip to ask if there was anything she could have done to make it work better. She invites regular clients to meetings in which she treats them "like guests in our home," soliciting ideas that will improve her service.

Administration. A quality circle made up of administrative assistants at Westinghouse initiated a plan to save time and money in dealing with office supplies. They pioneered the "stockless storeroom." They found a vendor who would deliver directly to each work station. Their scheme eliminated tiresome inventories, opened up some storage space, and allowed for a single invoice, which made the accounting department happy.

Production. Jim Gray was finding ways to save AT&T money even before it became one of many competitive phone companies. He devised ways of turning a repair job—say, a pole knocked down by a car—into permanent construction, by doing it all in one visit instead of the usual two or three. He also told his crews that, contrary to phone company policy, he was not going to call residences to check on the progress of installers or otherwise hover over their shoulders. "Here's the job," he would say. "Think it out. If you have a problem, get back to me." The crews rewarded his trust with high morale and better results.

MAKING USE OF OPPORTUNITIES FOR RESULTS

If we think of an innovator only as a pioneer, inventor, or company founder—a shatterer of some serene status quo—we miss the point about 95 percent of the high-achieving people who contribute to the world through their lives and their work.

Technological and social changes are appearing so fast today that the challenge, particularly in business, is not to shatter the status quo but to keep up with it. Practically all the men and women in our study who produce valuable results for themselves and their companies have proven themselves adept not only at keeping up with change, but also at anticipating future change.

A strong characteristic among them is that they can envision accomplishments beyond their immediate frame of reference. They see past the formal boundaries of their jobs, past traditional ways of doing things. They are flexible, active, creative, growth-oriented—in a word, innovative. As professor Ted Levitt of the Harvard Business School notes, their qualities give them the ability to "see opportunities before they become obvious." The question is, how do they retain these qualities under the pressure of day-to-day work? And how do they put them into action?

First of all, we learn from the peak performers that innovation is not an all-or-nothing characteristic which some have and some don't. Rather, as one might expect, it appears in varying strengths along a range of behaviors.

Toward one edge of the range are people we might call *consolidators:* They are at their best when they are improving—not changing—what they already know how to do.

Toward the other edge are the people we have been calling *innovators:* Confident of their ability to spot opportunity, they expect surprises and may even count on change as a source of energy for their work—rather like a sailor ready to use a wind shift for extra speed.

Most people operate between the two extremes. We notice that the peak performers are able to move, when necessary, from one edge of the range to the other. Their commitment to results keeps them from getting stuck in any one position. For example, they are able to move toward the consolidator edge when they want to perfect a set of job skills, reinforce the essentials of team functioning, or improve the basics of overall administration.

PEAK PERFORMERS USE BOTH INNOVATION AND CONSOLIDATION TO ACHIEVE A BALANCE THAT GETS RESULTS.

Innovation, with the consolidation it sometimes calls into play, requires precisely the sort of power—to initiate projects and follow through—that we see in people who rely on purposefully active behavior. Among their opposite numbers, where learned helplessness is more common, we see the phenomenon that Rosabeth Kanter summarizes: "In large organizations at least, powerlessness 'corrupts.' That is, lack of power (the capacity to mobilize resources and people to get things done) tends to create managers who are more concerned about guarding their territories than about collaborating with others to benefit the organization."

The contrasts we identified in our study of peak performers closely parallel some contrasts that Howard H. Stevenson and David E. Gumpert of Harvard described in a 1985 discussion of opposite types which they call "trustees" (our consolidators) and "promoters" (our innovators). Stevenson and Gumpert list the questions each type tends to ask in making decisions:

CONSOLIDATOR: "What resources do I control?"
"What structure determines our organization's relationship to its market?"
"How can I minimize the impact of others on my ability to perform?"
"What opportunity is appropriate?"

INNOVATOR: "Where is the opportunity?"
"How do I capitalize on it?"
"What resources do I need?"
"How do I control the resources?"
"What structure is best?"

Watching peak performers reminded us in many ways that the same person can act as innovator in one set of circumstances and as consolidator in another. Let us look for a moment at how the innovator's questions produce results for peak performers.

Where is the opportunity? It is not necessarily in the unknown or breaking new ground. Innovators, while good at going outside the current frame of reference, are also good at going deeper into it and seeing new uses of familiar ideas. Despite occasional dramatic surprises, a quarterback on a winning football team seldom does anything really new. He often does what everyone else is trying to do, better than they do it. The great quarterback is a peak performer because he has learned to go deep into his specialty by competing with himself—by bettering his own past performance through disciplined practice and by obsessively paying attention to detail—and by having the resilience and staying power to acquire experience.

How do I capitalize on it? Here the peak performer organizes around results. There are innovative thinkers who never get anything done. Peak performers, however, *move* in pursuit of an opportunity. Beth Milwid did not content herself with "doing the best I can under the conditions" when she found herself not getting the results she wanted in the bureaucracy she worked in. She had organizational skills, but she needed more. So she got a doctorate in psychology with an emphasis on organizations. Several years later, when she went to work for Crocker Bank in organizational development, she was well versed in organizational problems from her previous jobs and well equipped to deal with them.

What resources do I need? Consolidators tend to budge only when they have all their ducks in a row and can go first-class. Innovators—people who start businesses or make major contributions within companies, as peak performers frequently do—often make their moves without all the resources in place, and make imaginative use of what they do have. Maryles Casto didn't hold off her travel-agency venture while trying to raise a lot of capital; she figured the resources she needed were her personal touch, her willingness to provide an unusual level of service, and whatever money she had saved. That was $3,000. She might have wished she had more to commit, but made do with what she had. She discovered selling skills and organizing skills she didn't know she had, and in putting them to use along with her savings she resolved the tension that always prevails between the adequacy of resources and the chances for successful results. Handling that tension is part of the challenge and the excitement for a peak performer.

How do I control the resources? There is a one-word test to distinguish innovators from consolidators, and it is the word *control.* Consolidators think control is adequate only when they own the resource or have it on the payroll. Innovators figure what they need from a resource is the ability to use it. If it belongs to someone else, fine; the innovator doesn't have to carry that overhead. Big magazines in the past, such as *Look* and *Life,* had hundreds of in-house staff people to do most of their writing, editing, and selling. Successful new magazines like *American Health* and *Science* start with a lean cadre of staff people, as few as half a dozen, and farm out assignments to independents. Buying or hiring is still an option when that would be more effective.

What structure is best? Here an innovator looks at formal boundaries and traditional ways, and balances them against his or her desire for results. People are at the heart of the innovator's decisions about structure: *Who* is most affected by a decision? *Who* can make this project work? Consolidators are more likely to put formalities at the center of things: *What* actions are authorized? *What* are the responsibilities? Consolidators often take action without much contact with the people the action will affect. Innovators depend on close contact with the principal actors to give them their "feel" for the way results can be made to emerge. Jim Gray would take construction plans for miles of rebuilding on telephone company lines and say to himself: "They want five people to go in there? One of my guys could do it." He would get one of his guys and say, "Here. As long as the work is done right, I don't care where you are at the end of the day." Administrators would criticize Gray for not checking off all the procedures boxes on the plans—"people who wouldn't even know what a pole is unless they ran into it"—so he and his men operated a lot, as he says, "under the table." Since divestiture, as the company has begun changing in Gray's direction, he sometimes shifts to acting as a consolidator to promote much of the work structure he improvised as an innovator.

STAYING ON TRACK: AVOIDING ACTIVITY TRAPS

The importance of producing useful results may sound obvious, yet in practice it is not, even for the hardest-edged manufacturing companies. Being busy often passes for being productive. Andrew Grove, president of Intel Corporation, a leading U.S. maker of microprocessors and other semiconductor products, observes that the purpose of any organization is to produce output, whether it is silicon chips manufactured, insurance sold, bills mailed out, or tax returns processed. Yet, Grove says, "In one way or another, we have all been seduced by tangents and by the appearance of output, when what we were really looking at was activity."

Many people are committed to activity—to motion that is too often tangents and appearances. For them, the urgent crowds out the important. They can initiate action and they do achieve results, but what they do is seldom oriented by a clear mission. And it is seldom as productive as it might have been for them and their organization.

My first manager at the Apollo 11 project impressed on his subordinates—many of them extremely bright young scientists hired to make creative contributions to the space program—that his three main values were Arriving Early, Staying Late, and Looking Busy. He was interested in seeing bodies at desks, in case he was visited by his boss or any other senior manager. He worried about having people out of sight doing experiments or research in libraries. We knew he checked the coat rack when he came in to see who had arrived early; I hired a janitor who started work at 6:00 A.M. to hang up my coat so that I could go to the library and work.

That manager asked a bunch of inquisitive, independent-minded scientists for behavior that correlated not in the least with the heroic challenges of the greatest technological mission in the history of the human species. Putting in the hours is necessary to peak performance, but working smart produces more results than merely working long—or appearing to work long.

There are people who know all of this, think they are doing all of it, and still aren't getting the results they think they should get. What happened?

Peak performers, the people who both innovate and consolidate, show high initiative. They can start a project, and make a productive response to someone else's project. Other people, those who are merely in motion, also take initiative and instigate activity—but without a sense of priorities based on purpose. They often see their projects careen off course. Some are motivated by a need to draw attention to themselves, others by a fear of trusting or developing co-workers. They jump in and solve problems that someone else could solve. They interfere with other people's ability to take initiative.

These are the people who redouble their efforts after they lose sight of their objective. Their work is often best characterized by the saying from the Foreign Legion: "When in doubt, gallop!"

The business world is full of goal-directed individuals who are not sure why they do what they do. I am thinking of people who focus on money as their primary goal, work very hard to get it, and have little idea of a real mission—a larger context for that goal. I have heard men talk about survival, and the financial welfare of their families, while they counted their third or fourth or thirtieth million. They are examples of a larger category of well-intentioned yet overzealous people who incessantly try to prove themselves by launching powerfully toward a goal with no conscious mission behind it. Frequently they produce; often they achieve a modicum of success; but, charging from goal to goal with no mission to guide them, they live with the disquieting feeling that they are not really going in a direction they find personally fulfilling.

They remind me of a man I hired several years ago as a research director. He arrived with superb credentials and technical skills but frequently launched efforts in unproductive directions. I noticed that what he was doing often did not fit the organization's game plan. We talked, and it seemed he was doing a great many things without knowing why, but I could not get a grip on the problem until the night a number of us went to a concert and heard an ambidextrous musician who put on a flashy show of playing two different instruments, one with each hand, looking straight at the audience. The research director was obviously impressed. A few minutes into the performance I heard him exclaim, "Man, I'd give my right arm to be ambidextrous!"

The peak performer sorts things out and takes not just action, but purposeful action, in the service of results.

NO FEAR OF FAILURE

The peak performers in our study move toward success, not away from failure—a fundamental difference that contributes greatly to freeing up their willingness to take risks in the service of innovation and results.

The self-confidence we noted in most of them clearly grew from their bias toward the "self-actualization" that Abraham Maslow described—fulfilling one's highest values and being all that one can be. Among consistent high achievers, we did not often see the fear of failure and its punishments, real or imagined, that may spur desperate short-range action. Nor did we see the aversion to risk-taking and innovation that leaves individuals frozen at the edge of consolidation, going through the motions, operating not on insight but on memory.

Even the founders of businesses are not the risk-taking daredevils that folklore has made them out to be.

There is a popular notion that an entrepreneur is a high roller who gets his kicks from risking the family house on a chance to get rich. In fact, Paul Hawken, an experienced founder of small businesses (his current one, Smith & Hawken, started as an importer and retailer of high-quality garden tools), contends:

> An entrepreneur is a risk-avoider. He or she usually starts by seeing a situation from an entirely different angle than someone else . . . a market, a niche, an idea, a product that is unseen or discounted by others. Whether this is a personal computer (Apple), a hub-and-spokes air delivery system (Federal Ex-

press), or exercise for housewives (Jane Fonda), the need is obvious to the entrepreneur. There is no risk because they are totally identified with the end result. They are not studying the market, they are the market. That's a big difference.

What an entrepreneur will then do is identify every possible obstacle that could prevent him or her from achieving that goal, and eliminate as many as possible. Entrepreneurs only appear to be daring.

Their self-confidence, their ability to engage in purposeful action, their decisiveness and effectiveness, is learned. It is a learned effectiveness guided by a commitment to innovation that produces results. Through repeated educated risks, the peak performers learn as they go along, and over time their confidence in their own judgment gains strength. It is not fear of failure that drives them along, but a strong desire for achievement.

Remember Warren Bennis's finding that the ninety leaders he interviewed would use almost any word—*glitch, false start, bug*—rather than *failure*. The reason goes beyond semantics. It has to do with learning. When high achievers get less than the results they plan for and work toward, they allow the normal human feelings of disappointment, or anger, or fatigue, to pass; then they start analyzing. They search for information in the situation:

Where are we now?

What went wrong? Why?

Where are we headed?

How do we get there?

They operate as both innovator and consolidator, and resume moving toward completion of their mission and goals.

Even when circumstances are totally beyond their control, peak performers learn what they can from an experience so as not to knock their heads against that wall again. They keep their eyes open so that they do not, as mythologist Joseph Campbell once put it, "get to the top of the ladder and find it's against the wrong wall."

There is a special quality that leads to learned effectiveness and the results orientation of the peak performer. It, too, can be enhanced by training, and it, too, distinguishes peak performers from ordinary performers. It consists of an ability to take charge of one's work and its progress. To a significant degree, peak performers manage their own development. First they examine their own capabilities. Then they take steps to fully utilize and further develop those capabilities. They practice self-management through self-mastery.

5

SELF-MANAGEMENT THROUGH SELF-MASTERY

People love to watch construction workers fitting together a new building. There is something magnetic in the scene: Dirt and iron and wood and cables collected in what could be a great mess, and through it all the workers proceed with an air of competence, seeming to know each next step without constantly looking around for a boss and asking, "Now what do I do?"

Within limits, they manage themselves. It is that aura of self-management, more than anything else, that attracts me to the windows in the fences around new skyscraper sites. Each worker who takes charge of his own progress frees the others to contribute to what they are all there for, to make the building rise, floor by floor, as if nothing could stop it.

I am not suggesting that every construction worker is a peak performer. But in every form of work, as opportunities expand and complexity increases, as the call for creative thinking and high performance becomes more insistent, the power of self-management emerges more and more dramatically.

When we study self-managers in their varied environments, we see them opening a lot of running room for themselves. They need less supervising than other people, and they free the time and energies of those who manage them. It is a neat double play: In liberating their managers' energies, they liberate their own.

The skills of problem solving and information seeking emerge most powerfully in self-directed people who thrive on the fact that they are accountable for the consequences of their behavior. As Richard Boyatzis of McBer and Company puts it, they possess:

> a sense of efficacy, the disposition to see oneself as the originator of actions in one's life . . . [viewing] events in life as opportunities for taking action and [seeing] themselves as the agents who must precipitate such action.

THE SELF-MANAGER AT WORK: CRISP THINKING IN THE WAR ZONE

My father, Ed Garfield, was a sales engineer—giving technical advice to customers who requested it—for Kester Solder Company, which has since become a subsidiary of Litton Industries. In the 1950s, a customer, a men's cosmetics company in New Jersey, had just developed one of the first pressurized shaving-foam dispensers. Kester got a substantial order for the solder that would attach the valves to the cans of foam. More orders came in; then they stopped. A panicky call came from New Jersey: "Your solder is no good. Send a man down to check what's happening."

The reason for the panic sounds, several decades later, like a scene from a Woody Allen movie. The cosmetics company had shipped thousands of cans full of shaving cream and Freon propellant to supermarkets, drugstores, and department stores, and within two or three weeks calls started coming in from the managers of warehouses and stores across the United States: "Your shaving cans erupted on the shelves! The cream is getting all over our merchandise! All over anybody who comes close! Send help, fast!"

When my father entered a conference room at the customer's headquarters, he was attacked almost physically by seven mechanical engineers and their company's top managers. "Your firm supplied us with the wrong solder!" one of them yelled. "Yeah!" the others yelled. "We're going to sue you," the first one said. This was clearly a war-zone atmosphere. If handled badly, the situation could hurt Kester's relationships throughout its industry. Caring for the customer was important. Still, this outright assault went a bit too far. Any number of responses would have been possible, from apology to indignation.

But my father had trained himself to handle such high-pressure situations on his own, and have them turn out so that everyone involved—not just one side or the other—felt the situation was resolved. Instead of allowing himself to flare up, he started asking questions.

Could he please see the valve design? He knew the customer had hired a number of engineers to help with the design, hotshots in too big a hurry to use the consultation Kester had been offering. He knew they had plunged into an area where they had little history. Some were in the conference room. They hesitated, then produced a blueprint. The valve was vertical, held in place only by soft solder, not a material that should have been used for strength. Any pressure working on it would loosen it in time. Well, what to do now?

From the logical point of view, the frowning, worried men in the room might have suggested a cover-your-rear reflex. My father, however, searched for clues from similar situations, from times in the past when he had handled high-stress situations well. He saw what to do. Attach a flange to the neck of the can to take the strain at the bottom of the valve, and use the solder as it should have been used all along, to seal the opening around the flanges.

"Recall all our shaving cream? Expensive . . . Embarrassing . . ." The cosmetics people wouldn't like his suggestion. So he offered it, calmly and surely, as the thing to do. Tempers flared as he expected. He did not argue the point; they would see it when they thought over what he had shown them.

A few weeks later they called him back. Could he go over the suggestion again? They made final designs for proper soldering, and the shaving product—and Kester's reputation—were salvaged.

The problem between Kester Solder Company and the cosmetics company was troublesome enough that it could have usurped considerable time and energy at the top levels of management. My father was not top management. He was a technical adviser. Yet under intense pressure, alone in a room with an important customer's top management, he took responsibility for the outcome, and accomplished as much as anyone would have expected of the highest-ranking company leader.

THE LIFEBLOOD OF AN EXCELLENT ORGANIZATION IS TO HAVE SELF-MANAGERS AT ALL LEVELS.

SELF-MASTERY

A peak performer's skills in self-management emerge from the personal, internal skills of *self-mastery*. Self-mastery is nothing mysterious. It means orchestrating and developing one's capabilities, after looking to see what they are.

Self-mastery calls for thorough familiarity with one's mental and emotional strengths. And it calls for sustaining a commitment to personal growth—the understanding of what makes you tick as an individual—as well as professional development.

Three major aspects of self-mastery vital to self-managers are:

1. Self-confidence
2. Micro/macro attention
3. Mental rehearsal

Self-confidence stems from the feeling, and the evidence to back it up, that you know what you are doing and do it well. You can see the arguments for and against any decision, but you do not hesitate to make the decision and live with it.

Self-confident people feel an internal authority to act, based on a sense of their own expertise and the knowledge that if something goes awry they will know what to do. They count on their capabilities' being equal to a task. In short, they trust their own effectiveness.

Self-confidence is internal mastery. Effectiveness is external mastery. Each supports the other.

SELF-CONFIDENCE ⟷ EFFECTIVENESS

The more effective a peak performer is, the more self-confident he or she becomes. The greater the self-confidence, the more likely its possessor is to be effective. Clearly, intervening variables can make a big difference. A person's level of skill, the quality of response from others, their personalities, and organizational environment all play a role in the results one gets.

THE ONE ELEMENT THAT STANDS OUT MOST CLEARLY AMONG OUR PEAK PERFORMERS IS THEIR VIRTUALLY UNASSAILABLE BELIEF IN THE LIKELIHOOD OF THEIR OWN SUCCESS. THEIR TRACK RECORDS REINFORCE THEIR BELIEFS.

Self-confidence is not arrogance or bravado. Such conceits are more frequently signs of personal insecurity and fear of inadequacy. If Ed Garfield had given in to doubts about his competence when the customers were shouting at him, he might have responded with bluster and made the situation worse. Instead, he knew he could land on his feet. The strength of the peak performers' belief in their own competence allows them to:

- Focus wholeheartedly on mobilizing their skills and capabilities.
- Align with a team or organization, fully expecting the environment to contain the resources and support they need to excel. They prefer to see their work environment as more nourishing than toxic; and more often than not, they see themselves as able to make it so.

People with the twin attributes of self-confidence and effectiveness put into practice the six major attributes we found in interviewing peak performers. They:

- Plan and act consistently, guided by mission.
- Get results.

- Take initiative and manage themselves.
- Build teams and motivate other people.
- Correct course to stay on track.
- Manage change to maintain peak performance.

AN INEXHAUSTIBLE SOURCE OF EFFECTIVENESS FOR PEAK PERFORMERS: THE HUMAN CAPACITIES THEY CULTIVATE IN THEMSELVES AND THE PEOPLE AROUND THEM.

Micro/macro attention combines worm's-eye and bird's-eye views. A *micro* mode of thinking involves logical, analytical computation, seeing cause and effect in methodical steps. It is valued by those who prize attention to detail, precision, and orderly progressions: "If we do A, then B must follow." It is the worm's-eye view without which science, technology, and industry could not function.

The *macro* mode, the bird's-eye view, is particularly useful for shaking out themes and patterns from assortments of information. Call the macro mode of thinking intuitive, or holistic, or conceptual. It is good for bridging gaps. It enables us to perceive a pattern even when some of the pieces are missing. In contrast, the logical sequences of the micro mode cannot skip over gaps. The psychiatrist and researcher David Galin points out: "Since we are usually trying to operate in this world with incomplete information, we very badly need to have the capacity to perceive general patterns and jump across gaps in present knowledge."

George de Mestral, the inventor of Velcro fasteners, got the idea while brushing burrs out of his wool pants and his dog's coat. He didn't say to himself, "First: We want a replacement for zippers. Second: I will invent a tape with hooks on one side and loops on the other." He was simply curious about the tenacity of the burrs, so he looked at them under a microscope and saw their hundreds of tiny hooks snagged in mats of wool and fur. Years later something made him connect the sight with a problem on which he was working, and his invention was born.

A peak performer has the confidence that is required to trust some of the valuable and, for some, less-familiar human capabilities, such as intuition. Many people override intuition—the moment when they just know they have the answer—because it does not seem grounded in "irrefutable" facts and because the information comes from a location they regard as questionable: inside themselves.

Creative problem-solving integrates the micro and the macro, keeping each available to the other. Ed Garfield kept a firm grip on his micro view of technical detail in the problem between Kester and the cosmetics company while he searched his past experience, in a macro mode, for an approach that might enable him to see a solution.

Mental rehearsal. Peak performers, particularly in business, sports, and the arts, report a highly developed ability to imprint images of successful actions in the mind. They practice, mentally, specific skills and behaviors leading to those outcomes and achievements which they ultimately attain.

Albert Einstein indicated many times that his most powerful theoretical problems did not yield readily to logical thinking about equations. He is reported to have said, in searching for a way to describe how he did approach such challenges, that it was more like feeling the equations in his muscles. First he felt a sort of muscular excitation or tension that told him he was onto something. Then came mental images such as the famous one, of a little boy riding a beam of light, that foreshadowed the abstractions of the Special Theory of Relativity. Finally, the follow-through: $E = mc^2$. "Feeling it in my muscles" is a metaphor, probably. But it continues to serve scientists, and the rest of us, well.

Most people use words to describe their plans and activities, even silently to themselves. Language is arguably the most powerful of all human creations. But even more than words, *images* motivate people to perform at peak efficiency.

Brandon Hall told me about a graph he kept on his office wall, depicting his sales goal. Its ascending line conveyed the direction he wanted to go in selling corporate training programs. His production in 1982 had been $175,000. Even in the recession of that early part of the decade, he decided to set his goal for 1984 at $1 million—a peak that was talked about but never scaled at Wilson Learning Corporation. Hall would envision himself topping it. He envisioned himself trouble-shooting each customer's training needs. He envisioned himself deciding which Wilson products were right for each situation. This was not mere wishful thinking. As he learned the ropes in his early, less lucrative days, and as he used the dual process of mental rehearsal and effective follow-through, he acquired expertise and confidence. The result? He was the first Wilson Learning account executive to pass the $1 million mark.

His position as salesperson and consultant requires a high degree of macro perspective: What's going on here? Where is this system stuck? What could it accomplish? It calls, as well, for a micro perspective: What is the exact product or system or service for the client? What steps do we take to implement it?

The graph on the office wall represented not only gross sales to Hall, but also a measure of impact—his own and his company's. Its ascent signified satisfaction of his needs for achievement and self-development. And it represented the payoff for Wilson's investment in him, an employee whose commitment to self-mastery overcame both difficult economic times and his own inexperience.

SELF-MANAGEMENT IN THE LATE TWENTIETH CENTURY

When asked, "What will be the biggest management changes in the 1980s?" Peter Drucker drew on the half-century of thought that has made him the most influential analyst of modern organizations:

> First, we will all learn that modern economies are owned by and run for the employees and that the only property rights in a modern society are the rights of the job. Every manager I know still sees in his mind's eye that "labor" is the unskilled, pre-literate sharecropper, black or white, who streamed into the munitions plants in 1917. But by 1990, we will have learned, I hope, what the Japanese learned from us. We taught it to them:

> People are a resource and not a cost. The Japanese have accepted that idea and we haven't.

The point is to look at the depth of people's capabilities, in terms of skills training and in broader terms—*the effective mobilization of personal resources by human beings who develop themselves as self-managers.*

CULTIVATING SELF-MASTERY: PARTICULARS OF SELF-CONFIDENCE, MICRO/MACRO ATTENTION, AND MENTAL REHEARSAL

Since peak performers see themselves not as finished products, or static identities, or simple job descriptions, they are *by definition* always on a hunt for increasing self-mastery. They are aware not only of change but of a particular kind of change—the growth of those capabilities linked to personally meaningful achievement. They see themselves participating in a process that never ends. Their commitment to lifelong learning and change has its roots in several assumptions:

- Creativity and inventiveness are natural to all people.
- An inner restlessness, also natural to all people, can release creativity and inventiveness.
- Survival and security are obviously legitimate concerns. Yet once a society or an individual becomes reasonably well fed and secure, those concerns are joined by "higher-order" needs—for esteem, accomplishment, contribution to others, fulfillment of potential—the "self-actualization" that Abraham Maslow described.

SELF-CONFIDENCE: A RESULT OF SELF-KNOWLEDGE

To the peak performer, the dictum "Know thyself" constitutes more than a general piece of advice from the Seven Sages of antiquity. In the same bottom-line sense that he or she understands "Know thy capital resources" and "Know thy organizational objectives" as pragmatic priorities, the peak performer accurately assesses personal strengths. Peak performers inventory themselves.

"What am I really good at?"

"What are my strengths?"

After decades of work with major companies, Peter Drucker proposes: "The great mystery isn't that people do things badly but that they occasionally do a few things *well.* The only thing that is universal is *incompetence.* Strength is always specific! Nobody ever commented, for example, that the great violinist Jascha Heifetz probably couldn't play the trumpet very well."

Among the things one research director put on a list of his strengths was "knowing when to abandon a project." For a research director, that may be at least as important as knowing what projects to start.

Specificity rates high with the most confident peak performers. They are only casually concerned with general assessments ("I get along well with people"), which they consider academic exercises. What they are really after is how their particular strengths fit with the demands of their work and their organization.

In this they often illustrate the real point Charles Darwin made when he equated "survival of the fittest" with "natural selection." Darwin did not mean "fittest" as in roughest and most domineering—the raw power interpretation that the phrase usually gets in modern corporate life. He meant the best possible fit between organism and environment. The organism that fits best is the one most capable of adapting and using its strengths to meet challenge and change. Dinosaurs were the dominant creatures of their day, but they did not fit in a changing environment. Looking for the fit, a peak performer asks the next question:

"What are the key activities in my work?"

Not work in general. As we heard repeatedly in our study, there is no such thing. *Their* work, specifically. "What do I do in *my* organization, to discharge *my* responsibilities?" A chief executive realized, after some thought, that "handing out work assignments" is a key activity for him. That seems obvious, except that until he asked himself the question and pursued an answer, he could not fathom why he was having trouble matching the right senior managers with the right jobs. He is himself a meticulously organized worker, so he appreciates careful planners and tends to assign them to important projects—even to those projects that call for people-handling skills that the planners sometimes lack.

In light of the earlier questions about personal strengths and key activities, the top performers ask a further question:

"What do I need to learn?"

They don't waste time berating themselves for doing something badly. They look for shortfalls that impede the use of their strengths, and for corrections. The chief executive who hands out work assignments saw in himself a habit of leaving unclear just what he wanted to accomplish with each assignment. To correct it, he got specific. He started asking, "What do I expect from this person?" He puts the answer in writing, for himself and his appointees. Three months and again six months later he reviews it: "Has he or she met the expectation? Come close? Missed entirely?"

From "What do I need to learn?" come a variety of follow-ups. "What am I doing that I should do more of? That I should cut down? In what areas do I need to improve? What is the most effective way to get up to speed? Or can I delegate any of these areas to someone else?" All of us, by birth or learning, have areas that hold little interest for us. They just aren't "ours." Peak performers see no profit in kidding themselves about their preferences.

Preference before expertise. Donald Burr of People Express likes airplanes, so he is not trying to run a bank. There are many fine missions, goals, and tasks that many fine people are not equipped, by preference and aptitude, to do. I remember one brilliant engineer-turned-manager who struggled to run a department until he finally admitted that he could not work up much interest in other people's triumphs and setbacks, and arranged to limit his relationship with his colleagues pretty much to technical discussions. Peter Drucker remarks, "You can learn good manners to deal with people, but you *can't learn* to trust people. And you *must* trust to be comfortable with them."

Most shortfalls that the question "What do I need to learn?"

uncovers can be corrected. For instance, I have met quite a few managers—in smokestack industries, service professions, high tech, communications, across the board—who came up through engineering or personnel, and who know almost nothing about accounting, and make no attempt to familiarize themselves with its principles. That is the tunnel-vision trap. Some make it worse. They fall into the arrogance trap and proclaim *pride* in not being a "number cruncher." Pride takes a fall when they find that the financial managers are walking all over them in meetings. The solution is easy, once the problem is acknowledged: Take some accounting courses. Then apply them to what you already know in other areas.

Or there are the line supervisors promoted to broader management positions who are used to talking to workers in shop shorthand, and may stumble when they try presenting their ideas to top management. Again, I have seen such men and women develop a strength: They learn to concentrate, when a presentation is scheduled, on polishing drafts and rehearsing talks to make them clear and sharp.

A Source of Confidence: Ego Strength. The confidence to ask questions about one's own performance—and to act on answers that are sometimes difficult—emerges from an attribute that psychologists call *ego strength.*

Ego is a term much misunderstood as a synonym for *narcissist* or *braggart* or *authoritarian.* Originally a term from psychoanalysis, the ego is the executive agency of the personality, the director of actions. As such, it is the part of ourselves that selects the features of the environment to which each of us will respond and decides how our needs can be satisfied. The ego is a normal and necessary part of human personality.

Andrew Grove illustrates a practical application of ego strength by describing high-achieving employees at Intel as "micro CEOs." The ability to take charge, to be effective in any surroundings, shows "executive" capability that stems from the deepest kind of personal authority. No matter where he or she is in the organization, the micro CEO possessing a strong ego feels self-authorized to perceive things accurately and make effective decisions—an internal executive sense that translates as self-confidence and self-esteem, poise under pressure, ability to learn from others and manage change effectively. People with such ego strength contrast markedly with people who are said to have "big egos," the macho, authoritarian types who flaunt their ability to "kick ass and take names."

Ego strength often shows up in business and elsewhere as *hardiness*—the energy to sustain long hours of work and the flexibility to adapt to change. Hardiness comes from a strong sense of being on course. Less confident co-workers spend significant amounts of their energy hiding behind pronouncements of policy and "higher authority" and maneuvering to protect their skins, which tend to be thin.

So we see the peak performers mastering both themselves and their environments. Lee Iacocca's well-documented response to Henry Ford II's summarily firing him after years of hard work and high achievement was not that of a superman but that of a man possessed of considerable ego strength. This strength did not ward off the blow. It did allow Iacocca to act successfully in his own behalf once the blow had fallen. Despite a temporary increase in drinking and some tremors in his hands (understandable under the circumstances), Iacocca did not collapse under the shock of the impact. He could have gone to pieces, letting his anger at Ford mire him in the past, lamenting the loss of the good old days. Instead, he made his painful departure a launch pad for greater accomplishment. His strength of character, so evident to people in Detroit, made him the obvious choice when the management of Chrysler went looking for a chairman to rescue their company from disaster.

Ego strength differs from egocentrism in a crucial way. While the egocentric person, positioned at the center of the universe, cannot let go of his or her own point of view long enough to see what others see, the peak performer can take multiple perspectives on any given issue. With an ability to see a situation from varying viewpoints, he or she can make sense of conflicting information. Egocentrism limits you to trusting only your own perception and judgment; the result is a closed system without feedback or alternative information.

EGO STRENGTH LETS YOU MAKE USE OF THE PERCEPTIONS AND JUDGMENT OF OTHERS.

Where do peak performers learn the skills that emerge from ego strength? Often from other peak performers they adopt as mentors. One reason Ed Garfield handled the cosmetics company crisis so well was that he thought back to times in his past with a senior engineer named Ed Kolman, and remembered something similar that Kolman handled well. Confident from past experience that he would find what he was looking for, he was able in the pressure of that conference room to assess his strengths and translate them into strategic decisions.

As a young man, my father had been a technician on a production line, a first-class mechanic. He was familiar with solder. Yet there were gaps in his knowledge of the full range of alloys used in it, the different melting points of each, their different uses in production. He was determined to fill the gaps. So he took night courses at City College of New York. Before long his interest turned to sales, and he and Ed Kolman frequently discussed the best ways to deal with customers. I remember hearing rules like "Never disguise the fact that you don't know an answer. Always tell the customer that you don't know, and you'll find out. Then go out and do the research, and make sure you follow up." Orders started coming in, traceable directly to my father's efforts and Ed Kolman's coaching. "Customers are human," I would hear. "They don't like to be rushed. They don't want to hear only why and how your product is better. They also want to know how it can be used to their advantage."

Years before the cosmetics company's cans started gushing foam, Ed Kolman had taken my father along on a problem call. A customer was having big trouble in soldering the bases of light bulbs. The joints were coming apart. Kolman said nothing when the foreman showed them the automatic soldering machine. "Your solder's no good," the foreman said. Still Kolman said nothing. He watched the machine where the problem was. The customer had already switched to a competitor's solder, but the same thing was happening. The flame, the brass base of the bulb, the automatic settings, all seemed correct. As solder was fed toward the base, it should have spread out to make a bond. Instead, it balled up. "See," the foreman repeated, glaring at Kolman. "No good." Kolman was too engrossed in the problem to be insulted.

Finally Kolman spoke. "Move the flame a little, that way," he said. Suddenly the no-good solder was perfect. Bulbs went through the machine without rejects.

Afterward my father asked how he had performed the miracle. Kolman said, "Always observe. You know the basics of what we just saw. The part being soldered must be heated, not the solder. We adjusted the flame so that it hit the lamp base and not the solder itself. Eureka, your miracle."

Peak performers possessed of considerable ego strength are drawn toward performance that reflects, in Maslow's terms:

> . . . greater efficiency, making an operation more neat, compact, simpler, faster, less expensive, turning out a better product, doing with less parts, a smaller number of operations, less clumsiness, less effort, more foolproof, safer, more "elegant," less laborious.

Daily Tactics and Long-Range Strategies. We noticed throughout our studies that ego strength is more than just a source of confidence in daily struggles. It is a distinguishing attribute of peak performers as they make the most basic of long-range decisions, deciding whether or not to follow a particular mission: Do I summon my energies for this, or do I say, "This isn't worth it"?

Such decisions are based not on whim, or desire for peace and quiet, or addiction to action, but on an assessment of whether the energies summoned will serve missions, goals, and values that add up to the true bottom line for peak performers: achievement and self-development.

At the inception of a mission, most people give a lot of attention and energy to clarifying their purpose; some even take the time to clarify their underlying values. Then what normally happens in the stress and complexity of work life is that individuals start to lose the original meanings, the values underlying the original mission. Daily action gets disconnected from deeper purposes. With that disintegration, an individual may lapse into activity that ultimately turns out to be aimless—putting out brush fires not because they are important but because they attract attention. Then we see what psychologist Oscar Mink calls "a tendency to forget the intended beneficiary. Justice gives way to the convenience of lawyers, judges, and clerks; industry to profit at the expense of environmental and consumer needs; patient health and well-being to the convenience of doctors, nurses, and technicians; student learning to the career ambitions of teachers."

A continual monitoring, an opting for growth choices, mark the awareness and skill of self-confident people. The peak performer is an executive in both the internal and the external sense. One reflection of a strong ego is the self-confidence and accuracy of perception that allows one to function as a micro CEO—that is, a person who, even in the roughest times, can make effective decisions based on his or her most objective conceptions of reality. The peak performer's confidence can always be renewed by focusing on "Who I am and why I am here."

MICRO/MACRO ATTENTION: PARTNERS IN CREATIVE WORK

One result of self-confidence is that it frees up people's common sense. Even in situations of crisis, confident people can stay relaxed enough to pay attention to the sometimes surprising conclusions that emerge from the dialogue between reason and intuition.

Micro analysis is so often the dominant point of view that one might have difficulty, unless one has an uncommon amount of confidence, basing a big decision only on the patterns one sees from a *macro* perspective. The people getting impressive results today in successful organizations, large and small, hold overall missions in mind while they also attend to necessary details. For the most part, the reason for their effectiveness is not that they are inspecting minutiae and finding new ways for computers to count things. They know how to count, all right. They also have a commitment to the aspects of their business that used to be regarded as "irrational" (translation: harder to quantify), such as people, quality, and service to customers.

Albert Einstein liked to underscore the micro/macro partnership with a remark from Sir George Pickering that he chalked on the blackboard in his office at the Institute for Advanced Studies at Princeton: "Not everything that counts can be counted, and not everything that can be counted counts."

Trying to maintain perspective on "everything that counts" isn't easy. "There's a special tension to people who are constantly in the position of making new knowledge," Dr. Peter Carruthers observes. He speaks from experience. As head of theoretical physics at the Los Alamos National Laboratory, he focuses on the frontiers of science, where, he says, "You're always out of equilibrium. Carruthers admits it feels "unnatural" to live on the brink of confusion. "At times, it's better not to push it. Your unconscious ultimately has to do a lot of the work. God only knows how that happens, but it really does. You have to stuff yourself—gorge yourself on a problem—and then go and leave it."

In other words, the peak performer tolerates confusion and ambiguity up to a point and is willing to let go of a problem now and then, trusting that creative, productive mental work will take place.

This trust in the uncontrollable is not the same as announcing, "I got intuition," and going off on every wild hunch or wishful thought. As Carruthers says, you work. You do the data-gathering and analysis that provides the "stuff" for the unconscious to chew on.

"To be creative," says Howard Gruber, "you need to know a lot and cultivate special skills." As a specialist in cognitive psychology, Gruber examines the lives of first-rank scientists for clues to the processes underlying breakthroughs:

> Darwin studied barnacles for eight years and came to know more about them than anyone else. Leonardo drew a thousand hands.

> . . . The most stable generalization about the creative life is that you work hard, probably for a long time. Of course, in working you transform yourself, and what would be hard for others becomes easy for you. . . . For the creative person, the greatest fun is the work. You have to take notice when Darwin says he read Malthus "for amusement."

Yet such people are not workaholics who fit philosopher George Santayana's description of those who "redouble their efforts after losing sight of the objective." The people we are talking about do not lose sight of their objectives.

One underlying goal is to use the micro and macro modes of thought with equal facility so that each supports the other. Much talk about intuition implies that analysis and logic are hostile to creativity. Peak performers demonstrate, and scholars such as Carruthers and Gruber confirm, exactly the opposite: Analysis and intuition are intimate partners in creative work.

Analysis helps to break down a problem into manageable elements. It is not particularly helpful, however, without its partner, synthesis. The value of the macro perspective is that it allows one to see innovative ways to combine the analyzed elements into a new whole.

People who cultivate these abilities also become skilled jugglers, able to change focus back and forth among a network of enterprises. Bertrand Russell was a mathematician and a political activist. When the British government imprisoned him toward the end of World War I for his antiwar writings, he used the time in jail to write articles and the *Introduction to Mathematical Philosophy.*

Such nimbleness, a direct result of the peak performer's tolerance for ambiguity, allows an expanded context in which to manage oneself.

People who will not relax their preference for concrete, countable information tend to pass by possibilities that do not fit into what they already know. The "special tension" of which Carruthers speaks may even strike some as irresponsible vagueness. At a minimum, it threatens their comfort zone.

William J. J. Gordon, founder of the brainstorming process known as Synectics, says:

> All problems present themselves to the mind as threats of failure. For someone striving to win in terms of a successful solution, this threat evokes a mass response in which the most immediate superficial solution is clutched frantically as a balm to anxiety. . . . Yet if we are to perceive all the implications and possibilities of the new, we must risk at least temporary ambiguity and disorder.

NEW DIRECTIONS: COMBINING SELF-CONFIDENCE AND MICRO/MACRO ATTENTION

The fact is that daily work does most often rely on concrete, countable tasks. The fact is, too, that survival needs—food and shelter—tend to emphasize the worm's-eye view over the bird's-eye.

The achievements of most peak performers in our study did not result from bypassing those intense and often complex demands. They came, instead, from fitting daily tasks and survival concerns into a larger context where they had less power to dominate the individual's life.

Bill Robertson, for example, is a man of ideas in a world of hunger and survival. From behind the wheel of his limousine, driving me from the Roanoke airport to a sales conference at the Greenbrier Resort in West Virginia, Robertson treated me to a description of the region we were rolling through. He combined geography, geology, and local politics with such clarity and color that I commented that he ought to teach in a local college. He was an uncommonly fine communicator. He told me that running his transportation service was a lot more interesting.

Robertson was born in the back hills, in a community so suspicious of outside ideas that in the 1920s and 1930s the local people had torched several schools. Knowing somehow that ignorance was not bliss and that he could do more with his life than scare schoolteachers, he moved to the city and started as a mechanic.

He would read hungrily at lunchtime—biographies, geology, history. "Being mediocre," he said, "is a drag if you don't want to be."

The possibilities for his life extended beyond merely being somebody else's mechanic. In his spare time he started bringing worn-out old limousines back to life, rebuilding them from scratch. Then he started his own limo service, contacting corporations for business, advertising in the Yellow Pages.

"I had to run my own company," he said, "because it was the only way I could be sure the customers were getting quality service." That feeling for service extended to an extraordinary empathy with the automobiles on which customers could count for comfortable, reliable rides. Robertson brought a fascinating bimodal approach to their upkeep: Not only would he conduct frequent inspections, eyeballing the cars and running mechanical tests, he also imagined himself inside the engines, feeling where the stresses might be, visualizing how the internal parts were holding up. His description of the process reminded me of the inventor Nikola Tesla, one of the most brilliant people who ever lived, who could see in his mind's eye every detail of a machine he was designing—not only see the machine as it would be, but mentally see it running, go on to other thoughts, then after a few days turn his thoughts back to check how the parts had worn in the interim!

Robertson knew his life had been a series of moves based on a sense of his own abilities and how they fit into a continuously growing larger picture. Moving on from the ways in which he was raised to become a mechanic, then an entrepreneur, and then, perhaps, delegating the operation of his transportation service so that he could make the next move. He wondered: What could it be? The talents he had shown me as we drove through the Virginia and West Virginia countryside suggested that he could teach the skills of entrepreneuring. He promised he would give it some thought.

MENTAL REHEARSAL: SEEING IT FIRST IN THE MIND'S EYE

Another aspect of self-mastery is the rehearsal of mental images. Mental rehearsal is far from casual daydreaming. Peak performers give it concentrated and repeated practice.

Many athletes create mental images of the exact movements they want to emulate in their own sport. The Boston Celtics' star player and later coach Bill Russell wrote in his book *Second Wind:* "I was sitting there with my eyes closed, watching plays in my head. I was in my own private basketball laboratory, making mental blueprints for myself."

Liu Chi Kung, who placed second to Van Cliburn in the 1958 Tchaikovsky Competition, was imprisoned a year later during the Cultural Revolution in China. During the entire seven years he was held, he was denied the use of a piano. Soon after his release he was back on tour, and critics wrote in astonishment that his musicianship was better than ever. "How did you do this?" one asked. "You had no chance to practice for seven years." Liu replied, "I did practice, every day. I rehearsed every piece I had every played, note by note, in my mind."

Research has shown that imagined events imprinted deeply in the mind are recorded by the brain and central nervous system as memories. With practice and repetition, one can imagine well enough so that these memories are not distinguishable from actual physical experience. Some years ago I was asked to rate participants in a double-blind study of people who were afraid of speaking in public and who showed an interest in attending a class on becoming effective speakers. They were separated into three groups:

Group 1 took a how-to course on techniques for public speaking, using what one might call a purely informational approach, reading and studying the techniques but delivering no actual talks.

Group 2 did some reading and gave two talks a week to small audiences of friends and other class members.

Group 3 did some reading on effective speaking, watched videotapes of effective speakers, and rehearsed mentally twice a day.

They delivered one talk a week to small groups of friends and class members. Raters who did not know which group was which evaluated their speaking ability both before and after.

Group 1, who took the course but did not practice speaking, did not improve. They simply learned the rules for improvement much as if they had read a book on riding a bicycle without getting on one.

Group 2, who actually spoke in public, improved significantly.

Group 3, however, improved even more. In our follow-ups we determined that one reason they did so much better was that, rather than merely trying to upgrade skills gradually, they had been practicing against a peak-performing norm: the excellent speakers they saw on tape, and, in their mental rehearsal, their own internal image of the best they could possibly be.

Peak performers may not notice that they are doing something called "mental rehearsal." When they do identify it as a distinct skill and put it into systematic, regular practice, the effect can be dramatic. The lesson I learned in Milan about intentionally orchestrating a substantial increase in weight lifting showed me what an impressive skill mental rehearsal can be. My success at lifting 365 pounds was only partially due to the mental training of the moment. Equally important, I discovered as I thought over what had happened, were the years of mental rehearsal I had conducted, unaware of what I was doing, throughout my weight-lifting career. Coaching by the Soviet-bloc scientists had focused and intensified a capacity that already existed—a capacity, as Maslow would say, "clamoring to be used." Whatever the activity—sports, business, or anything else—I am quite sure that a first attempt in unprepared territory would not yield the same level of results.

In business, peak performers report using mental rehearsal for specific micro situations: presentations at board meetings, a sales encounter with a difficult customer, a speech to a large group. They may be unaware of using a formally defined skill. Few in our study were acquainted with the term *mental rehearsal.* I frequently hear responses like "Yes, I imagine things in advance, sometimes over and over. But I never knew that had a name."

They use it, too, in macro ways to see how an altered situation might turn out, much as one uses the what-if capabilities of electronic spreadsheets.

Tom Henderson, a division manager in a large textile company in North Carolina, decided that his people would do better with less structure—but what would the reporting relationships in the new division look like? He reached for his yellow pad to start drawing the usual array of dangling boxes, and stopped. Instead, he summoned an image of each of his top people to mind and considered what he knew and felt about each. Mentally, he moved each into different situations and observed how the man or woman handled it. Then he determined to "bracket" the project—to turn his conscious attention to other things while letting the process he had started continue to work in his mind—after phrasing to himself specific instructions about the outcome he sought and when he needed to have it. Three days later, when he turned again to the yellow pad, the final steps of realigning and reassigning people according to their strengths and potential contributions came, as he told me, "as if I were describing a situation we'd been living with for months."

Magic? Hardly. The technique is based on some of the best and most current research in neurophysiology, and has been observed among peak performers for decades.

THE SELF-MANAGER AND THE ORGANIZATION

What happens to a peak performer, or budding peak performer, in a nonpeak-performing environment? Studs Terkel told in *Working* of dozens of people who felt trapped by their jobs: " 'I'm a machine,' says the spot-welder. 'I'm caged,' says the bank teller. . . . 'I'm a mule,' says the steelworker. 'A monkey can do what I do,' says the receptionist."

In the great organizational scheme of things, they feel little self-confidence or self-worth. "Who you gonna sock?" asks one of Terkel's steelworkers. "You can't sock General Motors . . . you can't sock a system." Yet, as Terkel points out, to maintain a modicum of self-worth, some add drama to their jobs, like the waitress who moves with the grace of a ballerina, pretending she is always on stage; others, like a Brooklyn firefighter, get genuine satisfaction from what they do: "You see them come out with babies in their hands . . . give mouth-to-mouth when a guy's dying. . . . That's real." And many in boring, exhausting, even humiliating jobs "perform astonishingly to survive the day," Terkel affirms. "These are not yet automata."

An individual must find meaning and a way to grow, or die on the job. So when I think of peak performers, I think of any person, in an organization or out, who discovers ways to be a distinct, contributing person—who refuses to give in to the system merely because it initially looks impervious to any individual's attempts to affect it.

Several years ago a large medical center in the Midwest had to deal with a couple of major problems simultaneously: a financial squeeze and a serious level of burnout among its nurses. Skilled professionals were showing the classic signs of occupational stress—high absenteeism, rapid turnover, and erratic performance. I was one of two consultants the hospital administrators brought in. We convened representatives of the major departments to open a discussion of working conditions.

At the first meeting an assistant hospital administrator declared that burnout is not only inevitable but, from the organization's point of view, advantageous. "If a senior nurse can't take it anymore," he said, "it may just be her time to leave. For her salary, we can hire two people right out of school. Of course, it's more likely that we will only hire one, and save the extra salary." His remarks revealed quite clearly to the nurses a viewpoint of at least several senior hospital administrators. After a moment of stunned silence, every nurse at the meeting got up and left.

While understandable if one considered only the short-range numbers, the man's peculiar approach guaranteed long-range problems. A continuing shift toward a staff of low-salaried beginners with a low level of skills and personal development would push the level of patient care, technical competence, customer satisfaction, and overall reputation at the center in one direction: down. The nurses, who knew that the development of a health care professional is very much a matter of on-the-job training, announced a strike.

Another assistant hospital administrator, James McInerny, was assigned to help get the medical center out of its predicament. From the beginning he felt trapped between those senior administrators who saw burnout as a secret ally to help them reduce costs, and the nurses who saw better working conditions for themselves as a necessity to provide better care for the patients.

The nurses wanted McInerny to visit the wards and see what produced their stress. Instead of reading reports in his office, he spent time with the nurses, hour after hour. In the coronary care unit he met a man who had just barely survived a massive heart attack; the man had his life, but was obviously still waging a desperate battle for it. McInerny wanted to be reassuring, but his hands got cold and his heart started pounding. "The whole scene made me quite nervous," he said later. "I began to see the toll it could take on a nurse, day after day." In an attempt to be helpful, he asked the heart patient: "What did you learn from your heart attack?" He hoped to hear the man say something about health, diet, job stress, perspective on life, and taking better care of himself. Instead, the man handed him a piece of paper on which he had scribbled some words from Ernest Hemingway's *A Farewell to Arms:* "The world breaks everyone and afterward many are strong at the broken places. . . ."

That, he thought, could be as true for the hospital as it was for the man.

McInerny noticed that administrators and clinical people did not just have different points of view; they actually spoke different technical languages. So he taught individuals from both groups to co-lead a weekly dialogue between the two camps. One financial manager said he didn't see why he should have to understand what the doctors and nurses were talking about: "We handle the money damn well, and if they want to get some for a new machine or some additional staffing, it's up to them to understand how we do things around here." That, as Peter Drucker once remarked, is like expecting all the natives to speak English. Not so fast, a doctor protested. "You figure this is just a business, and machines and people are all the same—just expense items. But we're talking about improved treatment of human beings. That's what's behind the technical terms."

McInerny started a broad array of self-management practices throughout the hospital. He provided the nurses with instruction on leading patient groups to solicit suggestions. Admissions, it turned out, was a place that patients hated because they were often treated so impersonally—an interesting bit of information, since admitting is one of the most obvious public relations jobs anyone at a hospital does. McInerny taught the nurses to conduct surveys. One revealed a pattern of patient complaints about some physicians' giving diagnoses of potentially life-threatening illnesses and then turning a shaken patient loose to drive home alone. Several of the patients had had accidents or near accidents. In response to such feedback, he set up courses in communication skills. The admitting staff learned to address a sick or injured person's distress, as well as the status of insurance. Physicians learned to suggest that patients about to be given a grave diagnosis bring someone in to keep them company and drive them home.

He got corporate trainers to donate time to teach health professionals a view of their hospital as a provider of excellent services and also a revenue-generating business, like any serious company. He set up sales and marketing seminars. "The times are changing," he told them. "We have to sell our services and compete with the other hospitals in town. High-quality service is great PR—the ultimate income generator." He encouraged personal networks—"Get your friends to talk to their friends about how good we are"—and initiated community education programs on self-management approaches to health, relaxation, nutrition, and fitness. He used the hospital's computer network to post messages, both clinical and quasi-social, that linked people in the various departments.

He persuaded the administration to pay cash bonuses for ideas on saving money and improving the quality of service. The move was important, both financially and symbolically. Underpaid staff members appreciated the money. They also appreciated the tangible sign that the administration, which they had so recently seen as callous, now valued what they said and did. Their willingness to take initiative and manage themselves increased.

The atmosphere in the hospital began to improve markedly for the staff and, more importantly, for the patients. It really jumped when word got around that the formerly intransigent financial manager was putting his formidable intelligence to work to learn the doctors' needs and concerns, and their language—and, conversely, to explain his work pressures to them.

McInerny and I met again recently at the annual meeting of the American Hospital Association. Life will probably never be easy at the medical center, he said, what with competition from other hospitals and changes in government regulations. But turnover and absenteeism are down. Morale is up. "We all believe we have the best hospital in the area—and that's a big difference from the days when some of us were not so much aspiring to greatness as expiring to it."

What happened at the medical center happens wherever there is a well-conceived and well-integrated commitment to enhancing self-management.

HISTORICAL MOMENTUM

Self-management is an idea whose time, in the 1980s in the United States, has come.

Roger D'Aprix, a business writer familiar with companies such as Xerox and Bell & Howell, points out that before World War II one of the values that supported our society was the notion that principles and things were more important than people. Throughout history, a result of that belief has been a definition of courage as the willingness to make severe personal sacrifices for "a greater good." In Japanese prison camps during World War II, ten-man work crews of Americans were often warned that if any escaped, those left behind would be shot. Yet often one would escape with the help of the other nine.

In the Korean War, however, not a single American prisoner is known to have escaped, even though some prisons had as few as a half-dozen guards. In the short span between the two wars,

D'Aprix observes, something had eroded the soldiers' willingness to sacrifice for an abstract principle. More recently in Vietnam, there were escapes and clear instances of heroism; also, however, there were prominent instances of soldiers' refusing to obey combat orders which they felt were suicidal. When people refuse to support an organizational mission that is destructive to individuals, they are sending a message that they are no longer willing to honor the supposed greater good as a useful principle.

One could make a point about a supposed decay of moral fiber, but there is another point we should not miss: the rise of a system of values in which people are more important than abstractions. This value system stresses each unique contribution, each self-managed achievement, instead of treating human beings as uniformly interchangeable parts. As D'Aprix sees it, a leader nowadays "recognizes the ultimate supremacy of persuading others to confront themselves and their contemporaries and to grow from their experiences. Any other kind of management style in the face of our new values and our new work force simply will not do the job." Considering our traditional measures of organizational success, he concedes, that is a tall order.

> If a company gets into trouble with its revenue and profit targets, self-actualization probably will be viewed as a luxury in the pressure to batten down the hatches and meet targets. It becomes a luxury, however, only if we believe that it is incompatible or inconsistent with other goals. But there is abundant evidence that it is possible to be profitable at the same time [*and I would add, for the precise reason*] that you develop and train the individual to seek his personal identity and to contribute to organizational success.

Among peak performers, we see people assuming that it is natural for individuals and organizations to share a responsibility for personal growth. The impact of that approach adds up. Paying attention to self-mastery leads to self-management, and the lessons of self-management are prized by people interested in success.

Most of the work done in society is done in organizations. More often than not, that means people pooling their individual strengths to operate as teams. The peak performer looks for leverage to bring out not only his or her own productive power, but the productivity of others. How does the self-managed individual use self-mastery when the challenge is to function as a team builder and a team player?

6

TEAM BUILDING/ TEAM PLAYING: GAINING LEVERAGE BY EMPOWERING OTHERS TO PRODUCE

Alvin Burger remembers the one time he was shouted down and driven off a speaker's platform. As a member of the Florida Pest Control Association, he got up during a meeting in 1960 to make a suggestion. Exterminators generally paid employees poorly, trained them erratically if at all, assumed nobody would stay long in such an unattractive job, and left definitions of "standards" pretty much up to the customer. In Burger's view, that added up to unforgivably poor service.

"I think it is unethical to take money for poor-quality performance," he said. "It doesn't have to be this way," he continued. "We can improve our service by paying more attention, and more money, to the people we hire." His colleagues and competitors hooted and whistled in derision. Burger listened a moment, then headed for the door. Just before he opened it, he looked back and announced, "I quit."

Those were far from his last words on doing the job right. He has made his personal standards the standards of an entire organization with the arresting name of "Bugs" Burger Bug Killers, Inc., known in forty-three states as the Mercedes of the extermination business—not the biggest company, but firmly considered the quality of the field. Customer after customer expresses confidence, as Bob Crooks, manager of Gallagher's Restaurant in Garland, Texas, does: "You have 'Bugs' Burger, and then you have to go waaay down to get to the second best."

POWER GIVEN IS POWER GAINED

Following a presentation to the Florida Pest Control Association, I talked with Burger about his operation. His comments said volumes about the daily behavior behind his reputation. To a person, his employees are dedicated to unwavering quality. And they see a key to delivering that quality: effective teamwork among themselves and teamwork with their customers.

Teamwork extends from the smallest one-to-one job with another person to the largest corporation or government. It includes work with customers who may use a product, in-house colleagues who use each other's services, members of the general public whose most casual contact with an organization leaves them with an impression of it.

Conventional exterminators have trained their customers over the years to expect little more than a holding action against roaches and rodents. Most of the industry still talks about "controlling" pests and holding them to "acceptable" levels. By contrast, "Bugs" Burger guarantees—unconditionally—to eliminate them. Not most of them. All of them. You don't pay until every breeding and nesting area in your hotel, restaurant, or hospital is gone. If the company slips after that, it will refund your last twelve monthly payments and treat you to a year's service by another exterminator of your choice. Of course, not even Burger will guarantee that a traveling pest won't try to move in from outside. There is always the chance that a critter born on somebody else's premises will hitch a ride in with your daily supplies. If that happens and the stowaway offends a guest, "Bugs" Burger pays for the meal or night's lodging and sends a letter of apology with a gift certificate for a return visit. As their part of the bargain, "Bugs" Burger customers agree in writing to have their places ready for monthly servicing. They pay a fine if it isn't ready. They also pay monthly fees that run four to six times higher than those of other exterminators, sometimes more.

All right, Alvin Burger has high personal standards. But so do a lot of other people you never heard of. If his only notion about living up to his standards had been "To get it done right I've got to do it myself," he would still be a locally respected small operator in Miami (not exactly a small feat in a semitropical climate so hospitable to insects). What carried him beyond that boundary is an ability, developed through years of experience, to extend the force of his convictions to more than four hundred service specialists all over the United States so that each of them is just as motivated, and just as effective on the job, as Al Burger himself. He developed the leverage that comes from teamwork.

"Give me a place to stand, and I will move the earth." Everyone knows Archimedes was talking about the principle of leverage. Al Burger's place to stand is his insistence on quality. His lever is the ability he has developed to bring out productive power in other people.

In a fiercely competitive business, Burger finds that high-level achievement often comes from assisting others in bringing out their own capabilities, instead of just ordering them to copy every move he makes.

Part of his strategy relics on pure contagion. When he talks to his troops about striving for "that elusive level of perfection," they catch his passion. "It's like he's right inside your head," says a routeman—the service specialist who goes to the customer's place and kills the bugs—in Boston. "He knows exactly what you're thinking out there on the route. 'Oh, I'm tired. Why not just cut this short and go home?' He's a good motivator."

Another part of Burger's technique relies on carefully structured management. The heart and soul of the "Bugs" Burger operation is a quality-control system as tough as any ever invented.

The one applicant out of fifty whom the company hires goes through a rigorous five-month training program. People who know compare it to boot camp in the army, only "three times as long and twice as difficult." Nobody has any difficulty understanding Al Burger's definition of acceptable performance. At some other companies, employees might wonder if they had killed enough roaches to "control" them. "Bugs" Burger service specialists suffer no such uncertainty. They are supposed to kill not some, not most, not enough, but *all* the roaches. That may not be easy to do, but it certainly is easy to remember.

A district manager in Massachusetts avers, "This is the only company I ever saw where the owner and the people on the job all think the same way." In fact, the people on the job have some reason to think like owners: They control much of the up side of their working lives. They work at night, often alone, on schedules they make for themselves. Their income (a salary plus a percentage of gross billings) goes up or down with the number of hours they choose to put in. They can accept or reject promotions as they see fit; nobody looks down on a routeman who would rather not be a supervisor. Unlike independent business owners, however, they risk little on the down side. Benefits include insurance, pension, profit sharing, and performance bonuses. If a major customer quits or—as sometimes happens—is dropped for failing to "stay clean" or to cooperate with the service specialist, the company subsidizes the lost income until the customer is replaced. If a new job requires a lot more hours than a salesman estimated, the company subsidizes the routeman's extra time rather than entertaining a possibility of skimping on service.

"Yeah, we get pressure," says a routeman in Boston, "but it helps you keep up your standards. Without it, I guess we'd be just like any other company."

Twenty-five years earlier, Al Burger had stalked out of the Florida Pest Control Association meeting. All these years he had been operating as one of the most visible pest exterminators in the country, but he wasn't a member of his own trade association. At their meeting in Fort Lauderdale in 1985 he returned, and he was royally welcomed back. Later he told me simply: "It was about time."

WORLD'S SECRET LEADER IN TEAMWORK: THE UNITED STATES

During the 1970s Americans looked almost everywhere but the United States for techniques to boost productive power: to Germany and its legendary obsession with work. To Japan and its intensely devoted individual industriousness that channels people into powerful organizations where everyone pulls first for Matsushita or Toyota and last for himself or herself. To the "Little Dragons" of East Asia—South Korea, Taiwan, Hong Kong, and Singapore—so called because of their location on the volcanic Pacific Rim and the fiery power they show in teaming up industrious people, low wages, and wide-open investment markets to snatch manufacturing jobs and foreign capital not just from the United States but from Japan as well.

For all the attention paid to productivity secrets from other countries, however, another secret is just now being uncovered.

THE COUNTRY THAT HAS BEEN LEADING THE WAY TO AN ENTIRELY NEW CONCEPTION OF TEAMWORK IS THE UNITED STATES.

We all know the story of this nation's cultural heritage and the frontier spirit from which it grew. Settlers moving across the continent thrived on self-reliance and individualism. These values became accepted as basic to business operations in the United States. What is often left out of this picture, though, is a value that was equally basic to American frontier life: a necessary *collaboration* in times of extreme stress.

The fact is that Americans have a history of innovation in the area of teamwork. Wagon trains and frontier settlements were a superb synthesis of self-reliance and interdependence, a synthesis basic to American character. So there is another culture besides Japan's that can look with pride at a history of team accomplishment. The quality control circle—symbol of the collaborative effort in which the hands-on people are the source of ideas for getting work done—was invented in the United States. From the 1940s, there have been leaders in U.S. industry who recognized the limitations of pyramidal hierarchies in which high-level thinking is reserved for the "head" and low-level doing is reserved for the "hands."

The United States will continue to lead the way into the twenty-first century. Why? Because the wheel of experience is turning full circle. In our much-publicized difficulties of the past decade, we have been confronting—and learning from—problems that our vigorous new competitors are just now beginning to face.

As modern societies evolve, we see them shift back and forth between emphasis on individual effort and emphasis on collective effort. The forms change to reflect the times:

1. *Survival.* In primitive situations, people live in fear of being defeated by nature. A crop failure, game migration, or monsoon can wipe out hedges against hunger and destruction.
2. *Individualism.* To secure a greater sense of mastery over the conditions of survival, the Horatio Alger spirit ("to better my lot") emerges in America and elsewhere.
3. *Uniformity.* Later on, vigorous industrialization promotes uniformity and conformity among workers who are persuaded to "stand in" for the organization.
4. *Self-Mastery.* As the collective effort of "standing in" thrives, further individual attributes aimed at "standing out" grow in value.

Focused on individualism are countries such as Indonesia, Malaysia, and the Phillippines, evolving their industries and looking up at the development of the Little Dragons. Cultures (such as Japan's) moving from an emphasis on standing-in toward our final stage (self-mastery) look ahead to the combination of standing in while standing out, and behind at anybody who might be gaining on them. Cultures at Stage 4 (notably the United States) have to draw their own maps as they explore ways of perfecting collaboration while enabling individuals to grow.

Of course all such talk about stages of development must be general and approximate. In large societal systems, different segments evolve at different rates. Surely the Little Dragons have people at Stage 1 and many at Stage 2, as well as those at Stage 3. Similarly the United States has people living in ways that reflect all four stages. Each stage grows as a response to the limiting conditions of the previous stage. Societies, like individuals, are organisms spurred on toward growth by a kind of inherent neurological restlessness of their own.

Peak performers in the United States and elsewhere obviously do not limit their missions to survival or conformity. Their broader purposes recognize the uniqueness and differing needs of individuals, as well as their desire to make a contribution to the team.

One consequence of that increasing awareness is a decreasing willingness to be mere cogs in a big wheel. Uniformity and conformity frequently do not elicit the most productive forms of teamwork. We see societies in which people are losing interest in conformity and moving toward individual development and contribution, in which people work harder and more creatively because they see a chance to stand out while standing in. We began the transition a while back in the United States. As that happened, the peak performers quickly noticed that a key to their own best interests, their own chances for achievement and development, was collaboration.

Why is collaboration obvious? If there is something you can't get done entirely by yourself, one response can be a frustrated individualism: You punch away harder at the prevailing forces and get angrier. Or you give up. Another response can be the one we see among peak performers: You *align with* the available forces—the job, the people, and the organizational environment.

This response is fueled by a desire to expand one's possibilities, to contribute to the organization and the world around one—in short, on the need for "self-actualization" that Abraham Maslow identified.

Maslow developed the ideas and coined the term *Theory Z,* which William Ouchi used to describe a particular management style that blends "Japanese" and "American" traits to produce companies that have it both ways. (From Japan, for instance: long-term employment, consensual decision-making, slow promotion and evaluation, concern for the whole. From America: informal types of control, specialized career paths, individual achievement.) Type Z companies like Cummins Engine, Delta Airlines, Cray Research, 3M, Procter & Gamble are known for high morale, low turnover, and company loyalty. According to Theory Z, the way to sustain higher levels of production in an affluent society is to assume that the workers have "higher needs"—for self-esteem, belonging to an organization one can be proud of, standing out while standing in, becoming everything that one is capable of becoming—and to aim at satisfying those needs by offering autonomy and responsibility at work.

Maslow saw this as America's great contribution to the future, a *Pax Americana* based on new methods of production rather than on militarism—workers sharing in the great enterprise, encouraged to feel themselves partners rather than subordinates.

In the United States, many peak-performing individuals and many peak-performing companies are starting to emerge because of the realization that higher needs are as basic as the lower survival needs. Satisfaction, then, may come from a much wider range of choices than making it alive to the end of the day. Choices such as making contributions to the larger community or developing leadership, communication, and other skills, occur within the context of a job. When they lead toward increasing quality along with revenues, mastering a profession, or managing innovation, the expanded choices can lead to genuine satisfaction.

But not always easily, as the United States has learned in passing through the stage where Japan is now and where the Little Dragons are headed. In North America, survival was a real concern for both the European immigrants and the native Americans who were here to meet them. People stuck together. As things eased up, some of the social glue softened. Although many individuals still struggle for survival today, large segments of the society as a whole feel themselves past that point. As Europe and Asia struggled to recover from the destruction of World War II, the United States became a society in which the primary concerns of the work force shifted from matters of survival to matters of satisfaction. Americans who work were free to concentrate on the three rewards with which we are now so familiar:

Recognition
Job satisfaction
Quality of work life

The result was not paradise, but a period of confusion. We had hit uncharted territory. In the early 1970s the American work ethic, the zeal to build and produce, went flat. Much of Europe is now exploring that same territory, and there are signs that even the formidable Japanese may be entering it.

Nobody yet sees any numbers that prove a slump in Japanese productivity or quality, but observers there are beginning to show concern about the stories they hear. The "working devils" of the older generation still have the habit of sacrificing their personal lives for a job well done, still come in early to warm the oil in their machines before their shift starts and then stay late to discuss ways to improve, still charge through a task and then scout for another. There are, however, fewer stories like the one about the Honda worker who straightened the windshield wiper blades on every Honda he passed on his way home every evening. The younger people seem less inclined to go the extra yard. It is not that they are rebellious. It is, as business writer Atsuko Toyama put it, that some "do what they are told and not one iota more."

The change is far from an epidemic, but signs can be seen even at prestigious companies that attract the most ambitious recruits. An editor at *Yomiuri Shimbun,* Japan's largest daily newspaper, was startled when three first-year reporters quit during 1983, complaining that the work was too hard. It used to be rare for such a thing to happen among people who survived the competition among hundreds of college graduates for those jobs.

Yasuo Sekijima, international personnel and labor relations manager at Hitachi, says he began to notice in the late 1970s that there was something different, not so much in blue-collar workers as in young businessmen: their ignorance of teamwork. He uses a baseball analogy: "The young fellow thinks, 'I'm the third baseman. This is my territory. That's the shortstop's territory.' So he doesn't cover when the ball is hit between third and short, and the ball goes through."

The most obvious of the forces behind all these changes is prosperity, and the attendant desire after a long stretch of hard work to enjoy its fruits.

The economic miracle of the Little Dragons began, like that of Japan before them, in the wreckage of war and the apparent hopelessness of poverty and overpopulation.

Thirty years ago, all four societies were as poor as most Third World nations today. In Taiwan, for instance, the director-general of the Board of Foreign Trade remembers that he went barefoot as a child even though his family was well-to-do, because the country had no shoe industry. The first thought, in short, was to survive.

Their growth has astonished observers who saw the wretchedness and powerlessness of the region after World War II. In pulling themselves up, they combined several major elements that resemble, at least in principle, those of the American evolution toward productive forms of teamwork:

Drive of the Working People: "You will not find harder working, more dedicated, intelligent people up and down the line than you will find in these areas," says Malcolm Kerr, managing director of Asian operations for Hewlett-Packard, one of the many American electronics firms that have moved manufacturing operations there. "It is a wonderful thing to work with."

The Confucian Ethic: stressing an individual's duty to family and society. Each family cares for its own. This facet of the tradition means, according to Professor Steven N. S. Cheung of Hong Kong University, "If you lose your job, you must find another. If your brother loses his job, you take care of him until he finds another. There is no unemployment insurance. You don't get paid for being lazy."

Cheap Labor: being satisfied with less than what workers in richer areas will take—and working to catch up. In South Korea twenty years ago, the average wage for an hour's work was the equivalent of 3 U.S. pennies. In 1983 it was $1.69 (compared to $8.93 in the United States and $6.34 in Japan). Factory workers are starting to buy cars.

And conditions keep changing. "There is a problem for the future," observes Taiwan's minister of economic affairs, Chao Yaotung. He referred to his own country, but the problem touches South Korea, Singapore, and Hong Kong as well. "Since we are no longer a cheap labor country, that work is going to Indonesia, Malaysia and the Philippines." A breakthrough in technology to rival Japan's robotics or some other adaptation will be needed to prevent a slide back into the misery, he fears. Past performance indicates that his country can adapt, as Japan is doing. And, to return to the point of the story, as the United States is doing.

America still has tough bosses who think that kicking ass and taking names, threatening people's survival, is the way to motivate them. But among our peak performers we see far more recognition of the motivational power of teamwork through alignment—alignment based on both the enlightened self-interest of an individual and the best interests of an organization.

THE PEAK PERFORMER AS TEAM BUILDER

American business has an understandable aversion to *teamwork* when the term stands for groupthink, me-tooism, or committees that design horses and produce camels. Individual hard work and flashes of innovation have proved too valuable for too long to be pushed aside in a rush to quality circles or task forces.

But when thoughtful, effective teamwork becomes available—not as the only way but as one context for multiplying individual efforts by providing assistance, backup, and cross-fertilization—it can win the hearts and support of the people who profit from it. When you see teamwork showing up frequently in an aggressive and prosperous company that stays abreast of change and challenges its competitors, you know you are looking at a company in which collaboration is prized at a fundamental level—the level of organizational values and procedures.

Sales at four hundred-employee Keithley Instruments in Solon, Ohio, have nearly doubled since 1979, when the company experimented with its first production team. In that same time, profits have moved from $1.3 million to $2 million, output per employee has jumped 90 percent, absenteeism has dropped 75 percent, and health-care costs have been contained. The company, which makes industrial and scientific instruments priced from $150 to $150,000, had started running into production bottlenecks when it grew to about three hundred employees. President Thomas Brick and founder-chairman Joseph Keithley concluded that "engineering-type" solutions were not going to make enough of a difference, and asked human resources specialist Mark Frohman to see what he could do.

"We were not exactly overwhelmed with volunteers," Brick recalls, and Keithley fielded just one production team in October 1979. It was designed to break down departmental walls between R&D, manufacturing, engineers, marketing managers, and materials planners. Planning, for instance, used to come from outside. A training program emphasized that planning was part of the team effort, not separate from it; the job of any supervisor included planning, organizing, and problem solving. To help them function with this broader perspective, new team members got eight hours of training on company time, studying the company's history and plans, product information, and basic business economics.

By June 1982 all of Keithley's production was being handled by twelve work groups, each turning out a complete product and responsible for its assembly, accuracy, and inspection.

The first team supervisor, since promoted to production manager for the company, soon noticed that well-informed workers responsible for their own output became extremely demanding about supplies, information, and equipment. Before long they were leading the way in making demands for productivity and quality.

"I adamantly refuse to have this thing labeled," Dr. Frohman says. "We had a certain set of performance measures and a set of values going in. We just try to focus on what we want to accomplish, and ask, 'What'll work?' "

One surprise to the company is a newfound flexibility among workers who are cross-trained and therefore able to adapt to changes in product lines and the twists and turns a company sometimes goes through in times of economic slowdown when it is committed to avoiding layoffs if at all possible. A surprise to employees is that the emphasis on team goals has actuall… them to develop in significant ways as individuals.

"The skills you develop here," Dr. Frohman tells employees new to Keithley's teams, "are applicable outside the workplace." They see that a team, and each member of it, is less vulnerable than an isolated loner. Taking the lesson home, many learn to express themselves more easily not only at work but also in their families.

THREE MAJOR SKILLS

When we examined the behavior of managers skilled at turning a random collection of people into a highly productive work team, we saw evidence of changes in the role that managers play in many organizations. The effective leader who can inspire followers and serve as a symbol for a dramatic turnaround of a department or a company is still a folk hero—look at the fame that Lee Iacocca's exploits brought him. Increasingly complex systems, however, are also making room for the type of manager that William G. Dyer, professor of organizational behavior at Brigham Young University, describes: "This modern manager has shifted from dealing with problems on a one-to-one basis to solving more problems collectively, involving everyone that has a contribution to make. . . . In this context, the manager is a coach, a facilitator, a developer, a team builder."

Peak-performing team builders develop and use three major skills:

- Delegating to empower
- Stretching the abilities of others
- Encouraging educated risk-taking

The three skills are not at all the private property of peak performers, not at all alien to others. Yet the skills are often underused. Many of us use them in our families (small teams) and see them used in our favorite sports teams, yet fail to use them on the job.

Delegating to Empower. It takes no genius to observe that a one-man band never gets very big. To conduct a symphony you have to let other people play. The men and women who conduct well concentrate on conducting, not on playing the oboe or the drums. For that, they find someone better at oboe or drums than they are, and give them the job of being better at it.

A peak performer delegates to other people in order to multiply his or her own strengths. That means, among other things, refraining from making decisions others might better make themselves, because:

- Hogging work that belongs to others will only distract the peak performer from higher-priority activities.
- Delegating is a way to stretch other people, build their confidence, and encourage them to take risks.

In brief, a peak performer understands *empowerment.*

The five often misunderstood letters in the center of that word—*power*—call for a clear understanding of what *empowerment* means. It does not mean giving away your strength to someone else like Samson to the Philistines. On the contrary, peak performers discover time and again that releasing the power in others, whether in co-workers or customers, benefits them in the long run. In developing, rewarding, and recognizing those around them, they are simply allowing the human assets with which they work to appreciate in value. The more they empower, the more they can achieve, and the more successful the whole enterprise becomes.

As chairperson of the board of directors of the Federal Reserve Bank of Kansas City, and of the Center for Business and Economic Forecasting at the University of Denver, Doris Drury influences the week-to-week economic climate in the United States. She knows that the power to affect events is not solely a matter of sharp intellect and blunt ambition: "I know that in order for me to look good, everybody around me has to look good."

One reason "Bugs" Burger Bug Killers, Inc., looks so good is its proprietor's determination to let the local service specialists make their own decisions and profit from them. The crews work at night, on schedules they set themselves, under their own supervision. To stay with the company you have to meet its standards, but from the first day of training you understand that the person responsible for getting to the job, doing it right, reporting accurately on it, and setting your own career path is you.

Alvin Burger almost held on too tightly. He had been trying to do too much himself and by 1978 he and the company were both in trouble. Sales were $6 million and the profit margin was 1 percent. Burger recalls, "I was panicking, beginning to make mistakes. I was disoriented. I actually had heart palpitations. Too many things were happening that I couldn't cope with." Having high standards was one thing. Making them work was another. He turned to Howard Roth, his executive vice-president, and listened to him. "You," said Roth, "have reached the limit of your ability to manage. You need to turn over that part of the job to someone who can do it better." Burger did. Art Graham, a former employee, came back and built a management structure, wrote the company's first business plan, put together its first annual operating budget, and within six months pulled the profit margin up to 12 percent—partly through Graham's knowledge of how to get those things done, and partly because Burger stayed out of his way and let him do them.

At Chaparral Steel in Midlothian, Texas, managers obviously understand the difference between working with employees and interfering with them. President Gordon Forward doesn't like formal meetings, and holds most of his in the wide-flange mill or a hallway—mainly because that is where he can see and hear the people who, by his reckoning, produce "more tons of steel per employee per year than any steel mill in the world." The average American steelworker produces 350 tons a year. In Japan, 850 tons. At Chaparral, 1,300 tons at full capacity. The plant has been running at full capacity, prospering in a time when the aging American steel industry was staggering to record losses.

Chaparral managers place decision-making power where it will be most effective. Often that is not in the executive offices. Foremen do all the hiring. Employees run the quality-control program and the safety program. Workers make decisions daily on the mill floor. With four levels of management (one fewer than the Catholic Church, thirteen fewer than General Motors), workers can talk to a supervisor or the man at the top with almost equal ease. As one mill hand who considers Chaparral a great place to work explains: "If you have a good idea, somebody's gonna listen to you and that tends to make you think a little harder, go a little further out of your way, do things a little better, 'cause you always know they're not afraid to try new things."

Stretching the Abilities of Others. The peak performers who delegate at every opportunity are not altruists. Nor do they shun making decisions; they like responsibility and control. From their perspective, however, they see their own power amplified by the presence of powerful, capable colleagues. They do all they can to stretch their colleagues' abilities. A Tom Landry would rather coach the Dallas Cowboys than the Pismo Beach Irregulars.

They keep a balance, holding co-workers to commitments and at the same time encouraging people to learn to take initiative, to trust their own judgment, and make effective decisions—to find their own ways of getting the job done better than before.

"I never had a boss that tried to sit on me, and I think that's essential. If you expect people to develop, you have to give them the responsibility, you have to tell them what their objectives are, and then you have to let them do it." That is how David M. Roderick remembers his rise to the chairmanship of a traditional smokestack industry, United States Steel. In a newer information industry, Ned Leavitt had an almost identical experience.

When Owen Laster, head of the literary department at the William Morris Agency in New York asked, "Who would like to expand into the computer software area?" Leavitt volunteered. Some literary people have regarded any intrusion of computer software into their domain with reserve, if not outright suspicion, but some look on it the way Leavitt did. He told me later: "I needed the stretch. The book area was getting pretty predictable."

The agency gave Leavitt time to start his stretch, to learn who was who in software development, get used to the jargon, explore the standards for evaluating programs. He took the time to develop the knowledge that leads to "a feel" for what will sell. "When I started in 1983," he says, "I didn't know a peripheral from a pothole. Very excited software developers would tell me their ideas, and I felt as if I were in a foreign country." An early memo to Laster said, "I feel as if my clients are speaking Turkish." Leavitt didn't know any Turkish, but he did know through the initial period not to pretend to knowledge he didn't have. He asked a lot of questions. The developers were only too eager to explain their technology to him.

He began to understand their language. One of his first successes was MusicWorks, designed by a company called Macro-Mind. The program turns a Macintosh computer, in effect, into a typewriter for music, freeing musicians for the first time from the drudgery of drawing notes on ruled paper by hand.

Leavitt's stretch was designed so that he could still spend time with his major literary clients. Maintaining his presence in the book field allowed him to take on the new computer-related information without feeling totally cut off from his earlier expertise.

Looking back now, he says that the experience provided one major surprise. Stretching into computers got him excited again about books. He likened the experience to flying on a trapeze. "When I swing back into the more familiar territory of books, I bring momentum and new ideas I've picked up on the software side of the arena."

Encouraging Educated Risks. A bureaucrat sees risk-takers as risk-*seekers,* gamblers who want a thrill. A typical high achiever in our study views them differently: as *opportunity*-seekers, the sort of people entrepreneur Paul Hawken described as "seeing a situation from an entirely different angle from someone else," identifying every obstacle that could prevent him or her from succeeding in a mission, and eliminating as many as possible. The high achiever gains additional leverage by opening up opportunities for other people who can help in achieving goals along the way to the team mission.

Delegating and stretching other people's abilities often takes the form of encouraging others to take risks—not foolhardy plunges, but the sort of educated risk that can build self-confidence in a couple of ways:

- By paying off with success
- By providing a chance for successful self-correction in the event of a setback

Al Campanis, vice-president of player development for the Los Angeles Dodgers, is the man whose hiring, firing, and trades have kept the Dodgers among the most successful franchises in professional baseball. He has never forgotten the lessons he learned from watching the legendary Dodger president Branch Rickey.

Campanis was a twenty-nine-year-old shortstop for the Dodgers' farm team in Montreal in 1946 when he found himself playing beside a second baseman who represented the biggest risk in the history of a hitherto all-white sport dominated by Southern players. Jackie Robinson was determined to become the first black player in major league baseball, and like every black person who had grown up in a society where the Ku Klux Klan could operate freely, he was educated to the risks in that. Rickey, too, knew there was risk of retaliation from segregationists in the baseball power structure when he hired Robinson. He encouraged Robinson's drive toward peak performance, promising—and delivering—support at every step. Robinson took the brunt of the punishment, becoming the target of flying spikes, beanballs, and red-neck bench jockeys in one stadium after another. If his talent, and his courage, had been any less, the attempt might have failed.

It was an audacious move, it certainly carried risk, but from Branch Rickey's point of view it was *not* a gamble. Rickey recognized ability when he saw it. Al Campanis remembers him not as a social crusader but as a man interested in winning baseball games. In Jackie Robinson and other players from the Negro Leagues, Rickey saw what writer Michael Leahy calls "a mother lode of talent that could bring him championships for years to follow."

Rickey knew his game and he had scouts who knew it also, and whatever risks he took were educated risks. So, "One of the many things that Rickey taught me," Al Campanis says, "was that you look for players everywhere, including a lot of places others don't."

Campanis looked in Puerto Rico and found Roberto Clemente. He looked at the University of Cincinnati and found Sandy Koufax. He went to Mexico and saw a portly eighteen-year-old pitcher named Fernando Valenzuela. He has looked at other baseball clubs, taken players who seemed to have forgotten how to win, and offered course corrections that brought them back. Dodger manager Tommy Lasorda observes, "A good scout can watch a guy through a bad spell and know that he can be molded back into a winner. Al does that better than anyone. And he's not afraid to go out on a limb."

Not many of us can play professional baseball. Many a peak performer, though, has been asked "for the good of the team" to step out of a comfortable niche into unknown and uncomfortable territory. A classic situation is the engineer or financial wizard who, upon being invited to join management, has to come out of a shell. Often after years of caressing their printouts they find themselves leading teams. Some take to it more naturally. Others have responded by freezing, simply unable to work as team players. Still others skim a description of "managing by wandering around" and start to wander without knowing what to wander into, and often lose focus. A company leader taking an educated risk with someone like that is not going to abandon the new manager any more than Rickey abandoned Robinson. He or she always follows up in ways calculated to make the risk pay off.

THE PEAK PERFORMER AS TEAM PLAYER: "WE" RATHER THAN "I"

As a chief executive officer in difficult times for the steel industry, David Roderick has been reorganizing the nation's fifteenth largest industrial company to get it into trim for the twenty-first century. Soon after assuming the chairmanship of U.S. Steel in 1979 he began ordering bold steps, selling off assets such as the company's headquarters building in Pittsburgh, diversifying with the purchase of Marathon Oil, closing some inefficient factories and upgrading the technology of others. He has a reputation for being strong-minded and mentally aggressive. Yet:

> I don't want to put any thoughts out there that I'm the indispensable man. Certainly one of my major jobs is to give people the opportunity and the breadth of experience so that if for whatever reason I cannot perform, there will be people ready to step into this job. And if I'm doing my job right, there should be three or four people that the board could look at to come in.

One essential characteristic of a team player shows up in problem-solving situations. Peak performers concentrate on solving problems rather than placing blame for them. As a result, they tend to ask key questions such as "What is the current situation?" "Where are we going?" "How do we get there?" They also make life as easy as possible for themselves by collecting people who are not afraid to contribute to solutions and are capable of action. Lower achievers pose questions such as "Who got us into this anyway?" They tend to drive even the most talented co-workers into defensiveness or indifference.

At a level far down the line from CEO, Ed Kolman at Kester Solder saw his customer's problem with light bulbs as a collaborative issue: *I* didn't have a problem with a customer, nor did *he* alone have a problem with the solder. *We* had a problem, and we solved it together.

CUSTOMERS ARE EVERYWHERE

Another characteristic of people skilled at developing the talents of others is their ability to serve customers—and their expanded view of who a "customer" is.

A customer, it seems, is anyone to whom you provide service, not only the usual cash-bearing member of the public outside the company walls but also co-workers inside those walls. Does your department provide a service—figures, machining, printed material—to another department? They are customers.

Even at the highest level, we find peak performers in senior positions looking upon subordinates in their own organizations as customers. Robert Townsend, the successful maverick who turned around Avis and wrote *Up the Organization* and *Further Up the Organization,* puts it this way: "A leader is not an administrator who loves to run others, but someone who carries water for his people so they can get on with their jobs." Conversely, the senior executive is also a customer for services from subordinates. In both instances, the leverage to increase an individual's effectiveness comes from the skills of collaboration.

"If you look," Ed Kolman told my father, "you see customers everywhere." That is not always easy to do, especially when a campaign to upgrade customer service may begin with a pronouncement issued from an executive suite and aimed at a lower level where the customers are presumed to be. Everyone knows that salespeople need skill at handling customers. So do receptionists, delivery and repair people, and the overworked people behind an airline counter. But senior managers and executives? Some insist they handle only the bottom line, not the customer. Peak performers, however, have discovered that there is no separating bottom lines from customers. For them, the skills of customer service and the skills of leveraging the capabilities of others stem directly from the same basic value.

The basic value is empathy. Empathy—understanding the customer's desires and needs—requires feeling your way into a situation by asking yourself: "If I were in that person's position, what would I need most?" There is at least one other person to ask: the customer. "What do you want and need?" is a question that many peak performers actually ask the people with whom they work, and that a surprising number of ordinary performers never utter. It is equally useful with outside and inside customers.

Jim Gray carried years of hands-on experience as a telephone installation technician into his promotion to first-line supervisor at Pacific Bell. He told me that he can depend on his people because they can depend on him: "The guys are always asking me to fix things, and of course I do. We're all in the same locker room, and I've got to take care of the guys on my team the same way I would take care of any other customer. I don't always have the answer, but if any of my guys asks a question, he knows I'll check it out and get back to him."

Gray's team also knows that he acts as a buffer between them and other levels of the organization, and that he would go to bat for them exactly as he would for a phone company subscriber who has a problem. "I act like I own the place because I feel that I do. In some ways my pride is attached to how well we do as a company, and I have to be ready to handle problems the same way both inside with co-workers and outside with customers. My pride is on the line."

COMBINING THE SKILLS OF TEAM PLAYERS AND TEAM BUILDERS

The essential challenge that Alvin Burger, Gordon Forward, Karl Kamena, and other peak performers meet in their work is to stand in while they stand out. They don't just lead the teams they build. They join them. They reason correctly that peak-performing teams inspire peak-performing individuals, and that peak-performing individuals build peak-performing teams.

That combination of skills is not something they keep to themselves. "Bugs" Burger Bug Killers, Inc., is effective, for example, because its people are both team players and team builders.

They know how to participate and how to lead. Alvin Burger stated the mission, set the standards, and then said to his colleagues: "There they are. Go get 'em." Service specialists use the standards to do their jobs. Managers keep checking the jobs against the standards. The company makes money. Its people make money. They do it because most of them care less about power and dominance over other people than about results in the service of a mission they all agree is worthwhile.

And since they see that empowering colleagues and customers is such good business, the people in the system communicate constantly—up, down, and sideways—about their accomplishments and needs in getting the job done. They put together three skills essential to success as team builder and team player simultaneously:

- Spirit—keeping the mission alive
- Peer pressure—enforcing performance, not through intimida-

tion but through frequent reminders of the mission and its associated standards and values
- Communication—keeping the channels open and clear

Spirit—Keeping the Mission Alive. I learned at the Dow Polycarbonate Kickoff that Karl Kamena and other team leaders had used a newsletter called "Launchpad" to keep up momentum on the team during the initial phase. After the kickoff, the newsletter, with its name changed to "Calibrator," continued to serve by giving each team member biweekly reports, along with cartoons and quips.

Teams, especially those composed of members from far-flung departments, have a way of bogging down in details, losing sight of the whole. Successful team co-leaders like Kamena hold intact a vision of the entire project and make sure that the vision keeps getting communicated around the team.

Alive also means infused with spirit, with enthusiasm. Kamena and the other team leaders made sure that on the polycarbonate mission "the hero is the team." They kept reminding their colleagues that allegiance to individual constituencies, such as manufacturing or marketing, was secondary to the overall camaraderie of the team.

We can also look at the way Steven Jobs chivied, inspired, goaded, and led a team known as the "A-players" to design and produce the Macintosh computer that saved Apple from being crushed by IBM's PC. Jobs handpicked the players and molded them into a team by using every carrot and every stick he could find. Not only did he issue slogans such as the reminder that at some point a product has to stop developing and start selling: "True artists ship"; not only did he have his artists sign their work (there are forty-seven team members' signatures inside the mold for the plastic case of the Macintosh). He got hardware wizards and software virtuosi to give up vacations, love affairs, and night after night of sleep for the fascination of pushing microcomputer technology to new heights. Through the whole project ran his evangelical message:

> Opportunities like this don't come along very often. You know somehow it's the start of something. . . . And it's being done

> by a bunch of people who are incredibly talented but who in most organizations would be working three levels below the impact of the decisions they're making in this organization. It's one of those things you know won't last forever. . . . It's more important than their personal lives right now.

To be sure, the opportunity paid well. Some young members of the team put down cash for houses in expensive Palo Alto. Yet programmer Andy Hertzfeld notes, "Apple isn't just the money—it's a giant magnifying glass that takes your great stuff and broadcasts it out to everyone."

Or we look at the 1980 U.S. Olympic hockey team, which should never have been able to defeat the Russians and did. Or the mill hands at Chaparral Steel, who boost production while the rest of their industry wonders what hit it. Or the IBM employees all over the world living by Thomas Watson's pledge: "We want to give the best customer service of any company in the world."

Peer Pressure: Reminders of Standards and Values. A team builder/team player needs no esoteric system of rewards and punishments to make sure that people support one another's goals as enthusiastically as they support their own. He or she simply makes certain that each member understands a simple fact of teamwork: "If my end of the boat sinks, so does yours."

On the positive side of that, *support* is a synonym for *motivate toward.* Depending on circumstances, as Jobs demonstrated, the motivation can take any number of forms. One form it seldom takes, however, on successful teams from "Bugs" Burger through People Express and Karl Kamena's team at Dow, is intimidation. Such fear may work for a while. Then it fails.

Wherever there are organizations there are stories about the dominators, the tough bosses. A demanding boss who honors employees by stretching them, insisting that they give their best and helping them do it, is one thing. A martinet who uses fear to extort compliance is quite another. John Patterson, founder of National Cash Register, punished one executive by having the man's desk and chair carried to the curb and burned. Robert Malott, chairman of FMC Corp., was quoted by *Fortune* in 1980 as saying, "Leadership is demonstrated when the ability to inflict pain is confirmed." In 1984 he made that magazine's list of the ten "toughest bosses in America"—men who, in the words of *Fortune* writer Steven Flax, have occasionally "carried toughness beyond the point where it's necessary or effective."

No question, intimidation can be an effective short-term motivator. "Get the report in by Friday morning or get out" is the sort of order likely to produce a report by Friday—or a resignation. In an environment that produces frequent dictates of that sort, employees who have adequate ego strength and a secure sense of their worth tend to cope by realizing they could do better elsewhere. Replacing them takes time, money, and training. On those grounds alone, it has been shown repeatedly that intimidation is a poor long-term motivator. There are other grounds.

The Center for Creative Leadership in North Carolina studied forty-one fast-rising executives, roughly half of whom peaked early in their careers and were fired or forced to take early retirement. The most frequently cited cause of their failure was a bullying, intimidating style. It worked for a while, but eventually got too expensive. One senior manager told the researchers: "You can be as mean as you like at lower levels as long as you get results. But it all doubles back on you."

Intimidation pushes people away from concern for the team, back down toward survival thinking—*my* safety, *my* future, *me*. It causes many individuals to lose their grip on the higher values of collaboration and affiliation. It leads to regression rather than growth.

The anthropologist Margaret Mead used to enjoy asking why grandparents and grandchildren tend to be such good friends. The answer fits right in with tales of corporate life: because they have a common enemy. This also holds for senior managers and lower-level workers. They have a common enemy, too: the poor middle manager, stuck between them, a handy target for everyone's frustrations.

In peak-performing teams, those antagonisms less frequently exist. IBM, for example, consistently ranks among the best-performing

…panies in the world. Most managers there understand that positive motivators in the form of recognition, reward, and self-esteem are far more effective than intimidation. Instead of using coercive "push" power, IBM managers are trained to rely far more on magnetic "pull" power. They set sales targets that 70 percent of their salespeople can meet, thus making most of them winners who work with winners. The consequence? Teams composed of individuals who identify themselves as winners, who generate their own motivation and are more comfortable collaborating with others because in their environment there is no scarcity of winning.

Organizations all over the United States started looking several years ago for ways to pull increasing numbers of their people up to peak performance. After a training session organized by Jim Liberti of IBM in San Jose, California, an even more challenging issue emerged. Jim asked, "How do we establish peak performance throughout the company *as the norm*?" Companies that attract a high proportion of peak performers are run by managers willing to give power to gain power, not by people who collect power in order to squelch and dominate others.

David Ogilvy, founder of the advertising giant Ogilvy & Mather, reinforces the importance of that in his company by sending a Russian doll to the person newly appointed to head an office in the Ogilvy & Mather chain. The doll contains five progressively smaller dolls. The message inside the smallest one reads: "If each of us hires people who are smaller than we are, we shall become a company of dwarfs, but if each of us hires people who are bigger than we are, Ogilvy & Mather will become a company of giants."

So the team builder/team player draws distinctions between a drive for achievement and a drive for dominance. Bulldozing and manipulating people to dominate them keeps them off balance. For short-term compliance, intimidation sacrifices long-term alignment and dedication. It certainly does not release the power and potential in others. If unabated, it leaves people with two options:

- They retreat into comfort zones where they take as few risks as possible in a self-imposed underutilization, and ultimately reduce their contribution to the team.

• Or, if they are peak performers or peak performers-to-be, they look for ways to leave the team altogether.

Actually, there is a third option: They stay and change the rules. Richard J. Boyle remembers that as he advanced to senior positions at Honeywell beginning in the late 1950s, "steely, no-nonsense executives were the norm." These General Patton types in a major defense contractor left many examples of their autocratic management in corporate legend: "One 'productivity initiative' from those days (long since reversed) was the removal of bathroom stall doors to discourage reading on company time."

As vice-president and general manager of Honeywell's Defense and Marine Systems Group, Boyle pushed the move toward greater employee involvement in productivity which his predecessor had already started. He discovered along the way that reform had run amok—one inventory of task teams among the group's eight thousand employees in 1981 found more than two hundred, and there may have been more "because the people responding didn't share a common understanding of what a task team was." As a result, he determined that "the participative process must be managed."

"We now have procedures for starting up task teams and for measuring their progress. We have means of disbanding teams once their work is done. And we have fewer task teams now." Formerly rigid procedures got informalized when it seemed that productivity would benefit. For instance, anybody could drop by anybody else's office to check out a work problem—no big deal in most companies, but an upheaval in Honeywell's quasi-military culture.

> By signaling in various ways that certain traditional practices would no longer hold, we helped prepare people to accept the next idea: that they could continue to look to management to define appropriate objectives and results but they could start looking to themselves for ways of achieving them. To paraphrase our vice-chairman, Jim Renier, management's role would be to set the goals and then manage the environment so people could achieve those goals.

…nication: Keeping the Channels Open and Clear. On a peak-performing team, everybody knows what is going on. There are no hidden agendas likely to sabotage the team's efforts. Among individuals on the team, effective communication calls for:

- Empathy
- Authenticity
- Concreteness

Empathy, for Jim Gray, Ed Kolman, Ed Garfield, and others, serves "inside" co-workers as well as "outside" customers. Authenticity means simply being genuine, not hiding behind a role; if you don't know an answer, you don't fake it. You say, "I don't know. I'll find out," and you find out. Concreteness keeps everyone's attention focused on the actual work at hand, not on big, slippery generalities.

Team builders "keep the spirit alive" and "remind others of values and standards" through clear, consistent communication. Team players need this information so they can translate it into results. They also offer constructive feedback on how things are going to team leaders, who circulate the information through the system to reilluminate the missions, goals, and standards.

That is how it works at every level of "Bugs" Burger Bug Killers. Burger service specialists (about 7 percent are women) call on clients every month. After each call they fill out an exhaustive report on what they did and what the customer did. Did they see any roaches or rodents? Did they kill any? How many? Do they need help with the account? They had better tell the truth, and all of it. At least four levels of supervisors, from local to headquarters in Miami, check each report and spend much of their time making spot visits to customers, looking to see if everything is exactly as the service specialist says it is. A full-time quality-control team checks *them.* If a customer ever calls with a complaint, the phone rings first not at the service person's house but at headquarters in Miami.

Why don't people resent having their performance monitored so relentlessly? Because of the spirit in which it is done.

A service person covered with dirt, crawling under the sinks in a hotel kitchen, knows that Burger and every other manager mean it when they say, "You are critical to the success of this company, and I'm going to make you feel that way from day one." Frank Perez, the vice-president in charge of service, insists, "Our service people are the privileged class." Asking for help to meet the standards is no disgrace; it is encouraged. One phone call will bring a manager to a job site, any time. A routeman in Fort Lauderdale confirms: "In this company, the serviceman is number one."

In that climate, people throughout the company see its rigorous quality controls not as a way to oppress them or intimidate them but as tools to support each of them—as individuals and as members of a team—in producing superior results.

The leverage of team builders and team players serves them well as long as they keep in sight the mission to which they will apply it. Sometimes, like everyone else, even the best of them get off course. Combining the skills of self-management with the benefits of a well-functioning team sets the foundation for the next major characteristic: course correction.

7

COURSE CORRECTION

The sound of a high-powered engine fills your ears. The rows of video screens on either side of you glow in your peripheral vision. Your hands test the sensitivity of the steering wheel, your foot the quickness of the accelerator. The challenge is to keep the little car on track.

It's the Speedway game that youngsters play in video arcades and that many of us played in the old penny arcades. You press the button and the images on the screen in front of you start moving. You steer your video car around obstacles. Speed up. Slow down. Adjust to quick changes. Watch out for that fire engine. Go left around the wreck ahead. Too far. You're off the road. Back on, step on it to make up lost time. You make it to the end, but not without a few crashes. For the next game you raise the skill level. The car goes faster on the track; more obstacles close in; you handle more changes per unit of time.

What it takes to stay on track in this game, no less than in work and personal life, is course correction.

Course correction is a "master skill," allowing its possessor to use more effectively his or her other skills. Its three prime components—mental agility, concentration, and learning from mistakes—supply the means to develop other skills further.

CRITICAL PATH: THE WAY TO THE TARGET

On a number of occasions I heard the late inventor Buckminster Fuller say that all physical movement is a series of small course corrections. The most graceful movement, he added, comes with the ability to minimize the jerks and jolts as one steers.

Fuller's observation applies to every aspect of performance. He loved sailing, and often used its metaphors:

> It is impossible to eliminate altogether the ship's course realterations. It is possible only to reduce the degree of successive angular errors by ever more sensitive, frequent, and gentle corrections. That's what good helmsmen or good airplane pilots do.

We used to hear in the space program that on their flights between Earth and the moon, the Apollo ships were off course more than 90 percent of the time. The spacecraft would wander off its trajectory and the crew would correct; wander off and correct, repeatedly. It was easy, mathematically, to come up with the perfect trajectory between here and there, but the lunar voyagers were actually on that trajectory only 10 percent of the time. And you know what? It didn't matter. What mattered was results. They got to the moon. They got home. They did it by having the control to get themselves back on course, repeatedly. They were not on a perfect path, but a *critical path.*

The concept of critical path is pivotal in course correction. A critical path is the most efficient or appropriate trajectory to take toward a target. Within it there is room for mistakes and corrections. While the people guiding the astronauts had to be precise and operate within strict limits of accuracy, they were not hung up on perfectionism—the dreaded "paralysis by analysis." On the trajectory between Earth and moon, they were not tethered to the mathematically perfect line. Speaking of the Apollo Project, Fuller remarked:

> There were obvious first things to be accomplished, and second things before third things and 7,308 things before 7,309 things. Some were going to take longer than others. There would be a pattern of start-ups and lead-ins of differing time lengths. This complex, shad-bone-like pattern would be known as "the critical path."

On course does not mean perfect. *On course* means that even when things don't go perfectly, you are headed in the right direction.

Whether one is headed for the moon or increased third-quarter revenues, there is always the unpredictable, the ambiguous, the surprise, the change that calls for course correction. Certainly luck is the residue of design, and peak performers are luckier than most others because they risk carefully and design boldly. They use devices such as contingency plans, strategic planning, feasibility studies, and the worst-case scenarios which I call "catastrophe reports." But no amount of planning can guarantee the result.

SUBJECT TO CHANGE WITHOUT NOTICE

Two skills shared by results-oriented people everywhere are the ability to initiate change, and to capitalize on change that is thrust upon them.

A fundamental reality for peak performers in business is that their capacity to change no longer hinges on their ability to get back to the status quo. Traditions used to last longer than they do now. The surrounding world used to move slowly enough that even the most daring adventurer had a sense of playing out his or her variations against an immovable background of habits, policies, and "the way we've always done things around here." Now that we are all participants, like it or not, in the age of computers, peak performers recognize that change occurs against a background that is itself in motion. Change—in the strategic planning of organizations, the level of sophistication in marketing and sales, and the technology we use to do our work—is an integral part of daily life on the job.

Reflecting after World War II on the basic qualitites of society and culture that his own work on the atomic bomb had helped to alter, physicist J. Robert Oppenheimer observed: "One thing that is new is the prevalence of newness, the changing scale and scope of change itself, so that the world alters as we walk in it, so that the years of a man's life measure not some small growth or rearrangement or moderation of what we learned in childhood, but a great upheaval."

Much thoughtful speculation is available on the "megatrends," "third waves," and exponential rates of change facing us as the twentieth century moves into the twenty-first—so much that it is easy to forget that only in the last two decades have businesses developed formal R&D departments to promote change rather than react to it. Writing some twenty years ago in *Fortune,* Max Ways predicted: "The main challenge to U.S. society will turn not around the production of goods but around the difficulties and opportunities involved in a world of accelerating change and ever-widening choices. . . . So swift is the acceleration that trying to 'make sense' of change will come to be our basic industry."

Making sense of change is a major occupation for those who excel in any field. We see peak performers actually dealing with two distinct types of change: *Rapid* change, in which familiar elements shift their relationship to one another, and *radical* change, in which entirely new elements appear.

The skill of course correction assumes that the basic rules of the game do not disappear while the game is in progress, even though rapid changes in the environment do require monitoring the process and initiating change to stay on course. If this were a game of cards, the markings on them would be the same tomorrow as they are today, but Nature would never guarantee to deal you the same hand twice. Course correction requires rapid, efficient adjustments as the dealer delivers an increasing number of hands per unit of time.

One attribute common to both rapid change and radical change is their unpredictability. The players are subject to change without notice. For both, as Max Ways put it in *Fortune,* "The movement is so swift, so wide and the prospect of acceleration so great that an imaginative leap into the future cannot find a point of rest, a still picture of social order." Given the fact that trying to stand still on a moving point is not productive, the peak performers are the people in business who constantly and effectively make course corrections.

The corrections don't have to be big, dramatic events. They can be daily little moves with immediate, short-term payoffs.

Jerry Gordé, the thirty-two-year-old president of Virginia Textiles, Inc., in Richmond, runs a $6-million company that grew at a compound annual rate of 94 percent between 1979 and 1984. His hands-on style includes delivering everyone's mail in the morning and pitching in to help load trucks. He shares his working office, down in the warehouse next to the soda machine, with four other people and two dogs. Though he prefers that style, there came a time when he knew he would have to alter it a bit. He had an official "president's office" fixed up in a former storage closet next to the second-floor conference room, complete with a polished mahogany desk, walnut paneling, rich brown carpeting, and recessed overhead lighting. It is a practical solution to an aggravating little problem. Too many times while he was working on the loading platform, one of his well-meaning sales people would rush up with a client eager to meet the president. The sight of him sweating in his cutoff jeans rattled some of the more traditional visitors. So Gordé wrote a memo. Give a few minutes warning, he said, he would be glad to assist in a sale by running upstairs to the "president's office," changing into a suit, and there receiving visiting bankers and customers in surroundings that would make them feel secure.

WINDOWS OF OPPORTUNITY

During World War II, General George Patton noticed an increase in cart tracks on the roads ahead of him. A timid analyst might have waited to see if anyone else noticed, or formed a committee to study it. Patton inferred that the Germans were out of gasoline, immediately ordered his troops forward, and shortened the war in Europe.

Such windows of opportunity open and close in the world of business as well. To stretch the metaphor close to the breaking point, I would say peak performers use windows of opportunity to keep sight of a critical path. As they gain information and expertise in the work they do, they tell us, they develop a "feel" for openings, for the points at which they can institute course correction to (1) keep them within the boundaries of the critical path and (2) leap ahead.

Those windows don't always show up on your computer, if you use one, or on even the best-designed business plan. Of course facts are important. Just as important, though, is that "feel." Herbert Simon and his colleagues in artificial-intelligence research at Carnegie-Mellon University have shown in a number of experiments that experts rarely use logic and reason to solve problems. Instead, a physicist, for example, might look at a complex situation and say, "Aha! That's a conservation of energy problem." Unlike novices, who doggedly follow procedures through to the end, experts seem to store the appropriate problem-solving sequences so that they are likely to be there when needed.

When looking for windows of opportunity, it helps to be good at seeing patterns in a rapidly changing environment. A consulting firm called Inferential Focus gathers intelligence for clients, including Fortune 500 companies, money managers, and the White House, by spotting what Carol Colman of its New York office calls "anomalies in patterns and [piecing] together the facts that don't normally fit into an information mosaic." Such as? Such as the time several years ago that a member of the firm spotted four lines in *The Wall Street Journal* and made an inference that proved profitable to clients. The four lines concerned Saudi Arabia's changing its shipping requirements for incoming goods, reducing by half the size of containers and inspecting all, not just 80 percent, of the shipments. The consultant suspected fear of terrorism. The Saudis were known to respond to fear by stashing their oil money in a safe place—gold. Inferential Focus told its clients to buy gold. Six weeks later its value had doubled.

A strictly rational way of thinking, therefore, becomes just one of several approaches to course correction, each consisting of mental agility, concentration, and learning from mistakes—the Big Three principles of staying on course.

Having the Apollo 11 module off course 90 percent of the time is not to say we did not know the perfect trajectory. We did. When we computed it, we produced an irrefutable fact: The dotted line from here to the moon and back curves just so. But did the fact relieve us of further thought? Not at all. There were possibilities that we could not anticipate, so the programming took *that* into account.

A ruptured oxygen tank in the service module of Apollo 13 showed why it made sense to have good pilots aboard the moon flights. The crew brought the ship back safely using oxygen and power from the lunar module, information from Mission Control on Earth, and their own skill. For them, the window of opportunity was definitely real. Fire the retro thrusters on time, and land safely; fire them too late, and skip off the atmosphere into space; too early, and burn up. Course correction there became a matter of life and death.

SEEING WHEN, WHERE, AND HOW TO MOVE UP

With half your lifetime invested in your career, you might hesitate before changing your clientele, your sales practices, your company's name, even the way you dress. At forty-two, Skip Kelley had built his Kustom House Company north of Boston into a $324,000-a-year remodeling business, and Kustom House had been growing steadily. Yet Kelley wanted something more.

Not just more money. More recognition of his professionalism ("only used-car dealers have a worse reputation than home remodelers," he would say), more maneuverability for growth in a big ($80 billion) and fragmented industry, more chance to show what he could do, more excitement.

Skip Kelley had dreamed of what he wanted. For ten years he had labored over a workbench, crafting kitchen cabinets for his uncle, before he got the confidence to go out on his own. For seven more years he worked as a jobber, driving from house to house with his tools in the back of a pickup truck. Then he took out a second mortgage on his house and spent $70,000 converting an old railroad station into a showroom where a prospective customer can browse through the various woods, finishes, cabinets, sinks, wine racks, and fine touches that Kustom House Company (with the "K" for Kelley) offers. He created a Kustom House logo, picked out yellow and brown for his company colors, ordered uniforms for his staff, and designed a marketing plan. Any day, a customer could find him on his knees with the carpenters, the sleeves of his T-shirt rolled up. Now he was thinking of exchanging the T-shirt for a maroon blazer with a gray name tag.

He knew where he wanted to go. He wasn't getting there at a rate that satisfied him. So in 1982 this independent operator, who had done all right calling his own shots, became the first remodeler in New England to join a franchise operation called Mr. Build.

He was doing what every competent navigator learns as second nature—correcting his course.

Mr. Build was the idea of Art Bartlett, who had earlier blazed a trail in "conversion franchising." Instead of starting would-be business people from scratch, as in older forms of franchising (McDonald's, PIP, Supercuts), conversion franchising puts together a national team with entrepreneurs who are already established. Bartlett made his mark with Century 21 Real Estate Corporation. Starting in 1971 with a single office and $6,000, he built the Century 21 system to 7,600 offices across the United States before selling it to Trans World Corporation for $90 million and retiring in 1979. Bored with retirement, Bartlett then changed course: He wanted to get back into "the day-to-day excitement of building a company."

Skip Kelley wanted to align himself with Bartlett's vision, energy, and marketing tactics. He wanted access to a national branch name, television advertising, the performance bonds and guarantees that a big national organization could provide to boost customer confidence, upgraded accounting skills, group discount prices. . . . He wanted to break through the limitations of the business he had been running.

Remodelers see themselves as craftsmen; most of them, for all their skills on the job, are weak in business sense and business applications. The designer of the Mr. Build training programs offered that opinion, and Kelly had to agree. He had been reading for years about basic business tools that he was too harried to use—selling a service rather than a product, overcoming the customer's initial resistance, identifying a market, generating leads. Now these things were going to start working for him.

Still, parts of the change were hard for Kelley and his staff. At a job site, the work was as good as ever. Elsewhere, though, they felt they were giving up parts of something they had built themselves. Their name was now "Mr. Build Kustom House Company." Kelley recalls:

> I was really upset. Mr. Build wasn't mine. It came from somebody else's mind. I already had my colors; I would never have chosen gray and maroon. I would never have chosen that name, either. . . . I already had a name. My name. It hurt a little bit to push that aside and take the back seat to Mr. Build.
>
> But that's the problem with remodelers. We romance the business to death. We forget we're in business to make money. I knew, if I thought about it, that the mass approach through Mr. Build was going to work—after all, would people rather buy a McDonald's burger or a Skip Kelley burger?
>
> That's one of the things they taught me in the training session. I shouldn't care *what* they call me. As long as they call me.

Kelley attended a series of classes that Mr. Build gave for franchise owners and came home with training manuals and new ideas. He used to do jobs all over, miles apart, trying to get all the work he could. Now he focuses on a ten-mile radius from his showroom. He sent five thousand mailers to homeowners in that area, concentrating on those making more than $30,000 a year. "I got out of the thirty-year-olds and into the forty-year-olds." When he hangs his MR. BUILD sign in front of a new job site, he asks the new customer if he can send out letters to the neighbors, inviting them to take a look at their friends' addition. He used to close one sale for every ten inquiries. Now he closes one out of five. His marketing costs dropped from 8 percent of estimated gross sales to 4.5 percent, and in the first six months after joining Mr. Build, his sales jumped to an annualized volume of $500,000. By mid-1984 they were headed for $1 million.

Skip Kelley is no less a craftsman than before. Now, though, he is also a businessman. He likes the growth, and he likes an unexpected luxury that came with it: time. He has learned to delegate. When the telephone at the showroom rings now, the call is usually for his production manager or his office manager, seldom for him personally. In the winter of 1983, he and his wife took the first vacation they had had in ten years. In 1984, for the first time in his life, he attended a remodelers' convention.

Even people who know where they are going sometimes have to adjust their course. From the beginning, Skip Kelley had his mission and his goals in view. He realized that he had to change the path by which he was going to reach them.

Do these people worry about getting off course? Not much. In fact, they expect it to happen. They know one way to avoid navigation problems is to stand still, and peak performers do not incline to that solution. They value progress toward their goals and their mission. Accordingly, they hone specific skills for locating where and when they need a course correction and how to make it.

READY TO USE

Morton Hunt's observations in *The Universe Within* on hard-wiring (mentioned briefly in Chapter 2) suggest strongly that the impulse to correct course is an inherent part of the human nervous system, not something we have to impose on it. In computer terms, hard-wiring refers to built-in characteristics, the results of fixed circuitry rather than programming. In human beings we might call it predisposition. Hunt contends: "The circuitry of the brain develops, under the biochemical guidance of genes, in such a way as to assemble incoming experience into realistic, useful concepts, and not the reverse." In other words, those concepts are not sitting out there in the world waiting for us to pick them up. From the scrambled incoming material of experience, we assemble concepts in our minds, each of us creating meaning in our own way.

If Hunt is right, and if human nature includes an "inherent neurological restlessness," we need to do something with the thoughts in our minds and with the world they represent.

People don't just sit in the mud when they find themselves stuck, because their hard-wiring for curiosity, restlessness, and growth shows up as a desire to correct course.

THE THREE BASIC SKILLS OF COURSE CORRECTION

Still, there are distinctions between men and women who make effective use of their hard-wiring and those who don't. The ability to correct course—to fine-tune their perceptions and then act on them—follows almost invariably from knowing how to apply three major skills:

- Mental agility
- Concentration
- Learning from mistakes

No peak performer I ever met gets up in the morning and says, "I really must correct course today." More likely, they say something like "Our share of the market is going to drop unless we toughen up the advertising." Then they start to tweak the steering wheel.

It happened at Nike, Inc., in 1984. After twelve years of rapid growth in which they sprinted to the top of the athletic-shoe market in the United States, the founders of the Beaverton, Oregon, company saw their sales starting to level off. Competitors were chipping away at their market with big television campaigns. Converse even got to be the official shoe of the 1984 Summer Olympics. So co-founders Robert Woodell and Philip Knight took a look at their operation.

Until the company went public in 1980, it had had no vice-presidents—a sign of its founders' determination to "be a little different from everyone else." By the time it got near $1 billion in sales and four thousand employees, could it still function in the informal, nontraditional way it did when it was a $2 million company with forty-five hired hands? Well, Woodell and Knight concluded, maybe not.

Until 1984, Nike had directed most of its promotional dollars into athletic events and athletes—"word-of-foot advertising," they called it. In 1976 the company spent its entire advertising budget ($6,000) to start Athletics West, an Oregon track-and-field club where Olympians such as Mary Decker Slaney, Alberto Salazar, and Willie Banks trained. In the Olympic year, Nike support for the club approached $2 million. That fit right in with the way Woodell and Knight wanted to do business. But if Converse and Adidas were taking away some of the domestic footwear market, then there had to be more. So for the first time, they appointed an advertising agency, Chiat-Day of Los Angeles, to put Nike-wearing athletes on billboards, murals, and television spots. They haven't given up their philosophy, captured in the Nike motto, "There is no finish line," or their emphasis on enjoying life while you win. But they have taken a new look at how they plan to sell it from here on.

MENTAL AGILITY

When Skip Kelley remarked that home remodelers tend to "romance the business to death," he was exercising an ability to see a situation from more than one perspective at a time. He was committed to his business; he was eager to make it grow; he was willing to give up some of his attachments in it, such as his name, his company colors, and his lone-wolf feelings of complete independence; and he was able to give up some shortcomings, such as the romancing that makes some remodelers and other craftspeople forget they are in business for profit.

Kelley had the mental agility to maneuver around entanglements that could choke his growth. Being so attached to one's own views that one cannot see the alternatives is a quick way to get off course. Mental agility is just the opposite: the ability to assess situations by evaluating various options. It's much like the CAD/CAM computer technology which lets engineers test various designs on the screen.

Peak performers talented at course correction will fall in love with a mission, but not with their own ideas. They are adept at getting out of their own way.

Mental agility does not mean dodging the thoughts, feelings, and positions—one's own and other people's—in a situation that calls for action. It means being able to see all of them accurately. It means being able to describe accurately each primary point of view—your own and those of others. Peak performers in such situations tend to say things like "Let me see if I've got that straight. What you want is . . . The major items on this agenda are . . ."

When the shaving-cream company called in my father to accuse Kester Solder of causing their aerosol cans to leak all across America, he could easily have become incensed, shown them how wrong they were, and corrected the immediate problem without correcting the unpleasant course of relations between the two companies. Instead, he stood clear of the melodrama, and got a double win.

So, too, did John Bookout, Jr., president and CEO of Shell Oil, in a more recent situation. Early in 1984, Bookout found himself trapped between two hostile camps. On one side of him were shareholders of Shell Oil of Houston, many of them company employees. On the other, directors of Royal Dutch/Shell of the Netherlands, owner of 69.4 percent of Shell's stock. Royal Dutch wanted to buy out the minority shareholders for $58 a share. Six outside directors and most of the shareholders opposed the merger, calling the price inadequate. Should they hold out for more? They turned to Bookout for advice. Officially, Bookout represented Shell Oil, the organization. But he had nurtured the loyalty of Shell employees for eight years before the confrontation, and those employees owned almost a third of the minority shares. Thus he also represented a special class of shareholders who looked to him for leadership.

There he stood, resolutely neutral, at the annual meeting in Wilmington, Delaware. That is not usually his style. Bookout is known for being "generous with advice" and willing to butt heads. "Every time he got promoted," says a former colleague, "there would be a confrontation between him and someone else. John always won. He settled authority issues quickly." But his job was to serve both sides, and he did it. Toward the end of the meeting a shareholder who had come from England to protest quoted a nineteenth-century couplet:

> In matters of commerce the fault of the Dutch
> Is offering too little and asking too much.

A Royal Dutch/Shell executive from the Netherlands in the front row, looked uncomfortable as laughter broke out. "Thank you very much," Bookout said casually. "I hope you won't mind if I don't include that in the record."

The peak performer in such a situation practices what management consultant James J. Cribbin calls "Force-Field Analysis":

> . . . a hard-headed analysis of the *driving* and *restraining* forces that the change must take into account. Driving forces are supportive of the change. They may be *external,* such as legislation that makes affirmative action programs necessary, or the fact that a competitor is gaining a larger market share. They may be *internal,* such as the active interest of key authority figures. . . . Similarly, the restraining forces may be either external or internal.

Effective course correction calculates the driving forces to capitalize on them, and the restraining forces to decide what to do about them.

A key to the strength that mental agility generates is *flexibility.* This is not the same as bending before every breeze. It is, rather, the kind of brainstorming one sees in original thinkers. These people do not keep running dumbly down empty tunnels. They look at what is in there, look from a dozen different angles, argue for things and against them just to see what happens. Skip Kelley could have gone on running his business as if he had never heard of Mr. Build. Nobody who is firmly glued to conventional categories of thinking, and to his or her own past attitudes, can be flexible enough for major course corrections. A reasonable detachment, a more objective view, is essential.

CONCENTRATION

For many, *concentration* summons images of frowning people gritting their teeth, dredging up the endurance to keep going many hours a day but, in doing that, losing their fine tuning. They end up not discriminating very well. They pound everything that comes up in front of them, with the result that they hammer down a lot of nails but bend a lot of them. For peak performers, concentration consists of:

Stamina, the strength to sustain long hours of work and maintain high performance under high stress;

Adaptability, meeting changes in work or surroundings with appropriate behavior, with imagination and confidence that they can cope, and even thrive.

People who combine stamina and adaptability so that they can concentrate behave in predictable ways. Management consultant and researcher Richard E. Boyatzis sums up:

> They can be seen working long hours when this is needed. They can maintain a high quality of performance through 14-hour days and 70-hour weeks. Throughout such a prolonged or arduous task, they maintain their usual degree of attention to detail . . . have energy and resistance to stress . . . remain relatively calm and patient . . . engage in activities specifically chosen to reduce the effects of the stress or fatigue.

Hardiness. Better than "resistance" to stress, we have observed, is *resilience* under stress. Resilient people recognize and then cultivate certain key aspects of behavior, notably what University of Chicago psychologists Suzanne C. Kobasa and Salvatore R. Maddi term *hardiness.*

People who thrive in high-powered jobs—while others in

seemingly easier occupations develop ulcers, hypertension, heart disease, and a gnawing desire to escape from it all—approach life with specific attitudes that Kobasa and Maddi define as:

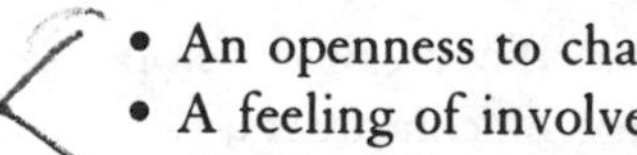

- An openness to change
- A feeling of involvement in whatever they are doing
- A sense of control over events

There are few better examples of concentration these days than the race between Japan and the United States to develop the "fifth-generation" computer, the breakthrough that could determine which nation will dominate in computers—and therefore in the worldwide economy—from the 1990s onward. The first generation of computers relied on vacuum tubes, the second on transistors, the third on integrated circuits, the fourth on very-large-scale integrated (VLSI) circuits. Each generation represented a leap in the speed with which computers process information. No matter how fast they have become up to now, all of them suffer from a bottleneck: They process information serially, one calculation at a time before going on to the next calculation. The fifth-generation computer will represent another course correction. With perhaps a million processors operating in parallel, it could be the first machine to emulate the functioning of the human brain. It could handle not only mathematical data, like today's conventional computers, but could also respond to spoken commands, translate languages, advise scientists on research strategies, actually make decisions. It would be a first step toward true "artificial intelligence."

In Japan, the job of developing the fifth-generation computer has been given to the Institute for New Generation Computer Technology. The government leaders who planned the institute gave it ten years from its inception in 1982 to complete its project. Its director, Kazuhiro Fuchi, has said that he doubts that his group will have a fifth-generation machine ready for the marketplace by 1992, but American competitors are nonetheless impressed and more than a little alarmed. "They will get a lot of payoff even if they don't reach all their targets," says David H. Brandin, a vice president of SRI International and the past president of the Association for Computing Machinery. One possible payoff, he suggests, would be a leap forward in making computers easier for people to use.

Fuchi has a clear view of his critical path. "If we can develop basic technologies that will lead to a new age of computers," he says, "the project will be a success." Underscoring the notion that intense concentration requires adaptability, Fuchi deliberately assembled a young team. "The question was who would adapt more easily to this research," he said. "Young people have fewer fixed ideas."

The United States has looked at the challenge from Japan and started some macro course corrections. Traditionally in this country, radical advances in technology have come from independent teams or, at the most, individual companies competing against the rest of the field. Legally, antitrust laws have been intended to keep corporations in the same field from conspiring with each other on products or prices. Politically, the electorate has been suspicious of the kind of government-industry collaboration that makes up the military-industrial complex against which President Dwight Eisenhower warned. But the economic muscle of "Japan, Inc.," in which the Ministry of International Trade and Industry (MITI) and the Ministry of Finance have combined public and private resources to knock the United States out of world leadership in one industry after another—autos, steel, consumer electronics—has spurred some changes. The necessity to concentrate corporate energies became clear to a degree unparalleled in American industry. In 1982, William Norris, founder and chairman of Control Data Corp., convened a meeting of top computer and semiconductor industry executives, and the result is a consortium of a dozen major corporations known as the Microelectronics and Computer Technology Corporation (MCC). Some industry heavyweights stayed out—IBM, reportedly because it feared antitrust action if it joined; Cray Research because, chairman John Rollwagen says, "That's not our style"; Texas Instruments and Intel for other reasons. Still, MCC is a new approach. Headquartered in Austin, Texas, and run by retired Admiral Bobby Ray Inman, former director of the National Security Agency and deputy director of the CIA, the new corporation plans to go straight for the frontiers of semiconductors, software, computer architecture, and artificial intelligence. One doesn't have to be a member of Inman's team at MCC or of Fuchi's in Japan to realize the race is on. From now until the fifth-generation computer is in place, thousands of individuals in both countries will be concentrating their energies toward this next stage in the evolution of technology. Whatever the outcome, the determinants of success for each team will be the stamina, adaptability, and hardiness of its members.

That is course correction, and concentration, on a large scale.

LEARNING FROM MISTAKES

Mistakes are not only inevitable, they can be made valuable.

Buckminster Fuller is most widely known for inventing the geodesic dome (the honeycomb sphere that protects many radar stations and held the U.S. pavilion at the Montreal World's Fair) and applying his ingenuity to almost every practical aspect of living. To the man himself, though, his inventions were less important than his lifelong refinement of the insights that made them possible. Fuller spent the last fifty years of his life delivering one urgent message:

> Humans have learned only through mistakes. The billions of humans in history have had to make quadrillions of mistakes to have arrived at the state where we now have 150,000 common words to identify that many unique and only metaphysically comprehensible nuances of experience.
>
> . . . Chagrin and mortification caused by their progressively self-discovered quadrillions of errors would long ago have given humanity such an inferiority complex that it would have become too discouraged to continue with the life experience. To avoid such a proclivity, humans were designedly given pride, vanity, and inventive memory, which, all together, can and usually do incline us to self-deception.
>
> . . . So effective has been the nonthinking, group deceit of

humanity that it now says, "Nobody should make mistakes," and punishes people for making mistakes.

. . . The courage to adhere to the truth as we learn it involves, then, the courage to face ourselves with the clear admission of all the mistakes we have made. Mistakes are sins only when not admitted.

That insight was underscored by Robert Maynard, owner and publisher of the *Tribune* in Oakland, California. He told me that he gets suspicious of people who imply that they have never made a mistake in their lives. "Life gives you a down quarter every so often, and a person who never acknowledges mistakes will fall on his face when he hits it. I look for people to hire who have the strength that life experience gives you when you've had your wins and losses. You learn how to capitalize on the lessons you've had so you can come back and do a better job the next time."

Discovery Toys founder Lane Nemeth is not exactly pleased by the mistakes she made on the way to building a $35 million company, but she knows what she learned from them.

I did things like run out of money. One time I borrowed money at 27½ percent interest . . . with a $7,000 prepayment penalty! I didn't know that I wasn't going to be able to pay that back, or that the interest was outrageous. I just didn't understand. So I just kept going through it. . . . I looked at where my problems were and tried to make constructive changes, but never felt that I couldn't turn it around somehow.

More than any other single element, what kept Nemeth going in the face of mistakes and the difficulties they raised was her commitment—to the product and to the people she had recruited. She refused to let herself think she would do anything but succeed.

We had every horrible thing happen, and I just kept thinking that it was perfect. Initially I would tell you it was the product I was committed to. Absolutely committed. I knew this product had to succeed. Then later on, and we had problems all the way along . . . I started realizing that I suddenly had a huge,

> huge responsibility to all these women [who were selling the toys at home parties] to whom I had said, "If you follow me, I will have a career for you and make you rich." I said to myself, "I can't face those people and say, 'Well, I got tired,' or, 'I'm burned out,' or, 'I don't like this anymore. Goodbye.' " I just can't do that. They have faith in me. They followed. So I'm stuck. That's really what happened.

Harry Truman once said, "The only things worth learning are the things you learn after you know it all." Baseball executives used to be so sure that black athletes should not play in the big leagues that they ignored vast resources of talent. It took a Branch Rickey and a Jackie Robinson to initiate a major course correction in that business, and an Al Campanis to learn from the errors of those who "knew it all." By the time Campanis heard sportswriter Roger Kahn eulogize Jackie Robinson ("He did not merely play at center stage. He was center stage; and wherever he walked, center stage moved with him"), he had learned that the issue is larger than admitting people of one specific race to baseball. The issue is locating and cultivating talent in general.

Many mistakes can be traced to a single source: inaccurate or outdated information. Incomplete or downright wrong information ranges from the narrowest specifics of a task to the broadest assumptions of a culture. The latter type of mistake, from which people in baseball and every other industry have been learning, includes racial, sex, and other forms of discrimination. Since these biases are based on erroneous information in our "collective data bank," what needed to be done to correct the mistakes—and correct course—was to correct the information. Black players are not bad for baseball; they help it immeasurably. Women are not inferior business people; many bring assets to their work that men find themselves hard-pressed to match.

A key to the success of peak performers such as Rickey and Campanis is that when they see misinformation, they go straight for corrections instead of using the mistake to blame others and find scapegoats. When Philip Caldwell, the recently retired chairman of Ford Motor Company, took control as CEO in 1979 and chairman in 1980, U.S. automakers were reeling from their own mistakes and the assault from Japan. He didn't look for somebody to blame. He looked for ways to correct course.

> Why kick the man downstream who can't put the parts together because the parts really weren't designed properly? We've stopped that kind of stuff. Now, two years before production of a new vehicle, the vehicles are taken to the plants where they're going to be made, and the people who are actually going to make them have a chance to go through the whole process and make suggestions.

Several years ago I served on the faculty of Control Data Corporation's Management Institute, giving one- and two-day public workshops on achieving and maintaining peak performance. Many participants came from companies other than Control Data, and I was consistently puzzled by the number of reticent, demotivated people among them. In similar programs sponsored by companies, associations, and universities for their own employees, I was used to vigorous response from top performers intent on improving already-impressive achievement and from rising stars intrigued by the possibility of significantly increasing their productivity.

Much puzzled, I started doing informal surveys in the workshops. "What brought you here today?" I would ask. "What results do you expect to produce from being here?" Answers from the demoralized group turned out to be remarkably consistent:

"My manager thinks I'm an underachiever and I need a boost to get me moving."

"They just moved me from engineering (or finance, sales, and other autonomous, self-managing work) to management, and I'm sinking faster than I'm swimming."

Here were people with the preferences and success histories of solo performers, deposited suddenly in managerial positions requiring team mastery, delegating, communication skills, sink or swim. And they had been offered the workshop not as a reward to support a significant career move, nor as advanced study consistent with their new responsibilities, but rather, they were sent, often after months of struggling alone, for remedial training, with a distinct feeling that they had disappointed their superiors.

I had been suggesting similar workshops to corporate clients, assuming they would send middle and senior managers and salespeople who were on a roll and eager to keep up their momentum, not worried, quasi-depressed people who assumed they had been sent for salvage. My contact at one life insurance company based in Hartford, Connecticut, was a regional manager; at a Pittsburgh-based industrial heating-equipment company, it was a division manager. To each I suggested offering the workshop to people at the time of their job change, calling it a recognition event, and linking it to their company's ongoing commitment to supporting their growth as managers. One of them saw the error in the earlier approach and corrected it. The other continued to know it all without learning anything new. The first let the people he selected know that they were being recognized as peak performers moving from technical or sales jobs to middle management. The other insisted on retaining the sink-or-swim model, letting his people know they were being sent because they weren't doing very well and needed remedial training.

The difference in results was dramatic. People from the first company showed up already feeling like winners, self-confident and ready to engage the new material. People from the second company sat through the same workshop but evidenced almost no change. They continued resisting, discounting any value they might produce for themselves, because it all felt like an unjust punishment that hurt their pride. "I'm a winner dumped in a workshop for losers," one said.

Needless to say, the experience of my workshop for the second group was largely a waste of time. It was a classic attempt by a manager to tack skills onto his plain old subordinates without considering the context for his action. The first manager reported that people returned to their company motivated and that they put their new information to good use.

A remark by no less a peak performer than Norbert Wiener, the father of cybernetics, captures my experience with the two managers: "The world may be viewed as a myriad of 'To whom it may concern' messages." Some of us pay attention, some of us don't.

COORDINATING PRESENT PATH AND CRITICAL PATH

Effective course correction depends on accurate information about (a) yourself, (b) the organization, (c) macroforces—the industry, the economy, the world situation. With impressions you form from a continuous stream of data inside and outside the organization, you can decide that you are

- on course and still able to rely on the original impulses, thinking, and timing that put you there

OR

- off course and in need of corrections ranging from frequent, subtle changes to real upheavals.

When an organization goes through upheavals of its own, peak performers are not just handy to have around but absolutely necessary.

In the 1970s, Sears, Roebuck & Co. was suffering from an identity crisis. High-priced specialty shops were clipping off top-end customers while discounters like Wal-Mart and K mart bit off a big chunk of the bargain hunters who had been a Sears mainstay since 1886. Newer, slicker catalogue merchants were even taking chunks of the catalogue sales. Sears' famous consistency and quality held the loyalty of many customers, but its stores were dowdy and the whole huge company was, in a word, depressed. Sears' share of the U.S. retail market dropped from 9.3 percent in 1967 to 8.2 percent by the late 1970s.

When Edward R. Telling became chairman and chief executive in 1978, however, the course of things began to turn. Depression gave way to exuberance. The customers are back, more of them than ever. The word went out that Sears had attractive new stores, faster service, and an expanded range of things to buy—from the traditional washers and dryers to personal computers, oxyacetylene welding outfits, designer clothes, and diverse services from auto insurance to stock purchases. For the first half of 1984, Sears earned $570 million, up 21 percent from the same period in 1983, on revenues of $17.8 billion. That performance followed a 56 percent earnings gain from 1982 to 1983, a year in which sales reached nearly $36 billion, more than Du Pont, General Electric, or Gulf, and just behind IBM and Texaco.

What happened? Sears and its traditions had been Telling's whole working life since he started as a clerk in 1946, yet he did not hesitate to embrace changes. He said, "Taking chances is a fact of economic life. Business must risk to grow. Fear of what may or may not happen is no excuse for avoiding challenges." To Telling, the Sears situation was not a threat but a challenge, and he felt considerable control over its outcome. One consistent finding of our study is that even in situations that challenge them severely, peak performers assume the type of control Telling felt. They have learned, in previous situations, to count on their mental agility, concentration, and ability to learn from mistakes. Telling sold off unprofitable stores and reduced the payroll by 82,180 employees—about 20 percent—most significantly in the bloated management ranks. After he eased out complacent old-timers and put younger, fresher lieutenants in key positions, he remarked, "It was very lonely. What I did had to be done, but I knew I wouldn't be very popular."

One particular thunderclap for entrenched executives was Telling's appointment of Edward Brennan, then only forty-six, to full responsibility for the huge merchandising division. That division has led Sears' return to robust health. Telling took Sears into areas where department stores had not operated before. Within a single week in 1981, Sears arranged to buy both a New York stock brokerage (Dean Witter) and a California real estate firm (Coldwell Banker). Adding them to its huge credit operation and its Allstate Insurance division positioned the old store to challenge the likes of Citicorp and Merrill Lynch in the financial big leagues of lending money and selling stock. As a reward for his efforts, Brennan moved into the chairmanship of Sears when Telling retired in 1985.

Mental agility. Concentration. Learning from mistakes. Telling proved to be strong in all three, to his company's great profit (and his own; he made $1.4 million in 1983). He, and Sears, corrected their course.

The capacity to correct course is the capacity to reduce the differences between the path you are on now and the optimal path to your objective—between your present path and your critical path.

SEEING POSSIBILITIES BEFORE THEY BECOME OBVIOUS

A member of the 100% Club of IBM's National Accounts Division reminded me of the answer Thomas Watson, Sr., gave when asked toward the end of his life: "At what point did you envision IBM becoming so big?"

"Right at the beginning!" Watson said. As early as 1924, when he changed the name of the Computing-Tabulating-Recording Company to International Business Machines, he envisioned what IBM would look like as a big, mature business (when it was "done," as he put it). Then every day he worked to correct the difference between maturity—the objective—and his present path. Recall the observation of Ted Levitt, business professor at Harvard: "The future belongs to people who see possibilities before they become obvious." Seeing possibilities before they become obvious is a talent that adds acuity to goal-setting. Skip Kelley turned around Kustom House Company, not from failure but from success that just wasn't the success he wanted. Steady performances such as his are so familiar among peak performers that they tend to be taken for granted.

But when somebody gets to the brink of disaster before pulling back, *then* the world hears about it. The famous stories—the legends about corporate turnarounds—grow up around inspired executives who revive ailing companies and restore them to profitability. Robert Townsend, for instance, took over Avis Rent-a-Car in the 1960s when it had not made a profit in thirteen years, and changed its course in six months. Townsend did not know any big secrets about how to rent cars. In fact, he insists in his influential books *Up the Organization* and *Further Up the Organization* that the material for a successful turnaround is in the people who are already with the company. At Avis, he went directly to the troops, telling them in his customary down-home language. "I don't know diddly-squat about the rental car business. I can't do it alone. Let's have some fun, build a good business, and get rich."

Like Skip Kelley, Townsend learned much after he "knew it all."

By talking to enough people, he spotted a pattern. Avis needed a fleet of new cars, a new computer system, a good advertising campaign, a bank loan to buy all that, and a larger share of a market in which it had 10 percent to Hertz's 60 percent. To make any of those externals work, it needed most of all a turnaround in the morale of its people.

Townsend made clear to the people at Avis his belief that a leader's job is to give power and responsibility to others, not to hoard it. "A leader is not an administrator who loves to run others, but someone who carries water for his people so they can get on with their jobs."

Second, he made sure that employees knew that they, not he, controlled the direction events would take and that dedicated work would pay them handsomely: "Look, you're the lowest paid in the industry. We're gonna try and get profitable. If we reach our goal—to be the most profitable with the highest growth rate—that will mean we keep six cents on every dollar we take in. We'll give one cent to you, which will make you the highest paid agents in the business."

In six months, with a slogan that became famous, "We're Number Two. We Try Harder," Avis shot up to 20 percent of the market. After three years, Townsend was ready to retire at the age of forty-five. When he left, the owners decided, "If you don't run it, we won't own it." They soon sold the company. It takes the skill of peak performers working together to create the alternatives and opportunities that inspire course corrections throughout an entire corporation.

What happens when the leaders of an entire city decide to course-correct?

A group of decision-makers in Cleveland in the early 1980s asked themselves: "What will happen if we don't take immediate, decisive action?" The answer was: "This city will collapse." Cleveland is America's fifth-largest corporate headquarters city, yet a declining industrial base, several years of enmity between the business community and local politicians, and widespread apathy had brought the city to the brink of bankruptcy. In 1979 a new mayor, George Voinovich, proposed that the private sector lead a program to streamline city operations, and E. Mandell de Windt, chairman and CEO of Eaton Corporation, spearheaded the effort.

Del de Windt tells of asking the president of a large company to take an important and involved role on the task force, and reminding him that it would commandeer many hours of his time and, in a very real sense, cut into the attention he could give his business. When the man immediately took on the job, de Windt asked in surprise why he had not done something like this sooner. The man said simply, "Nobody ever asked me." From that moment on, says de Windt, "I knew . . . I would be doing a lot of asking, not just to lend a name, but to lend a hand, some heart and spirit . . . without commitment and involvement at the top, there is no extraordinary effort from the ranks."

The CEOs de Windt recruited came up with ninety loaned executives and over $800,000 to investigate and present an action plan. The objective was to examine the sixty-three departments of Cleveland's municipal government and make recommendations that would result in both substantial savings and more efficient, more productive operations. A twelve-week study resulted in 650 recommendations. Some action began even before the final report was ready. In one instance, a loaned executive discovered that salt trucks, on alert for an impending snowstorm, had been loaded months before and the salt had solidified into one solid lump per truck. The salt trucks were promptly rescued and put to better use.

The bottom line of the recommendations showed a potential one-time saving of $37 million and potential savings of $57 million a year. Some 68 percent of the recommendations have been put into action. Another 26 percent are being implemented. Some $585,000 of the funds raised for the project were earmarked for action rather than for study—"probably," de Windt says wryly, "qualifying for the *Guinness Book of World Records.*" Cleveland is out of default. Construction has picked up.

What doesn't show on the bottom line, however, is de Windt's observation of "a sharply increased awareness of the problems of government by business CEOs." As one task force executive put it: "How would you like to run a business where your top management can change every two years, your revenue can depend on the whims and fancies of state and national government, and you have to convince more than half a million people that you can collect garbage, control crime, enhance safety, and brighten the future better than anyone else?" Del de Windt concludes: "Every city has the talent, the skills and the resources to help its community prosper. But nothing will happen until someone makes it happen."

Another city that needed to turn around not its finances but its image around the world was Dallas. After John F. Kennedy was assassinated, "Big D" felt itself marked by shame. Erik Jonsson was chairman of the board of Texas Instruments when he was elected mayor of Dallas in 1964, a year after the tragedy. The man who had built TI into an electronics giant made it his first order of business to pull the city together and show that it was not, as finger-pointers called it, a "city of hate." The result was Goals for Dallas, the first municipal goals program in the United States and by now the longest-running one in the country.

The Dallas goals, ranging from construction of the huge Dallas-Fort Worth Regional Airport, to judicial reforms, to block-partnership programs to help the disadvantaged help themselves, have gone through three cycles. The first cycle set the tone: High-level meetings, then neighborhood meetings; twelve task forces on government, health, safety, education, and other areas of major concern; additional neighborhood meetings to review task force proposals; three years of citywide effort to implement them. City officials claim achievement of 75 percent of the goals and progress on 98 percent in the first two cycles; the third began in 1983.

Giving the closing address at the annual Goals for Dallas Conference in 1984, I observed that John Kennedy in life helped a nation shaken by the Soviets' *sputnik* success pull a space program together, and in death provided the impetus for Dallas to pull a city together. Both situations required that people stretch themselves by using the three major skills of course correction.

PUTTING THE SKILLS OF COURSE CORRECTION TO WORK

Mental agility. Concentration. Learning from mistakes. With these three *general* skills, peak performers assess *specific* areas in which they occasionally go off course. These areas cover not only work but health and family relationships—major contributors to effective work—as well.

Spotting the indicators that it is time for a course correction can be easier for a company or a city than for an individual. Conversely, implementing corrections can be easier for an individual than for a large organization (big ships don't turn on a dime)—once the individual sees the need.

An individual's ability to start a course correction comes from looking and listening for cues to his or her position along a critical path. It may be obvious to other people that you are on the path or off it; but for an individual in the middle of a job, the cues can be subtle and easy to ignore.

I remember a meeting of the American Trucking Association where I met Larry Harris, a fifty-one-year-old company owner who had moved up through the ranks from driver to manager to proprietor. Larry was set, he told me at lunch. "I got where I wanted to get, and boy, it feels good." At that, his wife looked plaintively at him and asked him to tell me about the recent changes in his life.

It turned out that Larry had gained forty pounds. He drank more than he used to. He had developed hypertension. These were clearly not subtle cues, but he ignored them anyway. "No problem," he said. "I feel fine. This stuff just seems to come with the territory." He had seen it happen to friends. A number of them, in fact, had died or come close to dying of coronary heart disease.

I asked him how he liked his work. His tone changed as he talked about a guy who relished the autonomy and privacy he had in the cab of his truck, and who had learned to delegate a great many tasks as a manager. Suddenly this guy, as head of his own company, felt what he called "people poisoning"—too little privacy, too many people asking things of him. The computer age had brought him more information than he had ever had, but not nearly the wherewithal to interpret it. Management training to help him handle his present level of responsibility? Nah. He had moved up through the ranks, hadn't he? He knew trucking.

Larry was impervious to loud signals that he needed to change directions, in both his work and his health.

Recent studies indicate that job-obsessed people are actually as addicted to the adrenaline they produce as smokers are to nicotine. People addicted to intensity and activity and crisis respond only to a limited range of "loud" stimuli. Nothing short of an explosion and fire attracts their attention. Seeming emergencies (and everything starts looking like an emergency) deafen them to subtleties.

They miss cues. They literally do not hear what other people are saying, verbally and nonverbally. Information slips past them. Yet it is precisely the ability to pick up on subtleties that makes possible a timely course correction—being aware of things *before* they explode.

One of the most dramatic findings in our study has been the difference between peak performers and work addicts. Workaholics are addicted to activity; peak performers are committed to results. Job obsession or job addiction is not at all the same as intense effort in the service of a compelling mission.

Lately we have been seeing another problem. During a meeting in Phoenix of international Merrill Lynch account executives, then CEO Roger Birk, a slim, fit man of fifty-five, expressed to me serious concern over drug problems on Wall Street, particularly cocaine addiction. "Many of us know talented, successful people with a great deal going for them who are throwing it all away," he said. "Why would they do it?"

We concluded that the intense pressures of Wall Street, Silicon Valley, and other high-stakes arenas of competition can be breeding grounds for stress-related illnesses. When your sympathetic nervous system is in a state of chronic arousal, your production of emergency-related hormones such as adrenaline and cortisol stays at abnormally high levels which can damage the heart and blood vessels. With your system addicted to a full-throttle position, traditional stimulants—caffeine, sports, challenging work—no longer produce the kick you want. At the time Roger Birk expressed his concern, the fashionable alternative in some circles was cocaine. The use of that drug is an attempt to deal with job addiction in which everything feels like an emergency. Cocaine gives a temporary chemically induced "all-rightness" which compounds the problem by masking the emergency arousal state so that one begins to miss even the loud cues to which other people can respond. As Birk observed, high achievers in high-stress environments were attempting to beat intensity with intensity, and damaging their bodies, careers, and entire lives with their destructive addictions.

Even those doing extremely well are not likely to remain peak performers. They do not have the staying power. Their addictions burn them out.

The true peak performers, while capable of intense effort, retain an ability to relax that allows them to keep sight of results, long-range outcome, pacing, flexibility, and the importance of self-renewal. Peak performers in high-stress situations are what we might call positively addicted. Their intense commitment to their work—the addiction—is balanced by an extraordinary awareness of the need for careful course corrections to protect their physical and mental health. They know that successfully pushing the edge of one's capabilities for prolonged periods is a learned and carefully managed skill. In succeeding in extraordinarily stressful jobs, they make systematic course corrections to protect body and soul as they progress along the critical path toward their mission.

Our research also reveals the fact, surprising to anyone who thinks high performance ought to take a compensating toll, that they have better-than-average relationships on the job and at home. The reason is fairly obvious. Peak performers are self-starters with staying power. They are committed to their missions over the long haul, and they take all the help they can get. Deteriorating health or dysfunctional relationships can consume more of one's available energies than the work itself.

Besides, they are aware that if unresolved squabbles and resentments in the family or backbiting and jealousy on the job start moving to center stage, these distractions can consume disastrous amounts of time and energy. Peak performers are pragmatists. They value their relationships for the support they provide toward achievement, as well as for the fulfillment they provide in life.

Knowing that their personal effectiveness increases when their overall fitness level is high, many extraordinarily successful people decide at some point during their rise that they do not want to be vague about a matter of such importance to them. Frequently they devise specific ways of monitoring chronic work and stress overloads—not the occasional spikes of intense activity but the long-running, familiar, and therefore almost invisible destroyers. They might, for instance, monitor themselves for explicit symptoms of burnout and chronic stress overload, such as:

General physical pains
Insomnia
Hating your place of work
Hiding behind rules and formalities
Resisting change
Reduced productivity and performance
Getting along poorly with peers or supervisors
Increased personal and family distress

The list only begins to catalogue the ways in which job addicts devastate their health and their families as well as their productivity. But it puts up some warning markers.

SELF-RENEWAL: SURVIVAL OF THE FIT

By the time Tom Fatjo was thirty-six, he had turned $500 and a used garbage truck into the country's biggest solid-waste disposal company, Browning-Ferris Inc. Traveling, selling all day long and deep into the night, merging 160 local garbage companies into one giant, pushing constantly for growth, he was one of the youngest and most successful businessmen in the United States. But he began to realize he was using himself up physically. His hands shook. His family became "like shadows in the background," he said. "I needed to do something for myself before I ran down."

Fatjo made a short-term course correction: He took up jogging, then began running in races. Within a year he felt stronger and more energetic than before. Looking around, he saw other people "pressing as hard as they could . . . people who had a lot to contribute to their businesses, but it didn't appear their bodies would support them as they got older." The information clicked into place with Fatjo's experience of what he had been able to do for himself. He then made a major, long-term course correction.

He sold his BFI holdings to finance the opening of The Houstonian, an executive spa and fitness center in an eighteen-acre pine grove within easy reach of downtown Houston. It includes a condominium high-rise, fitness center, preventive medicine center, and the two-hundred-room Houstonian Hotel with twenty-four-hour room service for hard workers and twice the customary number of meeting rooms. Executives who use The Houstonian as a conference center get a close look at its fitness programs. Many come back for tuneups.

Once he got The Houstonian running, Fatjo made another course correction. A member of the President's Council on Physical Fitness, he wants everyone, not just a well-conditioned elite, to be fit. The top was a logical place to begin, but when he saw that executives who were enthusiastic about providing health programs for their employees still had no expertise for implementing them, the entrepreneur in him went to work. Drawing on advice from experts in the field, The Houstonian created Living Well, a twelve-week introductory health and fitness course run by a nationwide network of fitness experts, packaged so that a company buying it needs to provide only some space—and the employees who can benefit from the corrections Fatjo made in the course of his own life.

Since he started The Houstonian, testifies *American Health* editor-in-chief T George Harris, "Tom carries a workload past anything you'd expect from a workaholic. Yet he saves good time for family, friends, and for himself."

Fatjo did not kick back and turn into a placid loafer. To the degree that it is appropriate for his own constitution, he has stayed committed to work. He likes to work. Who can say that is wrong? Put this kind of man in a normal-intensity job and he would probably decay. He is one of those peak performers who graduated from a debilitating obsession to a positive, motivating mission.

COURSE CORRECTION AT HOME

The number one cause of guilt among ambitious business people in America is the ambitious one's feeling that he—and, increasingly, she—is neglecting the people back home. Thomas Shelton, the manager of market research at Deere & Company, remembers the time his wife told their four-year-old daughter, before a visit from Grandmother: "We're going to have a visitor, and it's someone you haven't seen in a long time. Can you guess who it is?"

"Dad?" the little girl ventured eagerly.

The next most common cause of guilt is failure to get control of one's work. Managers in particular berate themselves for failing to live up to an ideal that may be, in their circumstances, unrealistic. R. Jack Weber of the University of Virginia's Colgate Darden Graduate School of Business observes that many managers have been trained "to believe they should rationally 'plan, organize, lead, and control.' Yet . . . the work life of most of them is characterized by fragmentation, discontinuity, inadequate time for reflection, and relentless interactive demands." After a day of "interactive" pestering and firefighting, the manager sees a lot of uncompleted work around the office, concludes that he or she is not measuring up, and vows grimly to do better the next day.

None of this, of course, enhances anyone's performance. Peak performers—by contrast to their job-addicted colleagues—do not assume automatically that family and friends must take a distant second place to their careers. To the contrary, peak performers in our studies frequently talk about how important the support from family and friends is to them, and communicate that fact to their loved ones. Because their values are clear, when they inadvertently get off track and find themselves feeling guilty about it, they correct course. The job addict, never having clearly identified these values, often neglects family messages of discontent and feelings of personal guilt, and burrows deeper into work.

Peak performers pay attention. Guilt, like the ten items on the burnout list, is a sign that something is wrong. Nobody likes feeling guilty. Nobody wants to feel like a bad person. Feelings of guilt often surface as feelings of resentment against family members and friends who one thinks expect too much of one or don't understand what one is going through. At this point, two things can happen if the person with the feelings does not express them directly to the person at whom they are aimed. Resentment either gets discharged as anger: "Why the hell do I have to be the one who takes the kids to the park every Saturday? Joe and Harry get to catch up on their work. I need the time too." Or the guilt becomes intensified further: "How could I resent her? She's been so supportive all these years. This is making me miserable. This job is lousy."

To resolve such issues, or at least diminish their impact, peak performers are more likely than ordinary performers to talk with people at home and at work in an effort to see how they are doing and what course corrections may be necessary.

A cab driver recently took me in record time from Procter & Gamble's plant in Quincy, Massachusetts, to Logan Airport in Boston. He knew every shortcut, had known them for most of his thirty-six years, and was proud of it. But, it turned out after I expressed admiration, if I had hailed him just a few months before, we might have gotten lost.

For a while he had been jolted off course by a personal drama: a divorce and distress over how he would stay in touch with his children. He had lost track of his mission in life, "to be the best damn cabbie in the Quincy area." He started missing turnoffs, losing track of details. He would lose concentration when he was "ambushed" by certain songs that reminded him of his wife and his marriage. He finally decided to get some help. Going to meetings of the Parents Without Partners organization, he talked about what was happening and how he was handling it. "I never used to drive into dead ends on a run, and I'm starting to think life can be a dead end." With the feedback he gleaned from the comments of other members, he learned that diminished concentration after a severe jolt like a divorce is normal—and temporary. In time, his mental agility and concentration returned, along with an enhanced respect for the power of timely support.

The peak performer's ability to correct course is based on a talent for finding the anomalies in patterns—the data that seem out of place—and piecing together the facts that normally do not fit into a mosaic of information. That means, on the one hand, seeing deviations from the critical path, and on the other hand, seeing windows of opportunity (often before they become obvious). In either case, the peak performer acts to stay on track.

The temptation in studies like ours is to look for how-to-do-it prescriptions. Any such instructions would be false to what the peak performers showed us. Through experimentation and expertise, they develop a feel, an almost artistic appreciation, for the process in which one observation leads to another. There is a company called Inferential Focus, which gathers the data necessary for predicting trends, and peak performers often develop their information in much the same way the Inferential Focus team does: extracting meaning from their full range of skills—not just analysis, not just intuition, not just future vision, not just past experience. No one of them is enough, as Carol Colman of Inferential Focus points out: "The pace of change today is too great for analysis [alone] to help us understand what is taking place. We would rather be generally correct than precisely wrong."

A basketball metaphor applies to successful course correction. At the highest levels of involvement, a peak performer in business develops the combined skills of a great passer and a great shooter. The passer has to absorb the entire flow of action around him and still grab an opportunity for an assist as it arises. The shooter, on the other hand, has to exclude every extraneous element from his vision and concentrate only on the goal.

The passer: mental agility. The shooter: concentration. In great passers and great shooters, as in great business people, an added capacity makes the most of both: learning from mistakes.

So course correction is the skill that allows a peak performer to navigate through rapid change. What if the change is radical as well as rapid? What if nature, circumstances, or fate not only accelerates the rate of play but alters the rules of the game? In the age of information, how does one manage change to maintain peak performance?

8

CHANGE MANAGEMENT

In the good old days, telephones had hold buttons. Some still do. Chances are, however, that if you work in a large company you have encountered something like this:

> To hold a call press *9. If it worked, you'll hear an assurance tone, dee-dah. If it didn't you'll hear a sound like a European siren. To get the party back press *1 . . . unless you want to transfer the call to another department. In that case you press the switch hook (not too long or you'll disconnect the call), then press *7, wait for the assurance tone, dial the extension number, and tell the person who answers that you are transferring the call. To "park" the call at another station, press the switch hook and the correct three-digit number, and you can pick up the call at another location.

If your office has been switched to a computerized telephone system, you may have understood the above directions. Before you finally learned the system, though, it might have looked like something designed to drive you crazy.

Stephanie Bowers specializes in teaching people how to make constructive use of rapid technological change. She started work at Compath, a California-based telecommunications company, in 1978. As a project coordinator, she oversaw the installation of sophisticated telephone systems such as the ones that went into fourteen Macy's stores throughout the state between 1982 and 1984. A new phone system may not look like a threat. But when it requires thousands of people in scores of departments to divest themselves of habits they have comfortably taken for granted since they were children, it puts them in need of new habits—even new ways of thinking. Then it may throw even accomplished, intelligent professionals into shock.

NEW GAME, NEW RULES

Change is everywhere. That is no longer news. The accelerating *rate* of change—driven by technological jumps in fields from communication and information processing to utilities and banking—is not news, either. It has been twenty years since Alvin Toffler coined the term *future shock* in a *Horizon* article to describe the stress and disorientation that individuals undergo when they encounter too much change in too short a time. A generation has grown up since the scientist and novelist C. P. Snow wrote that, until this century, social change was "so slow that it would pass unnoticed in one person's lifetime. That is no longer so. The rate of change has increased so much that our imaginations can't keep up."

The real news comes from the men and women who excel, not *despite* a buzzing, blooming world of abrupt change and novel situations, but *because* of it.

Stephanie Bowers does not let change overwhelm her. Neither, she tells us, do her most adaptive customers. They do more than merely struggle to keep up. They know how to *manage* change.

The people who reach a peak, maintain it, and pass its benefits along to others share a major characteristic: They never stop learning new skills. They make their own luck.

The peak performers in our study do not regard change as something to resist, or even to understand fully. They see it, rather, as a source of opportunity they can guide. They know a horse is easiest to ride in the direction it's already going. That calls, of course, for considerable attention to the horse and to the precise skills for riding it, and for figuring out whether it's galloping toward a wall or an open field.

If the challenge were simply more choices and a faster flow, we could meet it with more organization and more speed—that is, with traditional time management and strategic planning. But we are also dealing with a rogue element: *new* choices, possibilities that have not been seen and dealt with before. Preprogrammed solutions, habits, and previous personal experience may not work. Peak performers recognize that they are making not merely *more* choices, but *new* choices as well. The skills for handling "more and faster" do not always work with "new."

"More" requires faster decision-making and quicker action in areas that remain, after all, familiar. "New" requires learning, training, experimentation, and integration. A surgeon who has more operations to do per day has to get faster or delegate more. But a surgeon who has new procedures or new equipment has an altogether different task, and may actually have to slow down while mastering the newness.

The combination of quantity, speed, and newness radically alters our sense of time. We do not just imagine that things are both different and moving faster. They are.

One reason is that it is the nature of technology to feed on itself, making more technology possible, in ever-shortening cycles. Over 90 percent of all the scientists who ever lived are alive now. So we have a bursting of old limits, not just of mechanical performance but of human performance. Technologies being developed are influencing the mechanical realm, of course, but their influence is far more powerful in the realm of ideas. We live in an "information society" that is making *knowledge,* not ingots or autos, the source of wealth.

WHO ADAPTS AND WHO DOESN'T

Before Stephanie Bowers could get up to speed, she had to master technical details of telephone equipment and its installation. The long-run usefulness of her work, however, came from a more extensive kind of knowledge: a feel for what it takes for people to divest themselves of old habits, move through "technoshock," and develop new ways of working.

Watching the impact of major change, Bowers noticed who adapted well and who did not: "People with generally positive attitudes, who respond actively in normal conversation and communicate freely with one another, are almost always the ones who will integrate any new system most easily into their jobs."

The process of integration at Macy's began when management distributed memos and put up posters. A change was coming, the announcements said, that would cut costs and at the same time increase each individual's power to communicate between departments, between stores, and with the outside world. The coordinating team from Compath and Macy's wanted people to see the computerized phones as a powerful new tool, not as a nuisance.

Soon, employees began attending training classes on company time. That is where people started to reveal themselves as change managers or change resisters. In one training session Bowers conducted,

> A man sitting in the back of the room wanted to know "why" and "what-if" about almost everything I presented. He was so active and inquisitive that he came across as a sort of tutor for the rest of the people. His questions were taking over so much of the class that I finally asked him to come up in front of the class to try out the features on the practice phone. People started laughing. The laughter puzzled me a bit, but it didn't faze him. He demonstrated the stuff for everyone and did it with grace. After the class I asked a couple of people what was so funny, and they told me he was a corporate vice-president. I wouldn't have asked him to do the demonstration if I had known that.

> But he showed everyone in the room how people who are leaders and have confidence in themselves can make any situation—even an awkward one—turn out successfully.

The most competent change managers, Bowers told us, were people whose commitment to the company, or their careers, or their own sense of mastery, influenced them to see the training as a way to make themselves more efficient producers. They incorporated it as a step toward the company's overall goals and their own. Other people had more trouble. Usually they were people with a less clear and compelling view of why they were there. They saw the training as a burden they had to bear to keep their jobs, and impressed Bowers as "unwilling to learn" :

> . . . the managers, clerks, anybody who acts as if everything they're doing is for someone else—for the boss, for their family—but who are not themselves committed to anything. They don't have a direction; they're just sort of there. When they start to deal with the new equipment, they tighten up, and when they finally ask for help, it is usually in a negative way.

These "negative" types are by no means the only change-resisters in organizations. Bowers has worked with plenty of upper-level professionals who act as if they were "insulted by the technology." At a brokerage firm once, she saw people with six-figure incomes so intimidated by a new telephone system that they decided "the best way to attack it was to claim that it didn't fill their needs. They couldn't really know that, since they were unwilling to venture out and learn it. I think they were afraid of being exposed—they who are so bright and accomplished couldn't put a call on-hold."

Of course, the attitude of a manager strongly influences the atmosphere in his or her department. Those interested mainly in concealing any ignorance from subordinates or superiors, and even from themselves, have a never-ending struggle on their hands. They are condemned to perpetuating the illusion of competence in an era when technological innovation, with its attendant realities of learning, is relentless. By contrast, Bowers found it easiest to work with the managers at Macy's who were committed to the success of all their people. These managers used all the ways they could to smooth the transition for their people and keep tabs on how things were working.

> When you walk up to someone trying to figure something out, and they say, "Oh, hi! I need some help," you know they are going to be just fine. Those types of managers ask questions until they are sure they have the answer they need, and don't sit on the information. When you see that, you can predict who will be the effective change managers.

GETTING FROM THE PAST TO THE FUTURE

Harry and I hadn't seen each other for fifteen years, since we worked together on Apollo 11. That didn't matter. When he took a seat in the front row for a talk I was about to give in New York, the smile we traded said, "Let's catch up on the news." Later that evening, at a quiet corner table in a restaurant, we did.

A lot had changed since our days with the Lunar Excursion Module. Harry had stayed in the aerospace industry through the Apollo flights of the 1970s, hoping to hook on to another compelling mission. But nothing equaled the excitement of the LEM project for him, and eventually he left to open a retail computer store, not so much for more money as to regain the feeling that he was, as he put it, "on the wave of the future. Think of the power we had in the IBM 360/75 mainframes during Apollo 11, and think of that power being available to anyone with a thousand bucks. That's change! Space age technology in your home study!"

Harry had not stood pat. He had altered some basic patterns in his life. He had initiated his own changes. The results had not been uniformly smooth sailing. Some of the passages he told me about sounded hard, even dangerous. Clearly he had prevailed. Not once that evening did he have to say, "I'm proud of what I've accomplished." His presence said it for him.

Before leaving to start the store, he had moved up through several promotions in the aerospace firm where he had worked and "learned to be a pretty fair manager." That meant listening to people, bringing them along, getting them to align willingly with the team effort instead of merely obeying orders—a big step, given the main influences in his life: the military, and before that, his father.

Harry's father was born before the airplane, raised on a farm. He moved to the city and, catching the wave of the future in his own day, opened an electrical-supply shop. As Harry remembers:

> He kept his nose to the grindstone six or seven days a week in a mom-and-pop retail store, taking no crap from anyone—except the customers. He had to be nice to the customers. He used to talk to me about the haves and the have-nots, the people in power and those who took the orders. He was pretty much a copy of his ancestors in terms of beliefs and point of view. Be the boss, work hard and make sure your employees do, and always do good work.

More than anything, he wanted Harry to enjoy the prestige of a professional career, to be an engineer.

So there was a certain irony to Harry's opening his own business. With all the talk about entrepreneurs and building a new world in the computer era, what it really meant to him was going back to his father's era: "My father was an immigrant from the old country, and now I'm an immigrant in the information society."

Harry is fifty-three years old. He smiled briefly across the table when he heard me say that people from now on could expect to learn new jobs two or three times in their lives. He had never thought he would be one of them. I elaborated. His smile came back, deeper and broader, along with an amused shake of the head.

> My children were born here in a new society, and I've gone back to working six, seven days a week, just like my father. The top-end possibilities are great: money and maybe even some freedom someday. Still, it's demanding. Sometimes it's lonely,

when there's nobody to bounce ideas off of. My er
much wait for my instructions. And the custom
from executives to ten-year-olds wants to discuss
The executives who come in don't know a thing about computers, technically, and a bunch of these kids know more than anybody else in the store. When you think about it, it's kind of funny. I'm getting where I want to go by dealing with the kinds of problems my father wanted me to avoid—except they're more complex than he knew about.

My father dealt with basic, practical needs: toasters, television sets. I'm dealing with people who are in the store because they're interested in developing their careers and their personal abilities.

The customers who come back to us or tell their friends about us are the ones who know we'll work with them to give them what they want. I've really learned to pay attention, not just to changing technology but to changing people and changing needs.

ANTICIPATE. ADAPT. ACT.

How does Harry stay alive to the opportunities that come to him in the guise of rapid, wrenching change?

The men and women who maintain peak performance in their careers as they move into the future are working out an answer. A love of mission is, it turns out, much like love of an individual. To keep it alive and effective, you *anticipate* difficulties and opportunities. You *adapt,* changing and growing as the individuals and the world around you change, and you periodically recommit yourself to your mission. You *act* to preserve what is best and discard the rest.

NO MORE SINK OR SWIM

An elegant summation of what we are beginning to face came from Alvin Toffler in this passage from *Future Shock*:

> Eons ago the shrinking seas cast millions of unwilling aquatic creatures onto the newly created beaches. Deprived of their fa-

miliar environment, they died, gasping and clawing for each additional instant of eternity. Only a fortunate few, better suited to amphibian existence, survived the shock of change.

Toffler's book of over fifteen years ago expanded the insights of his earlier magazine article and gave millions of readers not only an enduring term but also, in Toffler's own phrases, "a first approximation of the new realities" in the "human side of tomorrow."

In business, government, and individual daily life, people today are being cast upon unknown shores in even greater numbers than when Toffler first wrote about the shocks of change. The intervening years have, however, produced one major advantage that early creatures didn't have in the days of raw natural selection: Today in the world of work, sink-or-swim is not the only path to growth. Another path is learning—specifically, the methods that peak performers have developed, sometimes hit-or-miss, sometimes formally, since Toffler's book identified the major problems confronting them.

MANAGING CHANGE: FOUR BASIC SKILLS

Anticipating change is becoming a permanent feature of the human landscape. Acting on well-considered and innovative decisions is the choice many people are making these days. It's the adapting phase that's the challenge in managing change. Harry's success was due to his ability to incorporate four basic skills:

1. Being a student forever
2. Expecting to succeed
3. Mapping alternative futures
4. Updating the mission

Being a Student Forever. The now-familiar phrase *lifelong learning* implies a willingness to be sequentially ignorant—to know that having your degree or your title is by no means the end of the game.

Compared to kindergartners, first-graders look mighty big and smart. A time-honored Zen parable contains a useful caution, for the first-graders among us. A Buddhist sage offers tea to a visitor who has come to learn about Zen. The sage begins pouring, fills the cup, and continues to pour. Tea overflows the cup, fills the saucer, and he continues to pour. When the visitor finally rouses himself from a startled silence and asks the wise man to stop, he does. The point of the puddles of tea soaking what had moments before been a clean, elegant, inviting tray needs no words. A cup that is already full has no room for more.

Stephanie Bowers was fortunate that the Macy's vice-president in her telephone training class was one of those senior managers who is willing to be ignorant—to admit there are things he doesn't know—and is not afraid to show it by asking questions. His example helped her get the point across to a whole group of people. The stubborn account executives she came across later at the brokerage firm did her, and themselves, no such favor.

Along with their willingness to learn, peak performers enhance their skill in managing change by cultivating an unusual degree of tolerance for ambiguity. As physicist Peter Carruthers said, people who are making new knowledge live with a special tension. They may feel, as Carruthers does, out of equilibrium. That troubled him when he was young, until he realized that "if I understood too clearly what I was doing, where I was going, then I probably wasn't working on anything very interesting." An ability to tolerate ambiguity helps to avoid overdetermining one's goals. When I was growing up, my notion of a goal-oriented person had something to do with fixing one's eye on a distant target and never looking away. Of course, student pilots learn that such target fixation will surely lead them to fly into the ground.

"Tolerance for ambiguity" is close to "expecting the unexpected." It allows one to discover new information as one goes along. As they proceed, peak performers can adjust goals, always in the direction of more successfully completing a mission. What they are doing is balancing between change and stasis, between innovation and consolidation. They know that, in any event, change is inevitable. They know that linear goals without fluctuation provide a certainty that occurs in theory but not in real life. Much more genuinely certain is a selection of alternative futures, each a projected optimal accomplishment, each taking its shape from changes that are made along the way. A top achiever's willingness to keep learning makes possible a variety of steps at many points along a critical path, some of which can make obsolete the old ways of doing things, no matter how productive those ways may have been.

Being a student at every point in the management of change allows one to incorporate as much novelty as is useful in order to make sure one is making progress, and also enough consolidation (or repetition or practice) to confirm that one is actually learning the new facts and integrating them into the overall game plan. It makes use of the peak performer's openness not just to new bits of information but also to entirely new ways of handling information—new kinds of thinking.

A classic statement of the need for breakthroughs in the kind, not merely the content, of thinking came from Albert Einstein after World War II: "The unleashed power of the atom has changed everything save our mode of thinking, and we thus drift toward unparalleled catastrophes."

The new modes of thinking for which Albert Einstein asked do not mean that everything you learned yesterday is wrong, only that from here on, a greater proportion of the issues on which you spend your time will be novel. It means paying attention to *learning.*

As Toffler observed in *Future Shock,* the illiterates of the age of information will not be those who cannot read and write, but those who cannot learn and relearn. Estimates already suggest that people starting careers this year are likely to run through three or more major job changes during their working lives. Those committed to lifelong learning, who assume they can master the skills on which they decide to focus, can use each change of career to enhance their quality of life, not to threaten it. They can manage change, achieve goals, and update the critical path toward achieving a mission as often as necessary. Anticipate. Adapt. Act.

Expecting To Succeed. Some people make things happen, some watch things happen, and some wonder what happened. Most of those who make things happen are those who expect to be able to do it.

Stephanie Bowers could spot a Macy's employee who expected to succeed the minute she walked up to one who smiled and said, "Oh, hi. I need some help." Those were the people who took pleasure in the newfound power they had in their computerized touch-tone telephones. Bowers figures that "maybe three quarters of the people were delighted that they no longer had to wait for an operator to come on the line in order to transfer a call. They could do it themselves. They saw that what we were giving them was a new degree of independence."

As a way of ensuring success, peak performers develop powerful mental images of the behavior that will lead to the desired results. They see in their mind's eye the result they want, and the actions leading to it. They rehearse. They give new meaning, a positive excitement, to the statement "I can't take my mind off my work." They visualize—not as a substitute for thorough preparation and hard work but as an indispensable adjunct.

As we saw in the discussion of mission in Chapter 3, preference is a strong predictor of successful direction. Preference is more powerful than aptitude, yet often the two go together. People like to do work they are good at. People frequently get good at work they enjoy. They enjoy it more as their expertise increases and positive results occur. We like to win. Like anyone else, peak performers get excited about winning and performing well, about doing work they enjoy and are committed to, at least in part because they expect so firmly that it is going to turn out well.

By contrast, people who expect the worst (remember Stephanie Bowers's resisters) tend to be less willing to engage change, more suspicious, and even hostile when confronted with a new concept, method, or machine.

Expecting success is not merely a matter of attitude, of context. It also depends on mastering content. Before Bowers could accomplish significant changes for her customers, she mastered the details of the equipment she was going to show them. The better an individual understands the detailed workings of a situation, the more he or she can expect to succeed in it. Peak performers take this to mean a commitment to extreme thoroughness and mastery. Knowing their own commitment to such mastery, they have the further leverage of expecting realistically to succeed, no matter what work they happen to be doing. They put the *content* of a situation in an overall *context* of success.

Expecting to succeed, then, is a context within which to manage change in general. In all our observations, we see peak performers concerned not only with survival—with making it through the present—but with influencing the shape of the future as well. And that is not all. They anticipate that they will do it well. The psychologist Jean Houston notes, "They are not people of the breakdown but people of the breakthrough."

Mapping Alternative Futures. The purpose of mapping alternative futures is to get information from them that informs the present. We always have alternatives. More now, in fact, than ever. The skill is to pick out the one that gets you where you want to go.

The crucial question is: *"What will this situation look like when it is working perfectly?"* The time frame can be a month in the future, or two to three years or more, depending on the project. For a shoe salesperson at Macy's, the answer might be: "I can take a call out on the floor, park it on the phone back in the stockroom, and find a customer's shoes while I finish the call." For Harry, my old Apollo co-worker, it might be: "I've got a string of stores run by such dependable managers that I can think about new business, or not think about it at all, whenever and wherever I want to."

Subordinate questions build bridges from the future back to the present:

"What will I be doing in two to three years?"

"What kind of person will I be?"

"What skills will I have?"

"How will the 'me' of the future be affected by the choices made by the 'me' of today?"

The peak performer uses feed*forward* to learn from the projected future. Astronauts in a space flight simulator taught themselves to preprogram their minds and bodies to accomplish tasks in situations no human being had ever been in before. As everyone who watched the Apollo 11 moon landing on television knows, the preprogramming proved effective.

Most of the time in everyday life our nervous systems are programmed through feed*back*. Simulators pointed the astronauts in the opposite direction, feeding forward. Similarly, mapping alternative futures enables a peak performer to stand at a point in the future and consider events which, from that perspective, are already "past" and are therefore subject to the manipulations of hindsight. The point is to come up with optimal strategies and goals for getting "here."

The key is not to predict the future with unnatural precision, but to look about for clues to the general directions of change that are going to affect one's mission—and to follow the critical path for achieving it.

Updating the Mission. Two questions then follow:

Do any of the alternative futures reveal new information about the mission?

Do any of the alternative futures change the nature of the mission, or the critical path to it?

When the answer to either is yes, the next step is to incorporate relevant change so that the mission proceeds best.

I know at least three entrepreneurs who saw the physical-fitness boom several years ago as the wave of the future for membership health clubs. They built attractive training centers around an invention that captured the imagination of fitness experts, the Nautilus line of training equipment. The machines were expensive, the investment was large, and a swelling stream of customers made it look good. Then Joe and Ben Weider and others presented gym owners with a major challenge: high-quality fitness equipment for the home. In late 1984, moreover, the Nautilus company started using television commercials to sell home gym equipment directly to individuals. Other companies followed suit. Owners of some private health clubs started to fear that they might be the wave of the past. Time will tell. But at least one of those three gym owners has already updated his critical path. The mission remains what it was: to bring weight training and fitness to everyone. The form, however, has changed. He no longer demands that people come to him. He sends trained fitness experts to give personally tailored sessions in the homes of high-income clients. He also provides consultants for the design of home gyms ranging from modest to elaborate. Is this a replacement of private health clubs? For some clients, yes; for most, though, it is an increase in the number of options.

To stay at his peak, that fitness entrepreneur used feedforward. He made a rapid change in short-range goals and kept his mission alive. Rather than opening several more health clubs, he chose to target the home fitness market. A useful question for any update is: "What do I offer—service, quality, attention to detail—that still stands out?"

Reconnecting with the essence of a mission—the overall intent, the purpose and vision, beyond immediate goals and concrete steps—helps to provide direction in updating the mission. Entrepreneurs and people in small businesses encounter tempting opportunities they had not considered when they were starting out. So, too, for people within large organizations. New technology and new ways of performing old functions open up new job categories while expanding or eliminating old ones.

When Stephanie Bowers started at Compath in 1978, she knew she was skilled at meeting customer needs. She started by coordinating work that was already under way for existing clients. As she upgraded her knowledge of the array of equipment the company handled, she got opportunities to take on more responsibility. She began leading teams, coordinating big jobs such as the Macy's installation. She would probably still be there, handling larger and larger contracts, except that she continued to update her mission.

Recently Bowers realized what her most powerful attribute really is: taking charge in situations centered on rapid change. At Macy's she sometimes came upon a salesperson with four, five, or six customers lined up and calls to dispatch through the unfamiliar new telephone, and could see that the person was about to fall apart. She would step in and take the phone herself. To the customer on the line she would say, "We have a new phone system here and it will be a little while longer until all our people have it under control. Meanwhile, I can help you. Who would you like me to connect you with?" She was not snatching the phone away from a trainee. She was simply recognizing that beyond a certain level of stress, clarity and competence evaporate; at that point, she could not expect the employee to get much from an explanation of the way the phone worked. Once she took the pressure off, she had a grateful and receptive trainee, ready to learn.

> I found my favorite challenge is handling people who are frustrated or upset about a new phone system. All it takes to get them back on track is the right attitude and the right words: "All right, we made a mistake," or, "Somebody screwed up here and we'll handle it for you." Part of the effectiveness is in the way that you communicate it, and the clear assurance in your voice that the minute you walk out of the room, you are going to move to solve their problem immediately. It might not be you who solves it. You might have to get on someone else's case to get it done. But you communicate clearly that you are in charge and you know what to do. And then you do it.

DIVESTITURE: PERFECT CLIMATE FOR PEAK PERFORMERS

In May of 1985, I spent a half day with senior managers at Atlantic Electric in New Jersey. An executive said at one point: "A real challenge for us is getting our people out of the utility mentality. We can't sit around waiting for customers to come to us. Now we have to be entrepreneurs. Marketers of technology." I hear the same in other power companies, in banks and savings and loans, and of course in telephone companies. Institutions that were once *ex officio* pillars of the community—and about as nimble as pillars—are now learning to sell, to market, to compete. At all of them, senior managers are asking, "How do we get our people to go for it?"

E. Douglas Huggard, the president and chief operating officer of Atlantic Electric, remarked during the workshop: "In the fifties and sixties we were golden. We couldn't produce enough kilowatt hours. The more we produced, the lower the price got; the lower the price got, the happier people were with us. Then came the seventies, energy shortages, and higher expenses. People's utility bills shot up, and we were no longer the good guys. In the eighties we're trying to deal with those realities by making better use of technology and helping our people be more productive. We want them to see themselves as innovators."

The most visible recent example of massive change in American business, of course, is the divestiture of AT&T. The phone company has long been one of our most powerful cultural symbols. *Divestiture* refers to the central company's shedding its regional operating companies. The word can apply just as well to individuals ridding themselves of old ways of doing things. The AT&T divestiture shows us not just a corporation going through an upheaval, but the people who work in the corporation seeking ways to divest themselves of a lifetime of attitudes and procedures. This personal divestiture involves not just being willing to be a lifelong learner, willing to be ignorant when necessary; it also means being willing to relinquish ideas and practices that may have worked well in the past.

In the long run, the point is not "Will the regional phone companies survive?" The point is the liberating effect that the new status of those companies will have on the people in them, and on the people at AT&T. When Jim Gray joined the phone company in New York in 1970, the craftsmen around him joined up for life, for the security. "I never saw movement. We had no idea at all what it was like to be promoted, or to move to better yourself." By the time of the divestiture in 1984, Gray's early bosses had become AT&T's middle managers. Suddenly, their corporate aircraft carrier made a right-angle swerve. People who had grown up with a utility mentality were asked to become competitive, not just with upstart long-distance companies like MCI and Sprint but within their own areas; not nearly so insulated, now market-sensitive. For many, it felt like much more than being asked to learn a few extra skills. It felt almost like being asked to be another person. The external changes in the company demanded internal changes in its individuals.

People who prepare themselves as Jim Gray did can turn faster than the old aircraft carrier:

> Divestiture came. Now they say we have to run the phone company like a business. I'm sitting through all these classes saying to myself, "This is not new. I've been doing all this." All of a sudden I know why I've been getting awards. From the time they pulled me off a pole and said, "You're a manager, you start Monday," I'd been pulling my guys together like a family, saying it was up to them to do good work, showing them I wasn't going to look over their shoulders all the time and making sure they knew I'd always be there to help if they had a problem.

Jim Gray the individual stays hooked into the change process of Pacific Bell the corporation. He is attuned to the rate of change in the company. He keeps learning. He expects to succeed.

> I have so much responsibility now that I never had before. . . . I'm starting again, a rookie as a manager, so I'm writing down the things that have worked for me . . . and I know I'm going to fail half the time when I try something new, but I keep moving on. I remember back when I was just starting to make big moves, I'd make some big mistakes—cut a whole hospital out of the circuit—and my boss would pull me in, find out what I did, then say, "Jim, we expect this in somebody who's running at your level of results." I didn't understand it then, but what he was saying was that I was okay.

As he grows, Jim Gray divests himself of his own old ways, always in the context of the bigger divestiture. In a variation on that process, Stephanie Bowers left a company instead of allowing her mission to be limited by it. She took her skills out on her own. In yet another variation, my former colleague Harry set about developing an entire new repertoire of skills, deciding in the middle of his life that instead of staying with a corporation or going it alone as a consultant, he would build a new company in order to immigrate into this new land of radical change.

Each manages change in his or her own way. Each takes big changes and runs with them. All divest themselves of old ways and develop new ways.

Yet, as important as it is for individuals to make intelligent decisions about personal careers, there is something more profound going on here. As John Naisbitt put it in *Megatrends:*

> We are living in the time of parenthesis, the time between eras. . . . Those who are willing to handle the ambiguity . . . and to anticipate the new era will be a quantum leap ahead of those who hold on to the past. . . . It is a great and yeasty time, filled with opportunity . . . we have extraordinary leverage and influence—individually, professionally and institutionally—if we can only get a clear sense . . . of the road ahead.

That "extraordinary leverage" on an individual level belongs to the peak performers. In the short run, we will continue to see increasing demand for the specific skills of change management. But in the long run, the most effective way to manage change is a lifelong commitment to peak performance in all its aspects: to mission and the skills that make it a reality. To mission that aligns personal ambition, job, and organization; preserves health and family; and is grounded in the peak performer's *values*—those basic qualities that used to be known, in less ambiguous times, as character. Chapter 9 explores some of those values. The peak performers I have met do manage change by developing specific skills such as those we are examining here. Those skills are the visible extensions of a strong core of values that sustain the peak performers when the forces of change threaten to overwhelm all they have accomplished.

CAPABILITIES AND THE COGNICULTURE

The most abrupt shot of change that our culture is attempting to manage comes from the computer. Not all change points to computers, no matter how essential they may become; yet there is no denying that, as a simple extension of our own brains, the computer has in many respects given us a kick in the head.

Today, organizations and individuals are discovering ways to exceed their old capacities. One way they are doing it, of course, is delegating to computers the repetitious, fussy tasks that once made up much of "work." Until recently, many of those organizations and people could reasonably have regarded their capacities as more or less fixed. Certainly fixed within extremely modest limits. No more. Not when compared to current and future possibilities afforded by the computer.

In *Profiles of the Future,* Arthur C. Clarke quotes Professor Sherwood Washburn of the University of California anthropology department: "It was the success of the simplest tools that started the whole trend of human evolution and led to the civilizations of today."

Clarke then observes: "The old idea that Man invented tools is therefore a misleading half-truth; it would be more accurate to say that *tools invented Man.*"

In managing change that is so much a result of new technology, we confront the issue: What form of person are our inventions inventing? Simply a more efficient, functional human being who deals with routine tasks better than before? Or one who uses the time and leverage afforded by computers to cultivate capacities barely conceived of?

It was once a romantic notion that machines would allow people to develop into more knowledgeable, innovative human beings with a higher standard of living by taking off their hands much of the drudgery of daily life. As civilization moved from the agricultural to the industrial era, that is, in part, what did happen. Along the way, however, we created a new form of social organization called the corporation. Its benefits included pooled resources, shared risks, flexibility of exploration. Its costs included a numbing conformity, uniformity, and overdependence on rational functioning. Now, in the age of information, peak performers add other dimensions to the rational: They interpret feelings and hunches as information, and they assign considerable value to intuition as a complement to powerful rational processes.

Increasingly, peak performers farm out routine tasks to computers and cultivate the nonroutine aspects of their work. If agriculture is cultivating the land, and aquaculture is cultivating the sea, then *cogniculture* is what we might call this new kind of mental farming.

Not only do we see computerized telephones expanding the boundaries of independence for clerks in a department store, we see the information revolution changing the very nature of management. With access to information no farther away than the nearest desk-top microcomputer, senior executives no longer need legions of middle managers to gather and disseminate data. Significantly, many companies are now expanding the roles played by middle managers. Some decentralize, giving middle managers the sort of responsibility for results that used to go with more senior positions. Some cut back, putting more responsibility in the hands of fewer people. From now on, at every level, people with any expectation of peak performance are going to have to be lifelong learners.

LEVERAGING THE KNOWN, EXTENDING THE NEW

Citizens of a dawning age of cogniculture see the computer much as a turn-of-the-century farmer might have viewed a Ford tractor rolling through the front gate. The tractor was certainly a lever for known strengths, something that could do the work of fifty mules in half the time. It freed the farmer to do other things besides walking behind the mule, and ultimately freed 90 percent of the population to do other things than farming.

With computers, leveraging known strengths may be followed by even more dramatic moves toward extended mental capacities. Cogniculture includes both.

Computers take over data storage and number crunching. A suggestion of their further leverage for known strengths appears in software developed at the University of California at Berkeley. The Berkeley program, called MAGIC, allows any user to design special-purpose microchips—the "brains" of computers—without having to understand the basics of chip technology. John Gage, director of the science office of Sun MicroSystems, Inc., in Mountain View, California, estimates that prior to the introduction of this program, there were only several thousand people in the United States who understood the design principles of microchips. Now, high school students using the program may soon be designing uses for computer chips; any who find a company willing to manufacture the chip will have produced another application for some computer. The new software is available, free, to any higher educational institution inside the United States that requests it.

Beyond such known strengths, computers suggest ways of developing skills we are just starting to understand and for which in some cases we do not even have names—skills including increased concentration, better memory, more rapid decision-making, better hand-eye coordination. The learning vehicles are not all solemn and earnest. The Force, a video game from Behavioral Engineering of Santa Cruz, California, has you control a spaceship not with a joystick but with biofeedback signals transmitted through electrodes attached to your body. Tense up and the ship flies too high; relax and it settles to the ground. What might look frivolous at first can turn out to be an impressive way of teaching stress reduction and concentration.

The computer is a tool, like a tractor. It can leverage our strengths, or it can raise hell if not handled attentively. I would not be surprised to learn that some early tractors driven by well-meaning farmers leveled a few barns and scared a few recently unemployed mules out of their wits. One of the earliest acronyms around computers was GIGO, "Garbage In, Garbage Out." The computer is capable of helping us work better at all sorts of tasks, including those that are not useful to us. It has made us wizards at storing trivia. The key to using it well is leveraging not our weaknesses but our strengths, and thereby, so to speak, trivializing trivia. Peak performers who cut down the time they spend on low-priority tasks free time for (a) enhancing skills in traditionally important areas and (b) developing new mental capabilities. That is the essence of cogniculture.

How does anyone, peak performer or not, handle change on all those levels? Futurist Arnold Brown, interviewed in *The Tarrytown Letter,* argues that there is no longer any point in learning to do jobs that can be done by machines. A computer operator can do what it once took a Ph.D. in geology to do, search for subterranean mineral deposits. Brown suggests the computer may give us growing room to discover more uniquely human abilities:

> My son is entering the fourth grade and I'm trying to encourage him to write poetry. Why? Because the super-managers will be those having uniquely *human* competencies—ones that are not subject to replacement by machines. . . . The ability to communicate. The ability to resolve disputes among people. The ability to motivate and inspire. . . . In business and other fields, there will be a greater need for generalists. For people who have a profound understanding of how to think, how to evaluate, how to communicate. This requires a good solid liberal arts education—not the kind we're used to—but the kind that teaches people to use language, to problem-solve, and to understand the complex cultural context we live in. The counter-trend to this will be the development of new specialties, new combinations of skills like nurse-lawyer and space-biologist. But a broad vision will be required first.

CATASTROPHE AND BENESTROPHE

As we saw in Chapter 5, peak performers call on the skills of micro and macro thinking. At the micro level of change, most of us focus at one time or another on tasks like learning to put a computerized call on hold. At the macro level, we deal with changing definitions of work and organization that may well be, for some of us, disorderly or even chaotic. Peak performers see in such change a possible reordering of the elements that can lead to a higher level of functioning. Buckminster Fuller called it *syntropy.*

An example of people's reaction to tumultuous change was captured in a story by the columnist Pete Hamill. He describes a region in Puerto Rico where very poor people live in houses made of wood. Every so often a hurricane creates great waves that rip the houses apart. The receding waters drag the wood out to sea.

The homeless people wait while the storm subsides and the wood washes back to the shore. Then they use it to rebuild their little town. They use the very same wood that was in their old houses, but in different configurations.

For those people, a hurricane is a catastrophe. But for them it also calls forth qualities of creativity and collaboration. A powerful environmental mandate (from the weather, from Apollo 11, from a chief operating officer) can pull talents out of people to create cohesive units that may function at increasingly higher levels of performance. For just such reasons, the Chinese ideogram for *crisis* consists of the characters for *danger* and *opportunity*. Certainly there is much danger in a hurricane. The same was true for the Apollo missions. For some people, powerful contexts also present opportunity.

It is unfortunate that the only term we commonly associate with explosive change is *catastrophe*. Change can be powerful without being negative. For major, sometimes explosive change that has a positive outcome, we might start using the term *benestrophe*. The *-strophe* comes from the Greek *strephein,* to turn; we replace the Greek *kata,* for "down," with the Latin *bene,* for "good."

This is more than mere word play. One's expectations and orientation to change are crucial to peak performance. Many times while I was working at the University of California Medical Center, I talked with other researchers who worked with kidney dialysis patients. The patients who did best were those who "incorporated" the kidney dialysis machinery into their body image. They welcomed it into their lives as friend and ally, as if it were literally a part of their own bodies. Those who did worst regarded the machinery as a technological vampire, alien, preying on them. They did not invite it in as part of their body's support system.

All around us, human beings are establishing their relationships to major change. When I think of change involving technology, I cannot help thinking of Ted Vodde at Bellsouth Systems and his beloved Homer, his computerized home system of the future which will fix his dinner and remind him to watch the ball game. Clearly Ted has made peace with the idea of a Homer. On the other hand, I know a fair number of traditionalists, some highly expert in home management, who would greet Homer as comfortably as they would a boa constrictor. (I suspect that people who have never developed that expertise can't wait for Homer to get good enough to move in. I for one will give him free room and board.)

The issue is not Homer, or telephones, or computers. They are just there, like the hurricane. The issue is one's relationship with the change they bring. For the peak performer, the bottom line of that relationship is whether or not the change supports the mission.

GUTS AND VISION

New values seldom suddenly emerge without signs of stress. An unexpected occurrence once came close to stopping my old friend Harry in his tracks. But one characteristic of the peak performers in our study is their ability to turn stress into learning. That is what Harry did. His problem, as he described it, was:

> . . . kind of small. My doctor thought I had a mild heart attack. They kept me in the coronary care unit for a week to monitor me. That week, and afterwards at home while I was recuperating, I learned something that had never occurred to me before. I decided that most of the work that made this country great was done by people who were pressed for time, or were tired, or who didn't feel well—regular everyday people like me.

He did not by any means spend all his time thinking about himself:

> I thought about the people I've seen getting stymied by some change or other. After you pare away the little details, it looks as if people stall from one of two things—no guts or no vision. No guts, when most or all of the facts are in and they are still afraid to act, to put their judgment on the line. No vision when they allow themselves to get ground down by the details, the

> infernal interferences, and lose track of why they are doing something in the first place. They've got imagination, most of them. They could make things work. But they get ground down.
>
> That used to happen to me. I used to get furious about interruptions. Then I realized that my job *was* the interruptions. It took some imagination and some strategic vision to link up all those interruptions and see them as part of the main work.

"So," I asked, "what did you learn from the interruption your heart gave you?"

For all his ability to learn, Harry is no know-it-all. He talked about reassessing his own working style:

> It was what's-it-all-about time. I decided I'd been running on autopilot, thinking I was doing great but actually drifting away from what had worked so well for me before. I was burning myself up, so I got sick. I knew I had the vision, and the guts. When I finally realized those things, I got better.
>
> My father wanted stability. He needed it after the immigrant experiences he had. He values tradition. His kind of stability, having the one right way to do things, is not what works for me. I've learned to stabilize *while* things are changing. The vision—the mission, to use your term—helps me keep my bearings.

Harry found that blaming himself for lack of guts or vision served only to demotivate him further. Often, people think they don't have guts, or are not decisive enough, when what they really lack is a powerful enough purpose—a mission—to draw them into a future that looks complex. The mission might come from outside, as the Apollo project did for Harry and me when we first knew each other. But if the increasing rate of change leaves one uncertain about one's future, as more and more people tend to be, outside oneself is not a dependable place to look for a mission. The place to look is inside, to an area of preference and an internal decision to excel. Among peak performers, such a decision is most often based on an internal assurance that what one has chosen will allow for achievement *and* for self-development.

Peak performance does not apply just to a profession or career. It is a way of life. Certainly it has its professional aspects. Peak performers know how to lead people, to use numbers, to prioritize, to concentrate on goals, to form functional work teams, but they also know how to work on themselves. They remind me of athletes who know the mental part of their work is indivisible from the physical.

ACKNOWLEDGING THE HERO

Mastery of professional skills at work cannot be separated from self-mastery: Dealing honestly with ourselves, looking at the hopes and fears that make up the hidden machinery of performance, gathering information to formulate a mission, deciding what resources it will require, and following through.

Not a single peak performer I have ever met thinks that he or she can afford to let awareness tag along behind events. They do their best to anticipate, without getting hung up on having to know what *everything* means. Harry, after all, is no professor of philosophy. He is an engineer turned businessman. Peak performers keep an eye on possibilities for reinventing themselves. When meanings change for them, they consider the possibility that goals and missions, too, may change. Mapping alternative futures allows them to adapt quickly when change makes itself felt, and act with a speed that often looks uncanny to those who have not prepared as well.

But, one might ask, what distinguishes such foresightedness from attempting to dominate the future? Simply the awareness that the future cannot be dominated. Anyone at work in the world contends every day with changes that no one could have predicted or planned. Those are the moments when peak performers often move ahead of the pack. Having cultivated the skills to reflect on missions and goals, peak performers often see shifts that elude others and act on them with considerable mastery.

But is it accurate to say they *master* their development? That is not a verb Harry used during our talk, nor is it one I would use here. Perhaps he never will master his own development, any more than he can master change. He can, however, *guide* it. By continuing to pay attention, to monitor what he was doing, he gave himself an array of options—the luxury of choice.

> I may expand my business. Or sell it. Or retire. Or I may go into consulting. My son works for NASA, and he told me they may need a lot of help on some plans they have that are as big as the old days on Apollo 11. In the next twenty-five years, by 2010, they're talking about a permanent moon colony. My son is lucky, you see, because he has what we had—a mission big enough to cut through the annoyances, cut through the interruptions, cut through all the detail, cut through changes he doesn't want or understand, big enough to believe in.
>
> But even if "they" don't supply a big mission for him, I've learned that with enough guts and enough vision he could make his own mission. I have. I've paid my dues. I've learned my lessons. Everywhere I look now, I can see projects—some of them big, like Apollo 11 or the moon colony, some a lot smaller—that need people *like* me, if not me specifically. All they ask is, "Are you ready?" I am.
>
> My father made his own meanings and his own missions, and he didn't have any moon landing. I made mine, too. I became an engineer, and then a manager, and then a small-business owner in a powerful new field. That's plenty to feel proud of.

Yes. Harry learned to manage meaning for himself, and therefore to manage changes thrust on him. He reminds me of the contention by Joseph Campbell, the great scholar of legend and myth, that heroes—the best the human species has to offer—emerge in forms particularly appropriate to their time and their culture. They are emerging here and now, at all levels, in American business.

Harry would never put it this way, but I will: During his reassessment, he acknowledged his own heroism. He saw that he has learned many important lessons of the information society. He sees the continuity between past and future. He is a bit of his father and a bit of his son. What he has learned from each, overlapping as they do, allows him a kind of stability that enables him to manage rapid change. Harry has come through. He is one of Naisbitt's people of the parenthesis—tradition in part, future possibility in part, neither entirely. Where some would see only traps—rapidly changing technology, pressure from employees and customers, uncertainty—he sees a broad range of options.

In Stephanie Bowers, in Jim Gray, in Harry, we see people willing to be students forever. People expecting to succeed. People mapping alternative futures. People updating their missions. People who anticipate, adapt, and act. These are peak performers who have positioned themselves well in the age of information. They have learned to manage change with change.

9

MOTIVATING AND MAINTAINING PEAK PERFORMANCE

An ancient joke tells of a first mate on a sailing ship who wanted to become just like the captain, an imposing, respected patriarch of the sea. Noticing that at certain times on the bridge the captain would unlock a private drawer, glance at something inside, then relock it before giving a command, the mate became convinced that the drawer contained the secret of nautical success. One morning when the captain stepped away without locking up, the mate slipped over and peered inside. He saw a single piece of paper on which were written four words: STARBOARD – RIGHT. PORT – LEFT.

The way peak performers steer themselves in the direction they choose may at first imply some private advantage—an inborn gift of vitality, maybe good genes, or perhaps a confidential list of things to remember about having the will to win. There is nothing esoteric, however, about peak performers. What sets them apart is not knowledge possessed by only an inner group of initiates. What sets them apart is much simpler than that. They are people who are motivated by achievement in their work and full development of their human faculties.

The old secret-in-the-drawer approaches to motivation—speakers setting up flip charts of Five Steps to Success, expounding techniques to pump up confidence with variants on Coué's famous affirmation, "Every day in every way I'm getting better and better"—often don't work. Affirmations have to be supported by the behavior that makes them happen. An affirmation provides fuel; it is not a strategy. Motivational techniques can induce a "Hawthorne effect," a phenomenon named for a discovery made years ago by researchers at the Hawthorne Works of the Western Electric Company in Chicago. The researchers changed the working conditions of a group of women employees in various ways—starting and quitting times, rest periods, lighting levels, pay incentives, feedback and so forth. No matter what they did, productivity went up. Even when conditions were made worse than before, the women worked harder and more efficiently. How come? It turned out that they were responding not to the changes in their external environment but to the *attention* they got from all the experimenters and, by implication, their bosses. The attention meant validation. It told them they mattered. Can these increases be attributed to feedback or incentive pay alone? Not likely. When the attention shifted elsewhere, production slipped back toward the old levels.

The effects of most secret-in-the-drawer techniques are temporary because they are applied sporadically and outside the context of the real work. They seldom suggest a method for integrating the appropriate behaviors into the work life of an individual. When you see a change that lasts, you can be pretty certain that it took root within the individuals it affects, at the level of their own talents and motives. By contrast, many of the quick fixes treat motivation as if it were a fuel you inject into your system to make you run, and propose "solutions" that are external to the individual. Our peak performers consistently told us that external motivators produce the shortest-lived results. Such motivators work by promising reward or punishment; and when the reward is no longer novel or the punishment disappears, so does the behavior that was associated with it. The productive response is extinguished.

This is not to say that peak performers disdain temporary devices. "I need all the help I can get" has long been a favorite saying of the influential magazine editor T George Harris. Rather, they do not depend on external motivators alone. They reach beyond quick fixes that are quickly exhausted. Quick fixes are based on the notion that managers and consultants can supply some simple stimulus to produce sustained motivation in other people. The notion assumes that people are either naturally demotivated and waiting to be "pumped up" or, worse, enjoy being lethargic drones whose motivational batteries immediately run down if left alone. It assumes that people have no power of self-renewal.

You don't unilaterally motivate other people in the long term. We have been burdening managers for years with an impossible task, telling them they ought to motivate others singlehandedly, when the most a manager can do for others is to jump-start them—inspire them. Real *motivation* catches internally, after the mission is clear. Peak performers draw productivity from deeper reserves that are inexhaustible—from the *sources* of motivation.

VALUES: THE PIVOT POINT

You can tell people to value excellence. You can insist that they increase their productivity. You can emphasize the need for changing their behavior. You can attempt to train people and motivate them to upgrade their job skills and increase their effectiveness. But until an individual makes a personal commitment to achieving peak performance, makes that internal decision to excel, nothing much will happen.

What stimulates and sustains this transformation within a person, this internal "knowing" that he or she will move toward greater achievement? Insight? Not by itself. Insight does not guarantee results. Education? Not by itself. We all learn and relearn important lessons on which we fail to act, even in our own behalf. What is it, then, that moves the peak performers past the blocks to fulfilling their own best talents?

What I see in the committed men and women who fulfill the

impulse to improve themselves and who determine the direction a mission will take is a strong commitment to values. These values—the old-fashioned and very real qualities that make up a person's and an organization's character—put a mission on its critical path and keep it there.

In a peak performer we see the kind of person every one of us has been at his or her best. The peak performer has identified, or at least is drawn toward, certain values which underlie action. He or she consistently

- Values achievement, and finds his or her primary motivation through mission.
- Values contribution, and thus seeks results in real time, and assists in the development of others.
- Values self-development, and pursues self-management through self-mastery.
- Values creativity, and produces innovation through risk-taking.
- Values synergy, and looks for points of alignment among organizational, team, and personal objectives.
- Values quality, and pays conscious attention to feedback and course correction.
- Values opportunity, and meets the challenge of change.

Values are the leverage point for the whole internal impulse to excel, because they encompass not only *what* and *how* but *why*. Depth of calling—a strong feeling of commitment that a peak performer has for his or her mission—is necessary but not by itself sufficient for high achievement. Intensity is incomplete if you don't know what you're intense about: the worth to you and to others of what you're being called by. Why do human beings care so much about some things above all others that they will concentrate every resource on them? For an answer, look to their values. Values provide perspective in the best of times and the worst. People may be inspired to peak performance in a project like an Apollo 11 lunar landing or a new polycarbonate product launch. They may yearn for it (in full knowledge of what they are missing) like the chronically underutilized people in Studs Terkel's *Working*. They may mobilize all the strength and determination they have when life itself is threatened by cancer. In every case, their ability to sustain peak performance, whatever its definition may be for each individual, emerges from and is supported by their values. An older word rich with associations of its own may be used to capture the internal strength of the peak performer. The word is *character.*

We have focused on individuals, yet there are some dramatic examples of changes for entire nations that have come from conscious application of values. As a young Japanese businessman visiting the West in the 1950s, Akio Morita was deeply humiliated to learn that *Made in Japan* was an international synonym for shoddiness, a phrase that produced jokes. Morita returned to Japan determined to change that, and as chief executive of Sony, he is one of the business leaders who have made that determination a reality. Over the past thirty years, Morita says, "We have been striving to be the Picassos and Beethovens of electronics." Now, people ask of consumer products made elsewhere: "Is this as good as the ones made in Japan?"

People who take the trouble to create a mission based on values gain clarity about what they really want, independent of what seems possible. Had Morita told American acquaintances in the 1950s that he intended products from Japan to pose a worldwide challenge to those from the United States as a standard of quality, they would have doubted such an impossible dream. Creating a statement of an ideal reality allows a peak performer to start building bridges between the current state of affairs and the ideal one. In short: Values provide leverage for mission, and mission motivates achievement.

Motivation through mission frequently works through an apparent paradox, a freedom of action that comes from having "no choice." When you are shooting for the moon, or overcoming cancer, you devote the major share of your available energies to the task. As innumerable observers from NASA engineers to Scottish mountaineers to auto company chairmen point out, you find yourself overcoming obstacles that would, under ordinary circumstances, be insurmountable. Over and over in our studies we saw among peak performers that the power of such missions came from a strong internal drive that each individual managed to link with external opportunities. They were not just good soldiers; they were people following their natural inclination toward a passionate desire, a mission.

"When natural inclination develops into a passionate desire, one advances toward his goal in seven-league boots." So said Nikola Tesla, the brilliant scientist and inventor who designed the great power system at Niagara and whose discoveries in high-tension electricity and radio transmission still affect developments in electrical power. In the same vein, University of Pittsburgh professor Ian I. Mitroff researched the space program, and as he did so he began to suspect that

> the passionate, and often even irrational, adherence to ideas was . . . the norm or distinguishing mark of the creative scientist, and that this passion might be especially the case for those scientists who were bold, imaginative, and capable enough to propose theories of origin for something so huge and complicated as a whole earth-moon system.

One rule for creating a mission could be stated as "Don't juggle; choose." You turn away from some things you might like to do in order to focus on those you must do. For the man or woman with a mission, that is neither good nor bad. It is simply a fact. Within that fact are measures of achievement, a willingness and even a desire to test limits, a drive toward excellence and quality, and a desire for contribution. A mission is a message that motivates. It conveys a philosophy. And, as we've expressed throughout the book, it is senior to a goal.

John F. Kennedy expressed the most powerful motivations behind the moon landing as an assurance that it would be "impressive to mankind . . . important for the long-range exploration of space . . . not one man going to the moon, but an entire nation."

Westinghouse Furniture Systems, back here on firm ground, advertises its mission as "Expanding the limits of human performance." A section of the Hewlett-Packard corporate statement reads, "Objective: To honor our obligations to society by being an economic, intellectual, and social asset to each nation and each community in which we operate." Elsewhere, in its advertising, Hewlett-Packard announces tersely: "Performance. Not promises."

At the center of the whole constellation—self-management, results orientation, teamwork, course correction, and change management—is mission. And the mission of a peak performer gains its leverage from the values on which it pivots.

THE SIX ATTRIBUTES OF THE PEAK PERFORMER: AIDING AND AMPLIFYING MOTIVATION

It must be obvious by now that peak performers are people who evolve, grow, and change. I know none who considers himself or herself a perfect, finished product. In fact, a distinguishing mark of peak performers, besides their purposeful drive toward achievement, is their recognition of the dividends of virtually limitless self-development.

They develop their personal strengths in the six major areas I first outlined in Chapter 1:

- Missions that motivate
- Results in real time
- Self-management through self-mastery
- Team building/team playing
- Course correction
- Change management

Just making a list like that is, of course, misleading. As I hope I have shown in discussing each of the attributes in previous chapters, there is no sharp boundary neatly announcing the presence of one or the absence of another. Instead, what we see after eighteen years of studying peak performers is an overall pattern of attributes constituting a strong likelihood—not a guarantee, but a likelihood—that a peak performer will be motivated toward results by a personal mission; will possess the twin capacities of self-management and team mastery; and will have the abilities to correct course and manage change.

The original source of motivation is mission based on values. Once mission is identified and committed to, each of these attributes amplifies the motivation and contributes to maintaining peak performance over the long haul.

The attributes are not an inviolate sequence, not a recipe to memorize. They are, rather, deeply ingrained aspects of human beings who are imperfect. They are talents which have become second nature, often after years of trial and error. Most surely, they can be taught and learned. Yet they develop most effectively in the presence of something that is not so much learned as it is, quite simply, decided: The peak performer's deeply felt desire "to be the best I can be."

That internal decision to excel, a decision possible for all of us, leads one in time to experience these attributes as *needs.* Why needs? Because without them, one is not likely to achieve one's mission as a peak performer; and as a peak performer caring deeply about mission, one is not likely to be found without them. They emerge as a necessary collection of skills unified by the unassailable desire to achieve and develop to one's fullest. They are both needs and functional means to an end.

Are the six attributes the final word in what one needs for achievement? Hardly. They constitute a snapshot of what we have found to date. From that snapshot we can infer that without them, even the bravest and hardest-working man or woman handicaps himself or herself in the quest for peak performance. There is little doubt that additional research and general interest in peak performance will fill out the picture. For now, I offer the attributes as a dependable way to spot the peak performer at work and in other areas of life. They can be seen in the executive suite, sales call, and hiring interview. As our acuity of vision grows more equal to the task, we will see them with increasing accuracy and frequency.

One more time, the image of Poe's purloined letter comes back. The ways in which America's top achievers motivate and maintain their peak performance have been hidden in plain view.

MISSION ⟨-------⟩ RESULTS

As a partner of Arthur Andersen & Company said during a training session at St. Charles, Illinois: "Goals are dreams with deadlines." It is clear by now that a drive for achievement is not a trait with which peak performers are born. It is, rather, a state at which each one arrives as he or she focuses on a mission and on the results that fulfill it.

Jim Gray moved from telephone equipment installer to supervisor, taking care of the guys on his team the same way he took care of every customer, acting as if he owned the place because "my pride is on the line." He imagined his signature on every cable connection he made under every street in every city in which he worked.

James Rouse envisioned and then built the thriving Quincy Market in Boston because, to him, "It just seemed obvious that there was a human yearning for something like that in the heart of the city."

William Paley knew the broadcasting business and knew what it could do by the time he ordered his CBS Radio technicians in 1938 to put Vienna, Berlin, Paris, London, and Rome all on the air as the Germans invaded Austria. The technicians had more knowledge than he did about the particulars, and they said it would be impossible. What they did not have was the broader vision that compelled Paley to reject the impossible and thereby pull radio into a new dimension.

A distinction to notice here is the difference between *mission-driven* results and *goal-driven* results.

Every day, people with no particularly deep purpose achieve a lot of goals. They complete reports; make sales; ship orders; check off everything on their to-do lists. In the short run, those completions feel good. And they gradually fit together to make a trap. If, over time, the people checking off one goal after another do not see their work contributing to a larger pattern and an overall objective, they can develop the treadmill blues. Work begins to feel endlessly repetitive. There is little sense of mission. Little sense of growth. Satisfaction and desire decline. Performance deteriorates.

One characteristic of researchers is that they often study what they most need to learn. I am no exception. On more than one occasion, my secretaries have brought me up short. "We can't get this day's work done," they will say, "because we can't distinguish between all the things you want finished. You label everything urgent. There is only one category in here—emergency." What they're telling me is that we have slipped into organizing around short-term goals and started losing sight of our mission. When that happens, it is clearly time not just to look over our priorities but to reflect on whether, and how, immediate goals fit into a larger scheme of things.

Results themselves create motivation. Joe and Ben Weider knew that if people could be persuaded to try weight training and to persevere through the challenging early stages, the results would keep them going. The physical strength and muscle toning one gets from lifting weights are both rewards and added incentives. Finding the right amount of challenge is the key. Too much weight to lift, and one gets easily discouraged. Too little, and one gets bored with feeling no gain. The amount of weight on the bar that will make you exert, test limits, and still succeed—that is the key to results that motivate.

That key is what organizational psychologist Beth Milwid was looking for in applying strategies that get results. Her experiences with government bureaucracies left her discouraged. In themselves, the results were not motivating. Fortunately, Milwid developed a mission that was, and went after training aligned with that mission. Working at Crocker Bank as manager of career development allowed her to get satisfactions that contributed to her motivation: She could see how her workshops moved people along their career paths and how her counseling helped them fulfill their aspirations.

SELF/TEAM

Among individual peak performers, some characteristics are more evident than others. Different circumstances and challenges draw out different strengths, as do different jobs, projects, and organizations. All our peak performers are motivated by mission, and all prize results. But a Jenette Kahn might call on all her team-building skills in reviving a tired company, whereas a Brandon Hall might first develop his ability to self-manage in going for a new sales record. Each attribute is a capacity ready to be cultivated should a current challenge call it into use.

Some peak performers talk of a slow and steady development toward "internalizing" these most useful abilities as a natural part of changes they continually observe in themselves. Their experience presents us with the polar opposite of "tacking on" skills to the same old person. Others speak of single powerful occasions or periods, "sweet spots in time," that offer them a glimpse of themselves as capable of "a great deal more than I previously thought possible." All maintain that the potential for major increases in achievement and self-development exists in everyone, and that important keys to success are *commitment* and willingness to act *as if* the potential were moving powerfully toward its actualization. This "as if" quality, proceeding as a peak performer whether or not you have yet produced much proof that you are one, develops the habit of seeing oneself as the kind of person who readily uses the six attributes as valued parts of oneself. When the "as if" quality really is used to bring those skills into use, not just as a mechanical exercise with no passion, it allows a relatively rapid personal transformation into the real article.

These tactics show up strongly in the hand-and-glove relationship between self-management and teamwork.

Alvin Burger does not try to motivate his pest-elimination specialists with theory alone. He does it with action. He gets them down on their hands and knees, killing roaches and rodents, making money, and building their reputation as the Mercedes of the business. "As if" quickly becomes "as is." Their interest in achievement is particularly aroused by situations in which goals can be stated and performance can be measured: the determination to kill *all* the pests, the inspections, field reports, and feedback from customers. Each field technician is such an integral member of a team that he or she can easily say, "I did it myself."

A key to self-management is the capacity for self-observation. "A strong self-watchfulness, self-surveillance . . . that constantly searches for improvement, excellence, and respect," is what C. Jackson Grayson, chairman of the American Productivity Center, calls it. This is not overcriticism, judgmentalism, or the well-known paralysis by analysis. It is familiarity with your own standards of excellence, of what you consider to be quality, and maintaining enough of a detached perspective to evaluate your performance.

As Vince Lombardi told Lee Iacocca, every inch of the peak performer gets into the game, from the soles of the feet to the top of the head: "If you're lucky enough to find a guy with a lot of head and a lot of heart, he's never going to come off the field second."

One mark of the peak performer—one that usually draws other people's attention—is an ability to cut through obstacles without wasted effort. An eight-oared crew moves briskly when all its rowers' strokes are aligned, even when waves and current impede their progress. The crew might prefer calm waters, just as anyone would prefer to work in an excellent organization. But we see repeatedly that peak performers exist and even thrive in surroundings that are far from excellent. By comparison to ordinary performers, they shine particularly in volatile, shifting situations that call for skill in course correction and change management.

----⟩COURSE CORRECTION---⟩CHANGE MANAGEMENT----⟩

Peak performers have what psychologist Jean Houston, author of *The Possible Human,* calls "leaky margins." Their minds are not closed. They engage the ideas and experiences of other people while retaining the ability to generate their own. Information can get through in both directions. This is another way of describing the peak performer's capacity to grow.

Bill Robertson, the man who chauffeured me to the Greenbrier in West Virginia, knows how to create change and adapt to it, all within a plan of his own devising. His moves—first to the city, then to a job as a mechanic, then to rebuilding worn-out limousines, then to starting his own limo service, then to thoughts of branching out to other areas of entrepreneurship—show the "right stuff" calculation of a good pilot who may not know exactly what the weather ahead will be, but knows where he wants to land that night.

Planning, by itself, does not sustain high-level achievement. We all know what can happen to the best-laid plans. Planning by a man or woman skilled in initiating and managing change, however, becomes a powerful reinforcer to motivation. I make a well-thought-out change. It works! My work improves. I improve. I start looking for opportunities to build change into my game plan. As motivation thus turns over into remotivation, it (and the planning behind it) become components of an ability to maintain peak performance over time.

Even with that ability, the peak performer is still human. Motivated, yes. And sometimes ambivalent. A high level of accomplishment, along with the close monitoring one does in order to maintain it, can be simultaneously attractive and intimidating. "I want to be a peak performer, but it's a hell of a lot of work." We sometimes see a similar approach/avoidance attitude toward technological complexity, particularly while that person is watching the complexity march into his or her work life.

Large businesses such as Macy's have no choice but to adapt to the new technologies just to stay competitive. It isn't a question of whether they will do it, but when, and how fast. Small businesses, especially the newer ones, face tough decisions about when to accommodate a major change. At a conference of women entrepreneurs who had been running their businesses for more than two years, one of the speakers asked, "How many of you still keep your accounts receivable and payable in a shoebox?" Half the people in the room raised their hands.

So, when is the right moment to move the accounting from a shoebox to a computer program? Sometimes, course correction and change management are kick-started by considerations of survival. The shoebox won't tell me the tax consequences of different pricing strategies to move old inventory. A computer and Lotus 1-2-3 will. On the one hand, I must discard the shoebox at some point in order to grow. On the other hand, a change made too quickly, or at too high a cost, can kill the enterprise.

What about change that is thrust on one, as when an individual's position in an organization changes? During the last stages of research for this book, Dow Chemical asked Karl Kamena to move from the Polycarbonate Team, where he had been a key member, to Government Relations/Public Issues. His reward for doing so well on the product-launch team was a transfer to an area where he would again have room to grow and contribute his talents as a peak performer—in other words (mine, not his), where he would have to start all over. Kamena admits it was difficult to leave the position to which he felt so committed. Now he must once again find ways to align his personal goals with the requirements of the new job and the expectations of the Dow organization. But the motivation to do that comes from Kamena's overreaching commitment—to his own achievement and self-development.

Peak performers see the ability to manage change as a necessity in fulfilling their missions.

A PLACE TO STAND

If you have ever gone through a tollbooth, you know that your relationship to the person in the booth is not the most intimate you'll ever have. It is one of life's frequent nonencounters: You hand over some money; you might get change; you drive off. I have been through every one of the seventeen tollbooths on the Oakland–San Francisco Bay Bridge on thousands of occasions, and never had an exchange worth remembering with anybody.

Late one morning in 1984, headed for lunch in San Francisco, I drove toward one of the booths. I heard loud rock music. It sounded like a party, or a Michael Jackson concert. I looked around. No other cars with their windows open. No sound trucks. I looked at the tollbooth. Inside it, the man was dancing.

"What are you doing?" I asked.

"I'm having a party," he said.

"What about the rest of these people?" I looked over at other booths; nothing moving there.

"They're not invited."

I had a dozen other questions for him, but somebody in a big hurry to get somewhere started punching his horn behind me and I drove off. But I made a note to myself: Find this guy again. There's something in his eye that says there's magic in his tollbooth.

Months later I did find him again, still with the loud music, still having a party.

Again I asked, "What are you doing?"

He said, "I remember you from the last time. I'm still dancing. I'm having the same party."

I said, "Look. What about the rest of these people . . ."

He said, "Stop. What do those look like to you?" He pointed down the row of tollbooths.

"They look like . . . tollbooths."

"Nooo imagination!"

I said, "Okay, I give up. What do they look like to you?"

He said, "Vertical coffins."

"What are you talking about?"

"I can prove it. At eight-thirty every morning, live people get in. Then they die for eight hours. At four-thirty, like Lazarus from the dead, they re-emerge and go home. For eight hours, brain is on hold, dead on the job. Going through the motions."

I was amazed. This guy had developed a philosophy, a mythology about his job. I could not help asking the next question: "Why is it different for you? You're having a good time."

He looked at me. "I knew you were going to ask that," he said. "I'm going to be a dancer someday." He pointed to the administration building. "My bosses are in there, and they're paying for my training."

Sixteen people dead on the job, and the seventeenth, in precisely the same situation, figures out a way to *live*. That man was having a party where you and I would probably not last three days. The boredom! He and I did have lunch later, and he said, "I don't understand why anybody would think my job is boring. I have a corner office, glass on all sides. I can see the Golden Gate, San Francisco, the Berkeley hills; half the western world vacations here . . . and I just stroll in every day and practice dancing."

What is the essential skill that, when seventeen human beings walk to their offices and sixteen of them get into vertical coffins, allows one of them to have a party? Mission. Purpose. Some people do the same jobs as everybody else but have an unusual sense of mission, enjoy it, and have the energy to achieve at high levels. The dancing toll-taker had been given no special job, no change in the conditions that limited life for everyone else in the booths. Yet he had found a mission, and thereby discovered the will and the way to use the conditions of his job to support his mission. He had found what Archimedes said he would need, along with his lever, to move the Earth: a place to stand.

That place we might call a zone of peak performance, where he can align his personal mission with the specific demands of a job and the overall environment and objectives of an organization.

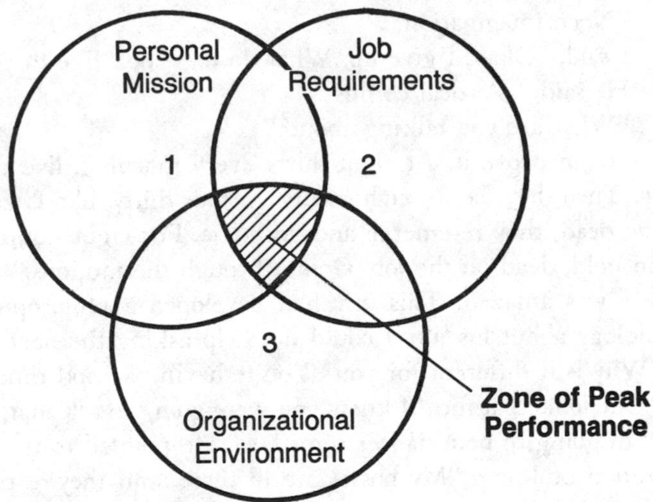

It is a place for major productive impact, an optimal leverage point for one's abilities. I don't know if the toll-taker has found the audience he was looking for, but I do know that when one observes peak performers long enough, it becomes increasingly clear that one of their major talents is finding such a place of personal power. And why not? Their desire for a place to stand is based on keen appreciation of leverage—on the knowledge that it is from such a location that their mission has its best chance to succeed. When they have the abilities that a job requires, and work in an environment that supports what they do, they encounter relatively little resistance.

Moreover, when a job provides the vehicle for accomplishing one's mission, when one's place to stand supports any task that may arise, one develops confidence in one's ability to complete the current mission and manage anything else that comes along. As Jim Gray grew in his various jobs with the telephone company, so did his realization that what he was doing because it was right for him was also right for the company. They let him know he was valuable. More to the point, though, he let himself know it.

What if the congruence is not there, and there is no solid place to stand, and you still have your job to do? Then it is tempting to force oneself, through superhuman acts of will, to overcome limitations in any of the three areas. We all know how hard it is to try to lift the weight with little leverage. People can be courageous, and tenacious, and often do try to do the job even though they know they aren't in the right spot. But often they know the spot is wrong, that they are not positioned correctly for their best efforts; and that weakens their willingness to take a stand and their ability to manage what occurs along the way.

The place to stand suggests an opposite to the Peter Principle and its tart notion of people being promoted to their level of incompetence. Here we are talking about positioning ourselves for considerable competence, arriving at a place from which all things seem possible. And whether our specific road to achievement leads to Wall Street, Silicon Valley, or Damascus, we could, with tongue in cheek, call it the Paul Principle.

People who locate their place to stand like what they are doing. They feel a commitment to it. They feel themselves growing, learning, and experiencing themselves through it. They have found not only their mission, but a firm standpoint, a situation—one might say an optimal context—from which to make it happen. They see concrete results emerging from what they do. They, not just other people, recognize the contribution they are making.

The plumbers in that aerospace company's thermodynamics plant who wore green surgical smocks and called each other "doctor" baffled and pleased their company's senior vice-president with their consistently superb performance. They took care of their pipes the way their foreman's son, the cardiovascular surgeon, took care of hearts. They recognized how important they were to the company's success, and they produced results accordingly.

Sony CEO Akio Morita says, "Sometimes a sense of mission, a sense of participation and a sense of achievement are great joys. A scientist or an engineer is like an artist completely caught up in playing the piano or creating a sculpture . . . he likes his job so much that he forgets about everything else."

And Lewis W. Lehr, chairman of 3M, a company widely admired for its ability to keep alive an atmosphere in which people can create new products, uses a vivid image: "I guess if the wheel is important, maybe it's important that *everyone* have a chance to invent it."

The opportunity that Lehr wants to keep open and the experience to which Morita refers come together in a comment on the fit between individual and job, made by Fernando Bartolome and Paul A. Lee Evans, professors of organizational behavior at the European Institute of Business Administration: "A perfect fit occurs when you experience three positive feelings at the same time: you feel competent, you enjoy the work, and you feel that your work and your moral values coincide. To express this in another way, a job should fit not only with skills and abilities but also with motives and values."

That is another way of describing the metaphorical place within oneself from which one can exert the powerful leverage of peak performance. In business terms, *leverage* frequently refers to the use of borrowed money to accomplish one's purposes. Victor Kiam's forty-to-one leveraged loan gave him a place to stand to turn Remington around and build the "enduring business" he wanted. Similarly, Robert Maynard leveraged his purchase of the Oakland *Tribune* and then revitalized the paper by leveraging the company's assets—including, most notably, the energy of its staff and the support of its readers.

The lives and achievements of the peak performers suggest that we can leverage assets other than real estate, securities, and similar collateral to obtain results other than company turnarounds. Jim Gray leveraged his track record as a technician and manager with the phone company to secure a series of promotions beyond what once seemed possible for a kid from Brooklyn. His accomplishments gave him a high "credit rating" as a substantial human asset to his company. He was able to position himself in a high-yield situation, based on his proven ability to produce and succeed. Kiam, Maynard, Gray, Beth Milwid, Jenette Kahn, all the high achievers we have described in some detail, leverage their human assets as well as physical or financial ones. Their talents and track record play a critical role in securing a place of power, an advantageous point from which to proceed.

With increased sophistication in leveraging such human assets, more individuals will insist on finding themselves a place to stand from which they can achieve and maintain peak performance.

A final dividend from finding that place to stand is that it unleashes hidden reserves of energy. The English author Colin Wilson makes the point somewhat poetically, yet precisely, in this passage:

> It is not the super effort itself that is important, but the energy we summon to meet it. The basic assumption is that man possesses far more energy than he realizes, a vast lake of vital reserves. What cuts us off from these reserves is a feeling of laziness—rather, of reluctance. We contemplate some effort and think, "What a bore." And this feeling of boredom instantly lowers our vitality. If I perform a super effort, like walking the additional two miles after a ten-mile walk, with a groan of self-pity, it would be completely useless. Yet if some sudden crisis or some sudden piece of good news—i.e., someone I love is waiting for me two miles away—made me decide to walk the two miles, I would do it with a springy step, prepared if necessary to go ten times as far. This, then, is the real aim of the exercise—to summon that state of optimism, of inner purpose, that makes the super effort easy. It is a trick of drawing on those vital reserves and overruling reluctance.

I would suggest that alignment of personal, job, and organizational needs—that place to stand—produces the "state of optimism . . . that makes the super effort easy."

I know of no one so fortunate that he or she always feels positioned on a place of power. For many, it is a rare experience. When I am in my own "place to stand," I feel like an athlete in the groove. There is a sense of being on top of things, whether or not this detail or that remains unaddressed. An internal knowing emerges that can best be described as feeling I am using myself, in George Bernard Shaw's terms, "for a purpose recognized by yourself as a mighty one."

When I am in my own place to stand I am not getting in my own way, selling myself short, or giving in to the many shortcuttings of values and outcomes that life presents as options. I have chosen what is best for me and, coincidentally, what is best for those with whom I work and live. I feel strong, physically, emotionally, and intellectually, because my place to stand allows me to perform and contribute at my best.

When I am on my own place to stand I feel like a gyroscope with a center around which the forces of work and life revolve. The forces may be tumultuous, but the center exists and I know where it is. Even if I am thrown off balance and bruised in the process, I know how to get back on course. The values that drive me toward my personally experienced "mighty purpose" are clear enough for me to engage the process repeatedly, to correct course, to motivate and remotivate myself, and, in the end, however long it takes, to achieve the best that my place to stand allows.

10

JOINING IN THE SEARCH

When Joe Frazier was heavyweight champion of the world, a journalist asked him, "Why do you box?" Frazier replied, "Because I'm a boxer," and seemed irritated that the interviewer didn't understand.

The critic H. L. Mencken declared in 1932: "I go on working for the same reason that a hen goes on laying eggs."

Are people like this trapped by blind instinct or relentless workaholism? Among peak performers, I see another answer. The peak performers, supported by their discovery of a place to stand, are doing what they feel best-equipped to do and are doing it very well. They find their life's work, their best expression, and are for the most part quite pleased with it. They know the joy of using themselves to the fullest, and the rewards, external and internal, that come their way as a result. A woman who attended a program for top performers in real estate wrote to me about her own search for a place to stand. She said, "When I'm functioning like a peak performer, I'm sure that I've really gotten on with it, that my essential life's work has swung into high gear."

In 1966, when I began a search to enhance my own career, I started with a purely personal question: "How can I do extraordinarily well?" Along the way I began to sense the shape of a critical idea: Peak performers are made, not born. As I grew more excited about studying the characteristics of peak performers, the details of the idea grew sharper, and the question expanded to: "What are the conditions under which *anyone* does extraordinarily well?"

I did not know at the beginning that the search would give meaning to my entire life. My mission emerged in the doing. Through the early work on Apollo 11, and with cancer survivors, then the meeting with Soviet-bloc scientists in Milan, extending now through nearly twenty years of learning from high achievers in corporations and other organizations, the study of peak performers leads to an inescapable conclusion.

What peak performers do is not abnormal. It is normal. Their achievements and skills clearly demonstrate qualities highly valued by human beings. Any of us, and all of us, can be peak performers.

We now have a picture of peak performance based on observation of formidable results achieved by formidable people. Among the key points that emerge from our study is one I never would have predicted: *Even the power of observation, the ability to spot a peak performer or potential peak performer, is a learned skill.*

Sir Arthur Conan Doyle was a young ophthalmologist in 1887 who found himself waiting much of the time, alone in his office, for patients who never came. To relieve his boredom he created Sherlock Holmes, the detective whose powers of observation would astound the people with whom he came into contact. The point of the story? That the fictional Holmes possessed an uncanny ability to observe, a cultivated ability to spot clues? Not really. What is more important is that Conan Doyle, an eye doctor whose mission naturally included improving the observational abilities of the patients he saw, heeded an intuitional summons to correct course, to fill empty hours by writing about what he valued most. In so doing he created the quintessential observer. Conan Doyle's course correction in the service of his overriding mission is every bit as impressive as the sleuthing of his creation, the amazing Holmes.

In the words of the Russian proverb, Conan Doyle looked first for "the horse he was riding on." Like more recent peak performers we have studied, he knew—as the pioneering psychologist Abraham Maslow put it in *The Farther Reaches of Human Nature:*

> We are not in a position in which we have nothing to work with. We already have a start; we already have capacities, talents, direction, missions, callings. The job is, if we are willing to take it seriously, to help ourselves to be more perfectly what we already are, to be more full, more actualizing, more realizing, in fact, what we are in potentiality.

The world would have lost plenty if Conan Doyle had simply endured his lagging medical practice or junked it, instead of observing and acting on his mission and thereby developing his potential.

Maslow vigorously promoted "growing-tip" research, taking his term from the fact that the growing tip of a plant shows the greatest genetic action. We already know that as he pored over his notes on "the healthiest people (or the most creative, or the strongest, or the wisest, or the saintliest)," he realized he was studying not aberrations, not supernaturally endowed anomalies, not "noncomparable individuals," but a *kind* of person.

Everywhere I look now, I see people joining the search for a kind of person, for the peak performer, observing and acting on mission and potential—within themselves, within their organizations, within humankind.

WITHIN YOURSELF

How do I know if I'm a peak performer?

I hear the question often, and frequently the people who ask seem afraid that the unspoken answer will be "You aren't. You don't measure up."

You begin answering the question by examining your current situation, "the horse you're riding on."

You may have chosen wisely and well. You may have known

intuitively that loving your work and being inspired by its possibilities were critical to a life filled with challenge and rewards and energy. You may have selected your job on those grounds. And still, in the midst of job stress, organizational politics, firefighting, and the frequent craziness of daily life, your mission may be nearby but nearly forgotten.

> I did love it once—or at least I knew I could love it. It feels far away now, that sense of being in the right place, working at the heart of things.

Anyone who feels that way will find it difficult to see his or her direction, values, and opportunities as part of a coherent mission. When the uneasiness becomes really pronounced, I see many of us redoubling our efforts when we have lost our direction, to paraphrase the philosopher George Santayana's remark about fanatics. The result is not necessarily failure. Not at all; there are some famous and wealthy people who have mislaid their original missions. The result is, though, that their redoubled efforts often secure gratifications not quite their own, at considerable cost to body and soul. So they have another question to ask themselves:

> *Is my place to stand true to my real passions, or have I traded my passions for security or glory, and settled for gratifications not quite my own?*

The key is to identify the stand you're taking—the current situation—without illusion, candidly, with what one peak performer called "ruthless compassion," and then to act in your own behalf. Peak performers assess the degree to which their abilities, jobs, and work environment coincide to move forward their mission—the degree to which their current stand gives them leverage.

Many of us know the feeling of being close but not quite there, having the mission in sight but a bit out of focus. We adjust; we move elements around; we struggle, perhaps for years. We fail to see that we are having difficulty not with adaptation but with growth and change. To others our struggle might seem puzzling. Those who know us well—or well enough—may feel that what is best for us is obvious. But, obsessed with the familiar trials of daily work life, we act like the insurance salesman who bends everyone's ear at his niece's wedding, relentlessly selling his wares; we continue to ignore the "real stuff" of our place to stand and the "right stuff" in ourselves.

> *Will I ever be able to discriminate between what really matters in work and life and what only seems to matter? Will I have the ability to judge wisely and the courage to act in my own behalf?*

For the peak performers, the answer to these questions is yes.

For some of us, our place to stand is yet to be found; we have not taken our best stand, have not fully engaged our mission. But old missions—real ones—don't die easily. They may recede into the background, but they are still waiting there, ready to move to center stage. Like an unrequited love, a real mission lives on in the mind of its creator, awaiting its resolution.

> It just didn't work out. I got pulled away by different interests and responsibilities. The circumstances changed and the passions cooled. It just wasn't practical to go on. Besides, something more reasonable came along.

Our reasoned, reasonable loves offer but shadows of the motivation and potential in our real ones. Hans Selye, the most prominent researcher of stress in human life, observed: " 'Realistic people' with 'practical aims' are rarely as realistic or practical in the long run of life, as the dreamers who pursue their dreams." This is a distinction well known among the peak performers we studied.

With work as with people, there must be fifty ways to leave your lover. But if the love is real, its feelings bone-deep and wholehearted, the fifty ways serve only as rationalizations and excuses. Many of us have major responsibilities: equity positions, family obligations, our friends' expectations, our familiarity with a place and a job. Instead of allowing themselves to be trapped in such situations, the peak performers talked realistically about the risks and temporary discomforts of challenging oneself to better one's situation. They talked of the courage needed and the difficulties, and of their fears and self-doubts.

But then came the conclusion that I learned to expect, when they smiled and spoke of times for reflection, the quiet times when a memory, an award, a picture, triggered associations with a face, a name, an old life plan. With missions loved, as with people, came a torrent of images. There is a certain pathos to such reflections, taking its origin as Wordsworth said poetry does: "from emotion recollected in tranquillity." Not sadness: Emotion. Emotion that reconnected them with the source of their motivation. The bottom line for the peak performers is that they went ahead and pursued their dreams.

Others might say:

> You know what I always wanted to be. . . . I wonder what would have happened if . . . I never fully understood why it didn't work out. . . . If only . . . If only . . . If only . . .

Such reflections, normal enough in anyone, trigger further reflection for the peak performer:

> *What did I learn from that situation? How can I recapture those old dreams, perhaps in an altered or updated form? How can I act in my own behalf?*

And how, the unstated question goes, can I ensure against being like those people unable or unwilling to learn from such reflection, who continue in their rut, riding the horse long after the race is over and the beast has died?

Searching for the peak performer within yourself has one basic meaning: You recognize yourself as a person who was born not as a peak performer but as a learner. With the capacity to grow, change, and reach for the highest possibilities of human nature, you regard yourself as a person *in process.* Not perfect, but a person who keeps asking:

> *What more can I be? What else can I achieve that will benefit me and my company? That will contribute to my family and my community?*

And answering for yourself.

In the final analysis, tackling the question *How do I know if I am a peak performer?* is like tackling the question "How do I know if I'm in love?" You just know.

As with love, the next most frequent question is:

Will it last?

The issue is not whether your lover will leave, but whether you will. It turns out that many people who work at less than peak performance are as afraid of success as they are of failure. Unspoken—almost never acknowledged—their thought is:

> Once I get there I'll be stuck. Out of excitement; out of gas. I'll have exhausted my potential for peak performance. I'll wander around in a kind of high-level comfort zone with no new challenges.

This fear is an interesting one, based as it is on the assumption that it is better not to achieve your dream because once you do, there is only one way to go from there: down. Or at best, sideways. Also unspoken, and all the more powerful for that, is the lingering thought:

> I'd rather dream than act in my own behalf. I prefer unmade music to a song that has an ending.

Peak performers, once again, see things a bit differently. They do not see accomplishment as a fixed state, nor as a safe haven in which the individual is moored, completed, finished. Not once have I heard a peak performer speak of an end to challenge, excitement, curiosity, and wonder. Quite the contrary. One of their most engaging characteristics is an infectious talent for moving into the future, generating new challenges, living with a sense of "more work to be done."

At a lunch at the Marriott Hotel in Berkeley in 1977, Linus Pauling agreed to talk with me about his life and work with one proviso: We had to avoid discussion of Nobel Prizes and other past glories. "My current work on Vitamin C is fascinating to me," he said, "and it's what I'm really interested in talking about." Abraham Maslow, at age sixty-nine and nearing death, expressed his regret for so short a life: "I'd conservatively estimate that I have two hundred years of good work in me."

The peak performers are not afraid of running out of ideas or challenges, of getting stuck at the end of the dream and merely idling along. They displayed no such fear of success. They know, as the well-known Nike running shoes poster says, that "There is no finish line." Psychologist Carl Rogers underscores the attitude of people I would call peak performers. For them:

> The good life is not any fixed state . . . of virtue, nor contentment, nor nirvana, nor happiness. . . . I believe they would consider themselves insulted if they were described as "adjusted," and they would regard it as false if they were described as "happy" or "contented" or even "actualized." As I have known them, I would regard it as most inaccurate to say that all of their drive tensions have been reduced, or that they are in a state of homeostasis. . . . If I attempt to capture in a few words what seems to me to be true of these people, I believe it will come out something like this—The good life is a *process,* not a state of being. It is a direction, not a destination.

An apt description of peak performers, who are far less worried about being stuck than about settling for too little. When I did hear them complain, it was seldom about people having too little talent or drive. It was often about a co-worker or friend—and at times even themselves—having too little imagination. It is imagination, the capacity to envision a desired state of affairs, that takes them beyond the plateaus.

So the peak performer's answer to *Will it last?* is often:

Can you imagine something even better?

Two other questions, never asked in public but often hinted at, are:

What if I do commit myself to a mission—can I do it?
What if my best isn't as good as someone else's best?

Assuming the mission has been carefully assessed, the desired results planned, and short-term goals outlined, the question still nags: *Can I do it?*

> I'm an average person from an average background with an average job. *On what basis can I justify these lofty expectations of myself?*

You may even hear the voices of co-workers and friends questioning your abilities: *Who do you think you are to concoct such grand schemes?*

The doubts and self-doubts are normal. Anyone, no matter how accomplished and self-confident, can elevate goals high enough to allow doubt to creep in. Mike Collins, the third astronaut on Apollo 11, the one who remained in the command module and didn't join Neil Armstrong and Buzz Aldrin on the lunar surface, admits that he estimated we had a fifty-fifty chance of completing the mission successfully. Hardly the guarantee that some people seem to require before they will engage a risk.

Peak performers do not paralyze themselves with obsessive worrying and self-criticism. They use doubt as a stimulus for purposeful action. It's a classic case of seeing the glass half full, not half empty. To a peak performer, a fifty-fifty chance is halfway home; he or she uses the uncertainty of the outcome to renew commitment and intensify effort. This is not to say that peak performers do not have doubts centering around personal inadequacies, fears that they might not be courageous or confident or talented or skilled enough, concerns about their ability to gather support. They do. But they make commitments and, once committed, use forward motion as the antidote to doubt.

Their purposeful action toward their objectives coexists with the doubts. Doubt exists side by side with motivation. The peak performers I have met focus, by choice, on the motivation. They derive their strength to persevere not from some secret fortitude of the heart but from a simple choice to move ahead, to get on with it despite doubts about personal limitations and possible shortcomings.

The fact is, peak performers know that doubt will eventually yield to mastery. They possess the ability to let go of something that paralyzes so many people—insistence on a guarantee of the desired outcome. They know such guarantees are most often illusory. They proceed instead with the conviction that they will grow, get the necessary skills and support, and be "big enough" to meet the challenge.

In Alvin Burger's need for management assistance, Lane Nemeth's early errors at Discovery Toys, Lee Iacocca's dark days at Ford and Chrysler, in every person we studied, the human doubts and fears existed. But when it counted, the peak performer moved ahead anyway, dealing from strength. When it came to their missions and their goals, the bottom line was: "A deal is a deal, and the show must go on."

What about the possible reality that the best I can be is less than the best of someone else?

No matter what I do, what skills I learn and apply, you might say to yourself, I'll never be an Einstein or a Mozart. In fact, what ticks me off more is that I can't even do as well as my sister Gloria, or Jim at work. You'd be half right. Einstein and Mozart loom as inaccessible models for most of us. Gloria and Jim? Well, that is probably a more accessible level of achievement. But why look at Gloria and Jim at all? This line of reasoning can lead down a dead end that even the most competitive peak performers want to avoid. They are far less concerned about competing with other people than about competing with themselves.

Al Oerter, four-time Olympic gold medalist in the discus, spoke for many peak performers in sports and business when he told me: "I don't compete with the other discus throwers. I compete with my own history." Acknowledgment for top performance, rewards for winning, please most of the peak performers as much as anyone else. Seldom, however, do they take those recognitions as absolute. No matter how valuable or gratifying the reward, they took it primarily as a benchmark in their current stage of development and achievement. Numerous wealthy achievers have been quoted as saying, "Money is just a way of keeping score," and for most that is more than just a clever remark. Money does tend to flow toward achievement in business; and it is surprising (though not to most peak performers) how the flow slows down when money itself replaces the original mission as the main object of desire. "Going for the goodies," as one put it, has distracted more than one former high achiever from the real source of achievement. Peak performers with staying power view the recognition they get, almost without exception, as calibration—a confirmation that they have reached a level preceding a further launch toward yet greater, or at least different, accomplishments.

They are certainly fierce competitors. But they focus their energy on the plans and actions required to exceed *themselves.* Their passion, and their motivation, is to better their own previous best.

But not all fierce competitors are peak performers. A superior example of competitive drive misdirected appears in Peter Shaffer's play and film script, *Amadeus.* Shaffer's drama focuses on the relationship between Mozart and his older rival as a composer, Antonio Salieri. Salieri decides that his best will never be as good as Mozart's. He responds by trying to sabotage the younger man's career. As Shaffer presents him, however, Salieri is not really a villain. He is just a man who finds it unbearable that an upstart with obnoxious manners and no greatly obvious intellectual capacity should be able to write music infinitely greater than his own. Salieri *wanted* to be great. As a young man himself, he had promised God his whole life if he would just be allowed to write sublime music. And the poor man had the misfortune of being able to appreciate just how great Mozart's music was, even though most of Mozart's contemporaries could not.

A classic story of the good being jealous of the great. Salieri certainly cared as much about his work as Mozart did, and certainly labored as diligently. He was rewarded: As chief composer at the emperor's court, he was czar of the Viennese musical world. And yet, the appearance of the genius Mozart seemed to reduce his accomplishments to fractions. Salieri's gratifications shrank; his jealousy mounted. All he knew was that God had betrayed him, that it was Mozart who would be immortal. He led conspiracies against the younger composer, undermined his position with royalty, in ways similar to the undermining we sometimes see in organizations today when someone is unfortunate enough to rise not to the level of his or her own incompetence but to the level of a boss's incompetence or fear.

Salieri's most serious error was in neglecting his own development as a composer while concentrating increasingly on subverting Mozart. The irony is that although Mozart's genius and subsequent immortality were indisputable, Salieri need not have been a negligible figure. During a recent family trip to Milan we saw a performance at the opera house, La Scala. The program's historical notes mentioned the composer whose work "Europa Riconosciuta" highlighted the very first performance ever presented at La Scala. That composer was none other than the self-deprecating, self-described "patron saint of mediocrity," Antonio Salieri. I could only imagine how far he might have gone had he not depleted himself so severely through jealousy and misdirected competition. To Salieri, Mozart must have seemed like an unclimbable mountain. But it is not sufficient for the climber to master the mountain. He must also master himself, or there will be little of him left to enjoy the view.

Let us hope there will always be the Mozarts, the truly unclimbable mountains. But as I keep reminding myself, it would be an error to see all peak performers as a different breed of people. They are you and me, frequently only a step away.

The step that makes the difference is most likely to show up in the peak performers' ability to keep their values in focus, fully visible during the workday, not just in rare moments of solitude or inspiration. Peak performers understand the influence such an awareness of values has on both performance and quality of life. Conversely, they are also aware of the danger of losing one's grip on higher values and reducing oneself to a collection of survival tactics driven by self-absorption, fear, and a depleting competitiveness.

When we look within ourselves for evidence of peak performance, what we see is a process—a value-driven process toward a desired state of affairs, toward the person we most fervently want to be. *When we individuals insist on our long-range development, not just as survivors and competitors but as human resources, our lives manifest a power that supports both our survival and our drive toward peak performance.* When we continue to invest in our own emerging powers, we develop as unique and increasingly productive individuals.

WITHIN THE ORGANIZATION

We have all seen much valuable analysis in the past few years of excellent companies, those peak-performing organizations that prosper while others in the same field do not. We also have much to gain by studying excellent *individuals.*

Organizational environment is an undeniable powerful variable that affects the performance, for better or worse, of every individual. To put it more colorfully, ignoring the influence of environment would be like comparing two people attempting to swim a river without noting that one is loaded with lead and the other with cork. In virtually every recent analysis of organization, however, a conclusion is drawn: "It all boils down to people." A confusion then arises that is never adequately resolved. What is the developmental bottom line—organizational environment or individual ability? The usual way out is to say, "Well, of course it's a combination of both." A safe intellectual position. And one that does not provide much guidance in daily life on the job.

We know by now that a peak-performing organization does not guarantee peak-performing individuals any more than a great school guarantees great pupils. The entire premise of this book is that peak-performing people bring something to the job, something valuable and necessary to the success of an organization. It is this something, the collection of qualities we can identify in people who are hired, trained, and promoted, which constitutes the lifeblood of an excellent company. Yes, it does boil down to people. But *what* about people?

Can we define what it means to be a peak performer at every level of an organization?

What most of us want, I assume, is a company led by peak performers who inspire peak performance from individuals at every level—senior or middle managers; sales, marketing, and technical people; corporate staff; everybody. Some of us, particularly in small entrepreneurial situations, have the opportunity to mold an organization's values from the top. For the rest of us, the challenge is to position ourselves on a team or in an organization at a point that gives us a chance to begin making a difference. In engaging such a challenge, the peak performer seeks other peak performers within the organization, for collaboration and leadership. The key then is to know who and what to look for.

How can you spot the characteristics of your company's most productive people? How can others use this data base of excellence to learn and apply those characteristics on the job?

As I keep saying, we begin with the pivotal notion that peak performers are made, not born.

Throughout this book I have maintained that the characteristics we observe in our most productive people, whether leaders or not, are learned. I have attempted to identify them. These characteristics are used as skills by people who have made that same decision to identify what is useful and valuable, and are implementing a decision to excel.

"It takes one to know one" may be more than a platitude in identifying, hiring, and promoting peak performers. The best selections are made by those who have achieved much themselves, who value their own development and that of others. Men and women who are themselves top performers are more likely than the Salieris of the world to be attracted to results-oriented descriptions of ambitious personal missions and goals. They are attracted to other people who evidence effective self-management, team leadership and participation, skilled course correction and change management. They are not likely to shy away from another peak performer's intensity or enthusiasm, or from an interest in innovative risk-taking, should such things emerge in an interview or discussion. They are more than likely to see these characteristics as assets, since they do not fear working and living intensely themselves.

A peak performer is not likely to see a strong desire in others for self-development and attainment of personal mission as narcissistic or antithetical to what is needed in a "good company man." In an era in which the controlling reality is the development of human capital, such value-based personal ambitions, when aligned with an organization's mission, qualify as the most desirable of all assets.

In such an atmosphere, generalities quickly become specifics. For instance, promotion procedures begin to home in on criteria such as levels of skill acquisition—particularly the peak-performer skills we discuss in this book—and to coordinate with programs designed to train and develop those skills. Top performers from within an organization become a valuable training resource. They are identifiable, and not just in companies famous for excellence. Careful observation in even the least impressive organization usually reveals outstanding individuals who have persevered in self-managing their pockets of peak performance. These individuals may serve as resident mentors, able to communicate skills they have developed and tested, while they also provide technical information about a specific job. Such a top performer—a Karl Kamena, a Beth Milwid, Alvin Burger, Jenette Kahn, Robert Maynard, Jim Gray—allows other individuals to learn new ways of thinking and acting. These peak performers serve as models for understanding our own best efforts, our own peak periods of productivity. They allow the rest of us to develop as peak performers in our own right.

WITHIN HUMANKIND

In 1920, the journalist and historian Hendrik Willem van Loon was writing his popular children's book *The Story of Mankind.* He was faced with the challenge of trying to explain to young readers the immensity of time. So he wrote:

> High up in the North, in the land called Svithjod, there stands a rock. It is 100 miles high, and 100 miles wide. Once every thousand years, a bird comes to sharpen its beak. When the rock has thus been worn away, then a single day of eternity has gone by.

Poetic insight and useful counterbalance. Most of us do not live each day with that expansive a view. Many of the places where we work give us the feeling that it will take an eternity for peak performance to become accepted as the norm. But increasingly, as America and other countries find the future being shaped less by the Organization Man and more by peak performers, evidence accumulates that quantum leaps and changes of great magnitude are taking place around us. And, unlike Van Loon's bird, those who share the perspectives of this book realize that, yes, things are changing.

A generation ago we were told we were not as smart as our parents. Today we are told we are not as smart as our children. Evolution, it seems, is now moving fast enough to be visible; this is an evolution as much pulled by the future as pushed by the past. Drawn by intense and opposite scenarios—major technological strides on the one hand, planetary extinction on the other—things are, as they say, heating up. We have arrived at a point where we have for the first time the capacity to participate in our own evolution, to function as co-trustees in the process.

> *What sort of models do we want for ourselves?*
> *Are the peak performers a useful starting point for the person we all could be?*
> *What kinds of work environments facilitate the development of future peak performers?*

It may be that our current peak performers represent a norm for the very near future, especially as their skills become available through company training programs and in schools. It would appear that such an upgrading of our collective effectiveness will be a necessity if we are to prosper in an era of increasing challenge and complexity. We live in a time, as science writer Albert Rosenfeld observes, "where not only anything we can imagine seems possible, but where the possibilities range beyond what we can imagine."

It is certain that we will extend the set of characteristics to include others for which we currently do not even have names. For example, the ability to see freedom as having no choice rather than many choices—"no choice" in the sense of being fully invested in a mission instead of juggling many intriguing (and therefore not very potent) possibilities at once. Or the ability to achieve a balance instead of a trade-off of seeming opposites like technological innovation and environment, rising work intensity and health, individual achievement and family life.

In *Frames of Mind,* psychologist Howard Gardner proposes that human beings possess "multiple intelligences" that combine in many adaptive ways as individuals and cultures change. Intelligence, by Gardner's definition, is more than the narrow rational functioning that an IQ test measures. His frames of mind include "personal intelligences" that enable individuals to grow and understand themselves. In the tradition of psychology that comes down from William James through the social psychologists who succeeded him, the purpose of self-knowledge is less to promote one's personal agenda than to ensure the smooth functioning of the wider community. Gardner sees two capacities here: one turning inward and the other turning outward. Of the internal, he says:

> The core capacity at work here is *access to one's own feeling life*—one's range of affects or emotions, the capacity instantly to effect discriminations among these feelings, and, eventually to label them, to enmesh them in symbolic codes, to draw upon them as a means of understanding and guiding one's behavior.

The other, more external, personal intelligence, he says:

> turns outward, to other individuals. The core capacity here is *the ability to notice and make distinctions among other individuals*

and, in particular, among their moods, temperaments, motivations, and intentions.

Help in defining such emergent skills and characteristics among peak performers has already come from observers like the Canadian philosopher Marshall McLuhan:

> The future of work consists of *learning* a living (rather than *earning* a living) in the automation age . . . as the age of information demands the simultaneous use of all our faculties, we discover that we are most at leisure when we are most intensely involved, very much as with the artists in all ages.

Intensely involved. The simultaneous use of all our faculties. The cultivation and application of current (and future) capabilities in the service of a compelling mission. Are we hard-wired for such an evolution, such new skills?

> The idea that every part of every creature is fashioned for and only for its immediate use . . . is a caricature of Darwin's subtler view, and it both ignores and misunderstands the nature of organic form and function. Natural selection may build an organ "for" a specific function . . . but this "purpose" need not fully specify the capacity of that organ. . . . A factory may install a computer only to issue the monthly paychecks, but such a machine can also analyze the election returns or whip anyone's ass in tic-tac-toe. Our large brains may have originated "for" some set of necessary skills in gathering food, socializing, or whatever; but these skills do not exhaust the limits of what such a complex machine can do.

If what paleontologist Stephen Jay Gould writes in *The Panda's Thumb* is correct, we are hard-wired not only for peak performance but for increasingly high levels of it. The motivational bedrock will continue to be achievement and external mastery on the one hand, and self-development and internal mastery on the other.

A final thought on the relationship between achievement and self-mastery. Anthropologist Loren Eiseley recalls in *The Firmament of Time:*

> There is a story about one of our great atomic physicists. . . . This man, one of the chief architects of the atomic bomb, so the story runs, was out wandering in the woods one day with a friend when he came upon a small tortoise. Overcome with pleasurable excitement, he took up the tortoise and started home, thinking to surprise his children with it. After a few steps, he paused and surveyed the tortoise doubtfully.
>
> "What's the matter?" asked his friend.
>
> Without responding, the great scientist slowly retraced his steps as precisely as possible, and gently set the tortoise down upon the exact spot from which he had taken him up.
>
> Then he turned solemnly to his friend. "It just struck me," he said, "that perhaps, for one man, I have tampered enough with the universe."
>
> . . . It was not a denial of science. It was a final recognition that science is not enough for man.

The magnificence of our scientific achievements in the external world has by and large not been matched by a corresponding personal development in our internal worlds. With their dual motivation and commitment—to external achievement and to internal self-mastery—peak performers offer us a point of balance.

The characteristics we observe in the peak performers emerge from their development of technical skills *and* personal skills. They may constitute a corrective to unmitigated agency and blind ambition, those disastrous demonstrations not of a need for value-driven, purposeful achievement but of a need for dominance.

What is that drive for external control, for achievement without awareness? A dysfunctional mutation masquerading as peak performance? Many who were inspired by Apollo 11 can surely see such a mutational character emerging in the following comment from editor Reginald Turnill's introduction to *Jane's Spaceflight Directory,* a source the military considers highly authoritative:

"The U.S. is developing a new breed of military astronauts, because generals fear that superpower skirmishing in space is 'almost inevitable' in the next 25 years."

A senior executive of a large defense contractor handed me excerpts from Turnill's introduction after a meeting in New York. He had worked in the Apollo program at the same time I had. His voice cracked as he said, "It is the ultimate in territoriality. We and the Soviets are both looking back at Earth as a prize to be won, not as our home. Besides, it is a lousy business decision, bad entrepreneurship, shortsighted. If we would only turn around and check out the limitless *constructive* possibilities in space . . ."

We discussed the difference between space skirmishes and permanent moon colonies such as the one NASA plans for the year 2010, less than a quarter century from now. He said, "All it would take is a shift in awareness, in context. Both nations, and the rest of the world for that matter, need to turn around and look at the amazing possibilities of space. It would stop us all in our tracks. We don't need to fight over Earth as if it were a possession. We don't need to kidnap it. I hope we mature enough in time."

"Mature enough in time." The phrase would not leave me. That man was talking about self-development and a clarification of values. About more of us *having* to be peak performers rather than *hoping* to be. As editor Don Fabun remarked in the Kaiser Aluminum *News,* it seems more than a curiosity that we have named two major areas of the moon The Sea of Serenity and The Sea of Tranquillity. Few such names exist for places on Earth.

When the atomic bomb, code name Trinity, split the air over Alamogordo in the first man-made dawn, one of its creators, J. Robert Oppenheimer, quoted from the *Bhagavad-Gita:* "Suppose a thousand suns should rise together in the sky; such is the splendor of the Shape of the Infinite God. . . ." "Thus"—Fabun notes—"bringing together the ancient wisdom of the Hindus and the newer wisdom of the Manhattan Project."

By now, we cannot doubt that achievement without awareness is hazardous. A head without a heart is nothing. At that first atomic bomb test at Alamogordo, twenty-four years to the day before the launch of Apollo 11, Western man may have felt for a moment that he had conquered the atom. In the woods when he set the turtle down, he conquered himself.

Yes, it boils down to individual people. People whose lives are a balance of achievement and self-development. We are growing ever more aware of the need for peak performance, not only for the rewards it offers but for the conscious evolution it allows.

To me, Apollo 11 represented a temporary end to a peculiar form of discrimination, the discrimination against being the best you can be. If the Organization Man was the gospel, the heresy was that uniqueness and personal excellence could be demanded—and achieved—by the many, not the few. The whole experience led to a new understanding of levels of performance, individual and organizational, that are available to all of us.

During a sustained rush of heightened performance—from America's Saturn 5 rocket, the twentieth century's version of the pyramids, to the July 16, 1969, launch of Apollo 11, humankind's most historic voyage—personal bests were elicited, expected, and attained. On July 20, when the module *Eagle* separated from the command ship *Columbia* and traveled for twelve minutes to the lunar surface, arriving with only thirty seconds of fuel left, the five-billion-year-old moon had—perhaps—its first visitor.

Finally, in July of 1975, the American/Soviet hookup between Apollo 18 and the Soyuz 19 spacecraft became the last Apollo mission, one described by astronaut Deke Slayton as a triumph that makes it "hard to imagine how you can keep fighting over borders on a little piece of paper on Earth"—clearly a different sentiment from the earlier rivalries of the U.S./USSR race to the moon.

Clues. Evidence. Experience. Contexts for learning about the values, skills, and characteristics that go into peak performance. We have seen cauldrons of development for a few become demonstrations of possibility for many. Some of us grew more, evolved faster, and became peak performers because it was demanded. Outstanding performance was no exception; it was normal. The search began in the past; it did not end there. Today, people at work in literally every corner of our country are creating—with less fanfare and glory, but with even more confidence that peak performance is the norm—their own opportunities for high-level achievement.

What are our greatest achievements really about? With all our most compelling challenges, the ones that demand that we grow, change, and evolve most, I have the feeling that the answers are bigger than the questions. What was going to the moon really about? Apollo 11 astronaut and peak performer Mike Collins once said, "It was about going to Mars, Venus, throughout our solar system and galaxy to the farther reaches of the universe. What was going to the moon about? It was about leaving."

Leaving means changing. We see it, again and again, in peak performers—leaving what is "known" about human limitations, leaving notions of which of us can be peak performers, leaving old structures of organization, leaving beliefs that have served us well and now hold us back. (Any asset pushed too far becomes a liability.) We will *have* to be peak performers to accommodate the changes that await us.

The Apollo program challenged many of us to change. We left behind, at least for a time, what we "knew" about our technological limits, our productive capacities, the degree to which we could work together. We now understand it was not just *a* change but a sequence of major changes, not just a marathon to run but a series of marathons that changed the nature of running. There was no way to do it without leaving behind things we once had valued; ideas and procedures appropriate to other times had to give way. We were not simply called to try new things. We were called to be our new selves.

As powerful as the Apollo 11 mission was for me, as powerful an influence as it was on others, it was like a period ending one sentence. And a capital beginning another. The ridged sole of Armstrong's boot left the bottom rung of a ladder to reach for the dust of the moon. It traveled a few inches. It also traveled the entire length of humankind's evolution on earth—a single day of eternity. Now, as we begin the next day, many more of us will be leaving.

BIBLIOGRAPHICAL NOTES

CHAPTER 1. THE SEARCH FOR PEAK PERFORMANCE

Page

28 "When a man knows he is to be hanged": James Boswell, *Life of Johnson,* ed. G. B. Hill, rev. L. F. Powell (London: Oxford University Press, 1953), p. 849.

28 "Most people live": William James, letter to W. Lutoslawski, May 6, 1906, *The Letters of William James,* ed. Henry James (Boston: Atlantic Monthly Press, 1920), Vol. 2, pp. 252–255.

31 "idiomatic rather than academic": Studs Terkel, *Working* (New York: Pantheon Books, 1972), p. xxv.

44 Fran Tarkenton's switch from sports to chairmanship: Roy Rowan, "Fran Tarkenton, Corporate Quarterback," *Fortune* (January 21, 1985), pp. 118–122.

47 "If DC isn't going to rejuvenate them"; Susan K. Reed, "Zap! Pow! Shazam!," *Savvy* (January 1984), pp. 72–73.

47 "all the talent that created them": ibid., p. 73.

48 "Zen rock garden period": ibid., p. 74.

Page

48 "creative rights company": Philip S. Gutis, "The Real Wonder Woman Behind DC Comics," *The New York Times* (January 25, 1985), III, 6:1.

51 Maynard emerged from a childhood in the Bedford-Stuyvesant area: Dwight Holing, "Pressing Business," *San Francisco Focus* (June 1984), p. 50.

51 "Tell me what it is you know now": ibid.

CHAPTER 2. ACCELERATING ACHIEVEMENT: THE FARTHER REACHES

53 the United States was in a recession and Remington had lost $30 million: Jim Powell, "Made in America," *United* magazine, Vol. 29(1) (January 1984), p. 45.

54 "Remington's business was declining": ibid., p. 104.

54 "I really wanted to buy the company then": ibid.

55 He realized a profit in his first full year: Donald K. White, "Marketing Genius," San Francisco *Chronicle* (January 19, 1984), Business p. 1.

55 "Every morning, we have to deliver": Powell, loc. cit., p. 105.

56 Kiam shuts down the factory: Irwin Ross, "Would You Buy an Electric Shaver from This Man?," *Reader's Digest* (January 1985), p. 18.

56 Kiam trained himself: Powell, loc. cit., p. 103.

56 "What's really important in life?": ibid., p. 45.

57 "Experience is not what happens to you": Aldous Huxley, *Reader's Digest,* Vol. 68(407) (March 1956), p. 143.

58 "An Origin is a person who feels that he is the director": Richard De-Charms, "From Pawns to Origins: Toward Self-Motivation," *Psychology and Educational Practice,* ed. Gerald S. Lesser (Glenview, Ill.: Scott, Foresman, 1971), pp. 381–382.

59 Richard Boyatzis of McBer and Company gathers the broad range: Richard E. Boyatzis, *The Competent Manager* (New York: John Wiley & Sons, 1982), p. 2.

60 "capacities clamoring to be used": Abraham H. Maslow, *Toward a Psychology of Being* (Princeton, N.J.: Van Nostrand, 1962), p. 152.

62 "a capacity to find things interesting": Morton Hunt, *The Universe Within* (New York: Simon & Schuster, 1982), p. 166.

62 "an intrinsic characteristic of our nervous system": ibid., p. 358.

63 Charles House, head of corporate engineering at Hewlett-Packard: John S. DeMott, "Here Come The Intrapreneurs," *Time* (February 4, 1985), p. 37.

Page

64 "Every time a football player goes out": Lee Iacocca, with William Novak, *Iacocca: An Autobiography* (New York: Bantam Books, 1984), p. 57.

66 "I realized in one wonderful moment": Richard Lowry, *A. H. Maslow: An Intellectual Portrait* (Belmont, Cal.: Wadsworth, 1973), p. 31.

67 "the tendency of every human being": George Leonard, "Abraham Maslow and the New Self," *Esquire* (December 1983), pp. 331–332.

68 "the difference that makes a difference": Gregory Bateson spoke and wrote of this notion in numerous contexts, including conversations to which I was occasionally a party, and in his last book, *Mind and Nature* (New York: E. P. Dutton, 1979).

70 In 1979, I got a firsthand demonstration: An account of this first meeting with Eastern-bloc scientists also appears in Charles A. Garfield, Ph.D., with Hal Zina Bennett, *Peak Performance: Mental Training Techniques of the World's Greatest Athletes* (Los Angeles: Jeremy P. Tarcher, 1984), pp. 11–22.

75 "I was talking about a *kind* of person": Leonard, loc. cit., p. 331.

76 "it will not be one man going to the moon": John F. Kennedy, speech to Congress, Washington, D.C., May 25, 1961.

CHAPTER 3. MISSIONS THAT MOTIVATE

78 "Strictly speaking, purpose is defined": Chester I. Barnard, *The Functions of the Executive,* anniversary edition (Cambridge: Harvard University Press, 1968), p. 231.

79 "What man really fears": Ernest Becker, *The Denial of Death* (New York: The Free Press, 1973), p. 153.

80 "Everyone has noted the astonishing sources of energy": John Gardner, *Self-Renewal: The Individual and the Innovative Society* (New York: Harper & Row, 1964), p. 16.

81 "Watson . . . was a uniquely American type": Peter Drucker, "Thomas Watson's Principles of Modern Management," *Esquire* (December 1983), p. 201.

82 "If you come to Apple, you can change the world": Michael Rogers and Jeff Conant, "It's the Apple of His Eye," *Newsweek* (January 30, 1984), p. 56.

84 "It's the imagery that creates the understanding": Warren Bennis, *The Unconscious Conspiracy: Why Leaders Can't Lead* (New York: AMACOM, a division of American Management Associations, 1976), p. 93.

85 Lane Nemeth recently issued herself a challenge: "Successful Woman of the Month," *Successful Woman* (June 1984), pp. 8–12.

Page

88 employees can spend 15 percent of their office time: John S. DeMott, "Here Come the Intrapreneurs," *Time* (February 4, 1985), p. 37.

88 "They do not give up their personal identity": Charles Kiefer and Peter Senge, "Metanoic Organizations: Experiments in Organizational Innovation" (Framingham, Mass.: Innovation Associates, 1982), p. 2.

88 "I give a businessman my card": James Gray (personal communication, July 8, 1984).

89 Lars-Eric Lindblad's innovations: James C. Simmons, "Traveling Salesman," *American Way* (January 1984), pp. 66–72.

90 "We have always found that people are most productive": Charles Kiefer and Peter Senge, "Metanoic Organizations," *Transforming Work*, ed. John D. Adams (Alexandria, Va.: Miles River Press, 1984), p. 73.

94 "Whatever you can do, or dream you can": Johann Wolfgang von Goethe, *Faustus, A Dramatic Mystery: Prelude at the Theatre* (London: printed for Longman, Rees, Orme, Brown, Green & Longman, 1835), line 303.

94 "If you respect people and give them a good deal": Lucien Rhodes, "That Daring Young Man and His Flying Machines," *Inc.* (January 1984), p. 44.

95 "I used to go into the candy store": ibid.

96 "Because I knew that's where the business would be": Scott Winokur, "The Entrepreneur," *The Executive of the San Francisco Bay Area* (February 1981).

96 "Part of growing up is realizing": Interview by Marion M. Burdick with Malcolm Forbes, ". . . Enthusiasm, not Expertise, is the Requisite . . . ," *Goodlife Magazine* (January/February 1984); reprinted in Malcolm Forbes, "Facts and Comments," *Forbes,* Vol. 133(7) (March 26, 1984), p. 22.

96 "Everyone who's ever taken a shower"; Jon Stewart, "The Rise and Fall and Rise and Fall and Rise of Nolan Bushnell," *California Living* (March 10, 1985), p. 14.

96 "near the heart of things": Warren Bennis, "The Artform of Leadership," in Suresh Srivastva and Associates, *The Executive Mind* (San Francisco: Jossey-Bass, 1983), p. 23.

97 Borrowing an idea that had worked well for his former employer: Jim Powell, "Made in America," *United* magazine, Vol. 29(1) (January 1984), p. 103.

99 Six chief executive officers of major companies: Harry Levinson and Stuart Rosenthal, *CEO: Corporate Leadership in Action* (New York: Basic Books, 1984).

99 From their studies of skills acquisition: Frank Rose, "The Black Knight of AI," *Science 85* (March 1985), p. 51.

Page

99 "The sense of certainty and revelation": Colin Wilson, *Frankenstein's Castle* (Sevenoaks, England: Ashgrove Press, 1980), p. 69.

100 "Vision needs no special gift or effort": ibid.

100 Martin Allen and his family; "The High Priests of High Tech," *Dun's Business Month* (March 1982), pp. 53–55.

100 "A structure this pretty just has to exist": James D. Watson, *The Double Helix* (New York: Atheneum, 1968), p. 205.

101 "I am a practical man": Dick Maurice, "Ted Turner: Ambition and Drive Conquer All Things," *Las Vegas Sun* (January 22–28, 1984), p. 29.

101 I just love it when people say I can't do something: ibid., p. 28.

102 Warren Bennis in a study of ninety leaders: Excerpts from a speech, "A New Definition of Success: Personal Empowerment, Quality and Love," *The Tarrytown Letter* (November 1983), p. 5.

102 "You can't be effective if you're just giving money away": "William Norris," *Industry Week* (October 27, 1980), pp. 56–58.

102 Control Data tapped an abundant pool: John Boal, "The Corporate Bottom Line: It's Better to Give Than to Receive," *Esquire* (March 1984), pp. 255–256.

103 "companies have to assume social responsibility": "William Norris," loc. cit.

103 In 1983, Dr. Ritchie Lowry at Boston College: Boal, loc. cit., p. 256.

105 In another city, Boston, James Rouse looked; Donald D. Holt, "The Hall of Fame for Business Leadership," *Fortune* (March 23, 1981), pp. 105–111.

107 "Let us think of life as a process of choices": Abraham H. Maslow, *The Farther Reaches of Human Nature* (New York: Viking Press, 1971), p. 132.

CHAPTER 4. RESULTS IN REAL TIME

110 "First I 'see' the ball": Jack Nicklaus, *Golf My Way* (New York: Simon & Schuster, 1974), p. 79.

111 Chesney has been setting goals: George Leonard, "Margaret Chesney's Affair of the Heart," *Esquire* (December 1984), pp. 74–82.

114 Landry watched the San Francisco 49ers: "Dallas May Deal," San Francisco *Chronicle* (March 14, 1985).

116 "The formula for an interesting life": Stuart Brand, *Next Whole Earth Catalog* (Sausalito, Cal.: Point, September 1980), p. 4.

116 Richard Byrne . . . uses the expression *leveraging your skills:* Richard B.

Page

Byrne, "When Do You Begin Computing?," *Personal Computing* (March 1985), pp. 37–42.

117 One area in which Burr and his three thousand team members: Lucien Rhodes, "That Daring Young Man and His Flying Machines," *Inc.* (January 1984), pp. 46, 48, 50, 51.

120 "learned helplessness": Martin E. P. Seligman and W. R. Miller, "Depression and learned helplessness in man," *Journal of Abnormal Psychology,* Vol. 84(3) (June 1975), p. 228.

121 Investment banker Felix Rohatyn: David McClintick, "What Hath William Paley Wrought?," *Esquire* (December 1983), p. 299.

122 "First, I believed it could be done": James E. Buerger, "May 'The Force' Work For You," *Travelhost National* (January 22, 1984), p. N-1.

123 "Until one is committed there is hesitancy": William Hutchison Murray, *The Scottish Himalayan Expedition* (London: J. M. Dent & Sons, 1951), p. 6.

123 Jobs had to maneuver himself into position: "Apple Launches a Mac Attack," *Time* (January 30, 1984), pp. 68–69.

125 "For years, hotel food was an inside joke": Jim Wood, "The Front Burner," San Francisco *Examiner* (March 6, 1985), p. E-1.

125 "She's phenomenal for her unending enthusiasm": ibid.

126 "the system by which able people are nurtured": John Gardner, *Self-Renewal* (New York: Harper & Row, 1964), p. 76.

126 Rosabeth Moss Kanter . . . calls the people . . . "change masters": Rosabeth Moss Kanter, *The Change Masters* (New York: Simon & Schuster, 1983), p. 237. Also, in slightly different form, in Kanter, "The Middle Manager as Innovator," *Harvard Business Review* (July/August 1982), p. 102.

127 "The essence of excellence": Thomas J. Peters (personal communication, September 1984).

128 "Many of the major changes in history": Gardner, op. cit., p. 31.

128 "Until we believe that the expert": Rene C. McPherson, "The People Principle," *Leaders* (January-March 1980), p. 52.

129 ". . . When I am in your 25 square feet": "Rene McPherson: GSB Deanship Is His Way to Reinvest in the System," *Stanford GSB*, Vol. 49(1) (Fall 1980-81), pp. 12–15.

129 "you have to know what the three or four steps": Joe Flower, "Those Visionary Entrepreneurs," *Venture* (March 1984), p. 46.

131 the ability to "see opportunities": Theodore Levitt, *The Marketing Imagination* (New York: Free Press, 1983), p. xii.

Page

132 "In large organizations at least": Kanter, "The Middle Manager as Innovator," op. cit., p. 97.

132 Stevenson and Gumpert list the questions: Howard H. Stevenson and David E. Gumpert, "The Heart of Entrepreneurship," *Harvard Business Review,* #2 (March/April 1985), pp. 85–94.

135 the purpose of any organization is to produce output: Andrew Grove, *High Output Management* (New York: Random House, 1983), p. xi.

135 "In one way or another, we have all been seduced by tangents": Andrew Grove, quoted by Robert B. Tucker in "Maximum Man," *United* magazine, Vol. 29(2) (February 1984), p. 113.

136 "When in doubt, gallop!": Michael LeBoeuf, *Working Smart* (New York: McGraw-Hill, 1979), p. 25.

137 "An entrepreneur is a risk-avoider": Paul Hawken, "Surviving in Small Business: Random Notes from a Small Business Junkie," *CoEvolution Quarterly,* No. 41 (Spring 1984), p. 15.

138 "get to the top of the ladder": Joseph Campbell at University of California at Berkeley Extension Symposium, titled "Joseph Campbell at 80: A Symposium on the Hero's Journey," Palace of Fine Arts, San Francisco, March 24, 1984.

CHAPTER 5. SELF-MANAGEMENT THROUGH SELF-MASTERY

141 "a sense of efficacy": Richard Boyatzis, *The Competent Manager* (New York: John Wiley & Sons, 1982), pp. 71–72.

145 "Since we are usually trying to operate": David Galin, M.D., "The Two Modes of Consciousness and the Two Halves of the Brain," in *Symposium on Consciousness,* ed. R. E. Ornstein (New York: Penguin Books, 1977), p. 30.

145 George de Mestral, the inventor of Velcro: Carol Orsag Madigan and Ann Elwood, *Brainstorms & Thunderbolts* (New York: Macmillan, 1983), pp. 239–240.

147 "First, we will all learn": interview by Warren Bennis with Peter Drucker, "Invention of Management," *Directors and Boards,* Vol. 1(6), No. 3 (Winter 1982), p. 19.

151 "micro-CEOs": Andrew Grove, *High Output Management* (New York: Random House, 1983), p. xi.

156 "Not everything that counts can be counted": Professor George Engel, University of Rochester School of Medicine and Dentistry (personal communication, Berkeley, Cal., 1977).

Page

156 "There's a special tension": William J. Broad, "Tracing the Skeins of Matter," *The New York Times Magazine* (May 6, 1984), p. 54.

156 "To be creative": Howard Gruber, "Breakaway Minds," *Psychology Today* (July 1981), p. 69.

157 Bertrand Russell was a mathematician: ibid.

158 "All problems present themselves to the mind": Eugene Raudsepp, "Profile of the Creative Individual," *Creative Computing* (October 1983), p. 202.

160 "I was sitting there with my eyes closed": Bill Russell and Taylor Branch, *Second Wind: The Memoirs of an Opinionated Man* (New York: Random House, 1979), p. 68.

162 Studs Terkel told in *Working* of dozens of people: Studs Terkel, *Working* (New York: Pantheon Books, 1972), p. xiv.

162 "Who you gonna sock?": ibid., p. xxviii.

166 one of the values that supported our society: Roger D'Aprix, *Struggle for Identity* (Homewood, Ill.: Dow Jones-Irwin, 1972), p. 7.

167 "recognizes the ultimate supremacy": ibid., p. 135.

167 "If a company gets into trouble": ibid.

CHAPTER 6. TEAM BUILDING, TEAM PLAYING: GAINING LEVERAGE BY EMPOWERING OTHERS TO PRODUCE

169 Alvin Burger remembers the one time he was shouted down: Tom Richman, "Getting the Bugs Out," *Inc.* (June 1984), pp. 67–72.

173 To the "Little Dragons" of East Asia: Robert W. Gibson, "Asia's Little Dragons Spew Economic Fire," *Los Angeles Times* (July 15, 1984), Part V, pp. 1, 6–7.

175 Maslow developed the ideas: Abraham H. Maslow, *The Farther Reaches of Human Nature* (New York: Viking Press, 1971), p. 282.

177 The "working devils" of the older generation: Lee Smith, "Cracks in the Japanese Work Ethic," *Fortune* (May 14, 1984), pp. 162–168.

177 There are, however, fewer stories: Charles G. Burck, "A Comeback Decade for the American Car," *Fortune* (June 2, 1980), p. 63.

177 An editor at *Yomiuri Shimbun:* Smith, loc. cit., p. 164.

177 "The young fellow thinks, 'I'm the third baseman' ": ibid.

Page

178 The economic miracle of the Little Dragons: Gibson, loc. cit.

179 Sales at four-hundred-employee Keithley Instruments: Perry Pascarella, " 'Change Champion' Builds Teamwork," *Industry Week* (March 19, 1984), pp. 61–64.

181 "This modern manager has shifted": William G. Dyer, *Team Building: Issues and Alternatives* (Reading, Mass.: Addison-Wesley, 1977), p. vii.

182 "I know that in order for me to look good": Jonathan Stone, "Doris Drury: Woman on the Move," *Frontier* (June 1984), p. 35.

183 "I was panicking": Richman, loc. cit., p. 72.

183 President Gordon Forward doesn't like formal meetings: Doug Fox, "The Mavericks of Midlothian," *Muse Air Monthly* (June 1984), p. 31.

184 "If you have a good idea": ibid., p. 35.

184 "I never had a boss that tried to sit on me": Gary Tuma, "David M. Roderick, Chairman & CEO, U.S. Steel Corporation," *Sky* (June 1984), p. 88.

186 Al Campanis, vice-president of player development: Michael Leahy, "The Artful Dodger," *Western's World* (July 1984), pp. 47–49, 92–100.

187 As a chief executive officer in difficult times: Tuma, loc. cit., pp. 84–90.

188 "I don't want to put any thoughts out there": ibid., p. 87.

189 "A leader is not an administrator who loves to run others": Laurie Sue Brockway, "Further Up the Organization," *The Tarrytown Letter* (August 1984), p. 14.

191 We can also look at the way Steven Jobs chivvied: Michael Rogers and Jeff Conant, "It's the Apple of His Eye," *Newsweek* (January 30, 1984), pp. 54–57.

191 Through the whole project ran his evangelical message: Interview with Steven Jobs in *Macworld,* the Macintosh magazine, Vol. 1, No. 1, p. 135.

192 John Patterson, founder of National Cash Register: John A. Byrne, "In defense of fear," *Forbes* (June 4, 1984), p. 194.

192 Robert Malott, chairman of FMC Corp.: Steven Flax, "The Toughest Bosses in America," *Fortune* (August 6, 1984), pp. 18–23.

193 "You can be as mean as you like": John A. Byrne, loc. cit., p. 194.

194 The message inside the smallest one: David Ogilvy, *Ogilvy on Advertising* (New York: Vintage Books, 1985), p. 46.

195 Richard J. Boyle remembers: Richard J. Boyle, "Wrestling with Jellyfish," *Harvard Business Review* (January-February 1984), pp. 74–83.

196 Burger service specialists (about 7 percent are women): Richman, loc. cit., p. 69.

CHAPTER 7. COURSE CORRECTION

Page

199 "It is impossible to eliminate altogether": Buckminster Fuller, "Mistake Mystique," *East/West* (April 1977), p. 28.

200 "There were obvious first things": Buckminster Fuller, *Critical Path* (New York: St. Martin's Press, 1981), p. xviii.

201 "One thing that is new": J. Robert Oppenheimer, quoted by Don Fabun in Chapter 1, "The World Alters as We Walk in It," *The Dynamics of Change* (Englewood Cliffs, N.J.: Prentice-Hall, 1967), p. 2.

201 "The main challenge to U.S. society": Max Ways, quoted by Fabun, ibid., p. 3.

202 "The movement is so swift": ibid.

202 Jerry Gordé, the thirty-two-year-old president: Lucien Rhodes, "Will Success Spoil Jerry Gordé?," *Inc.* (February 1984), p. 73.

202 During World War II, General George Patton: Bennett Goodspeed, *Tao Jones Averages: A Guide to Whole-Brained Investing* (New York: E. P. Dutton, 1984), p. 90.

203 Herbert Simon and his colleagues: M. Mitchell Waldrop, "Machinations of Thought," *Science 85* (March 1985), p. 44.

203 A consulting firm called Inferential Focus: "Wall Street Applies Intuition to Buying, Selling," *Leading Edge* (February 18, 1985), p. 3.

204 At forty-two, Skip Kelley had built: Curtis Hartman, "The Conversion of Skip Kelley," *Inc.* (February 1984), pp. 41–48.

206 "I was really upset": ibid., p. 47.

207 "The circuitry of the brain develops: Morton Hunt, *The Universe Within* (New York: Simon & Schuster, 1982), p. 166.

208 "inherent neurological restlessness": ibid., p. 358.

208 It happened at Nike, Inc., in 1984: Ruth Stroud, "Market forces Nike into a new ballgame" (syndicated from *Advertising Age*), San Francisco *Examiner* (July 11, 1984).

210 Early in 1984, Bookout found himself trapped: Peter Nulty, "Shell Oil's Man in the Middle," *Fortune* (May 28, 1984), p. 182.

211 "Force-Field Analysis": James J. Cribbin, *Leadership: Strategies for Organizational Effectiveness* (New York: AMACOM, 1981), p. 196.

212 "They can be seen working long hours": Richard E. Boyatzis, *The Competent Manager* (New York: John Wiley & Sons, 1982), p. 170.

212 University of Chicago psychologists Suzanne C. Kobasa and Salvatore R. Maddi: Maya Pines, "Psychological Hardiness," *Psychology Today* (December 1980), pp. 34–35.

Page

213 "They will get a lot of payoff": Steve Lohr, "The Japanese Challenge," *The New York Times Magazine* (July 8, 1984), p. 39.

214 "If we can develop basic technologies": ibid.

214 "The question was who would adapt more easily": William D. Marbach, et al., "The Race to Build a Supercomputer," *Newsweek* (July 4, 1983), p. 59.

215 "Humans have learned only through mistakes": Fuller, loc. cit., pp. 26–28.

216 "I did things like run out of money": "Successful Woman of the Month," *Successfsul Woman* (June 1984), p. 9.

216 "We had every horrible thing happen": ibid.

217 By the time Campanis heard: Roger Kahn, *Boys of Summer* (New York: New American Library, 1971), p. 358.

218 "Why kick the man downstream": Jeffrey Zygmont, "Philip Caldwell: Chairman & CEO, Ford Motor Co.," *Sky* (August 1984), p. 54.

219 "The world may be viewed": Norbert Wiener, quoted in Paul Watzlawick, Ph.D.; Janet Beavin Bavelas, Ph.D.; Don D. Jackson, M.D., *Pragmatics of Human Communication* (New York: W. W. Norton, 1967), p. 258.

220 In the 1970s, Sears, Roebuck & Co. was suffering: John S. Demott, "Sears' Sizzling New Vitality," *Time* (August 20, 1984), pp. 82, 84.

221 "Taking chances is a fact of economic life": ibid., p. 84.

222 "The future belongs to people who see possibilities": Theodore Levitt, *The Marketing Imagination* (New York: Free Press, 1983), p. xii.

223 "I don't know diddly-squat about the rental car business": Laurie Sue Brockway, "Further Up the Organization," *The Tarrytown Letter* (August 1984), p. 14.

223 "Look, you're the lowest paid": ibid.

223 A group of decision-makers in Cleveland: E. Mandell de Windt, "When the Chief Executive Gets Involved," *Chief Executive,* No. 22 (Winter 1982/83), p. 11.

225 "Every city has the talent": ibid., p. 12.

225 The Dallas goals, ranging from construction: Tom Nelson, "How Dallas Put It All Together," *On Target,* San Antonio, Texas (October 1983), pp. 4–5.

229 By the time Tom Fatjo was thirty-six: T George Harris, "Health Baron of Houston," *American Health* (January/February 1983), pp. 56–58.

229 "I needed to do something" and "pressing as hard as they could": "From solid waste to physical fitness," United Press International, 1984.

Page

230 "Tom carries a workload past anything you'd expect": Harris, loc. cit.

231 Thomas Shelton, the manager of market research: Walter Kiechel III, "The Guilt-Edged Executive," *Fortune* (May 28, 1984), p. 220.

231 The next most common cause of guilt: ibid.

231 "to believe they should rationally": ibid.

233 "The pace of change today is too great": "Wall Street Applies Intuition . . ." *Leading Edge,* loc. cit.

CHAPTER 8. CHANGE MANAGEMENT

235 It has been twenty years since Alvin Toffler coined: Alvin Toffler, "The Future As a Way of Life," *Horizon,* Vol. VII(3) (Summer 1965), p. 109.

235 "so slow that it would pass unnoticed": C. P. Snow, quoted in Alvin Toffler, *Future Shock* (New York: Random House, 1970), p. 23.

236 Over 90 percent of all the scientists: Toffler, *Future Shock,* ibid.

241 "Eons ago the shrinking seas": ibid., p. 289.

243 "if I understood too clearly": William J. Broad, "Tracing the Skeins of Matter," *The New York Times Magazine* (May 6, 1984), p. 54.

244 "The unleashed power of the atom": Ralph E. Lapp, "The Einstein Letter That Started It All," *The New York Times Magazine* (August 2, 1964), p. 54.

246 "They are not people of the breakdown": Jean Houston, *The Possible Human* (Los Angeles: J. P. Tarcher, 1982), pp. 213–214.

252 "We are living in the time of parenthesis": John Naisbitt, *Megatrends* (New York: Warner Books, 1982), pp. 249–252.

253 "It was the success of the simplest tools": Arthur C. Clarke, *Profiles of the Future* (New York: Holt, Rinehart and Winston, 1962; rev. 1984), p. 228.

253 "The old idea that Man invented tools": ibid.

256 "My son is entering the fourth grade": Interview with Edith Weiner and Arnold Brown, "Supermanaging in the 80's," *The Tarrytown Letter* (August 1984), p. 6.

261 the contention by Joseph Campbell: Joseph Campbell, *The Hero With a Thousand Faces* (New York: Pantheon Books, 1949), p. 217.

CHAPTER 9. MOTIVATING AND MAINTAINING PEAK PERFORMANCE

267 "We have been striving to be the Picassos": "Akio Morita—Candid Conversation," *Playboy,* Vol. 29(8) (August 1982), p. 77.

Page

268 "When natural inclination develops": John J. O'Neill, *Prodigal Genius: The Life of Nikola Tesla* (London, Granada, 1980).

268 "the passionate, and often even irrational, adherence": Ian I. Mitroff, "Passionate Scientists," *Society* (September/October 1976), p. 52.

268 "impressive to mankind": John F. Kennedy, speech to Congress, Washington, D.C., May 25, 1961.

268 "Expanding the limits of human performance": Advertisement, "The 25-foot pole vault?," Westinghouse Furniture Systems, 1984.

268 "Objective: To honor our obligations": Objective No. 7, "Citizenship," Hewlett-Packard *Statement of Corporate Objectives,* Palo Alto, California, September 1983.

274 "A strong self-watchfulness, self-surveillance": C. Jackson Grayson, "Commentary: Productivity and Human Values," *ReVision,* Vol. 7(2) (Winter 84/Spring 85), p. 54.

280 "Sometimes a sense of mission": "Akio Morita—Candid Conversation," loc. cit., p. 84.

280 "A perfect fit occurs": Fernando Bartolome and Paul A. Lee Evans, "Must Success Cost So Much?," *Harvard Business Review* (March–April 1980), p. 142.

281 "It is not the super effort itself": Colin Wilson, *The War Against Sleep: The Philosophy of Gurdjieff* (Wellingborough, Northamptonshire: Aquarian Press, 1980), p. 48.

282 "for a purpose recognized by yourself": George Bernard Shaw, *Man and Superman: Epistle Dedicatory,* in *Seven Plays* (New York: Dodd, Mead, 1951), p. 510.

CHAPTER 10. JOINING IN THE SEARCH

283 "Because I'm a boxer," (personal communication, Rob Hughes, sportswriter, *The Times,* London, March 1983).

283 "I go on working for the same reason": H. L. Mencken, *Home Book of Quotations,* 10th ed., 1967, arr. Burton Stevenson (New York: Ray Long & Richard R. Smith, Inc., 1932), p. 30.

285 "We are not in a position": Abraham H. Maslow, *The Farther Reaches of Human Nature* (New York: Viking Press, 1971), p. 53.

285 Maslow vigorously promoted "growing-tip" research: ibid., p. 7.

285 "the healthiest people": ibid.

287 "'Realistic people' with 'practical aims'": Hans Selye, *The Stress of Life* (New York: McGraw-Hill, 1950), p. 294.

Page

290 "The good life is not any fixed state": Carl Rogers, *On Becoming a Person* (Boston: Houghton Mifflin, 1969), pp. 185–186.

292 "I don't compete with the other discus throwers": Al Oerter (personal communication, Bethpage, New York, 1966).

298 "High up in the North, in the land called Svithjod": Hendrik Willem van Loon, *The Story of Mankind* (London: George G. Harrap & Co., 1922), p. 1.

299 "where not only anything we can imagine": Albert Rosenfeld, "Will Man Direct His Own Evolution?," quoted by Don Fabun in Chapter VI, "Foreseeing the Unforeseeable," *The Dynamics of Change* (Englewood Cliffs, N.J.: Prentice-Hall, 1967), p. 21.

299 "The core capacity at work here": Howard Gardner, *Frames of Mind* (New York: Basic Books, 1983), p. 239.

299 "turns outward, to other individuals": ibid.

300 "The future of work consists of *learning* a living": Marshall McLuhan, *Understanding Media* (New York: McGraw-Hill, 1964), pp. 346–347.

300 "The idea that every part of every creature": Stephen Jay Gould, *The Panda's Thumb* (New York: Norton, 1980), pp. 56–57.

301 "There is a story about one of our great atomic physicists": Loren Eiseley, *The Firmament of Time* (New York: Atheneum, 1967 paperback), p. 148.

301 "The U.S. is developing a new breed": Reginald Turnill, *Jane's Spaceflight Directory* (London: Jane's, 1984), p. 4.

303 "hard to imagine how you can keep fighting": "One Giant Leap," *Space Flight,* PBS Video No. 103 (May 1985).

304 "It was about going to Mars"; ibid.

INDEX

About the Author

DR. CHARLES GARFIELD

Peak-performing individuals are at the core of an excellent organization's success. Dr. Charles Garfield has spent his entire career studying peak performers.

While other researchers were examining excellent companies, Charles Garfield was studying the people who made those organizations prosper. Over eighteen years, in America's longest study of its kind, Dr. Garfield identified the skills and strategies of more than fifteen hundred high achievers, comparing those in business to their counterparts in science, sports, and the arts.

Based on this research, Dr. Garfield came to two landmark conclusions:

- First, regardless of age, education, or profession, America's most productive people share the same set of basic skills.
- Second, and most important, these skills are learnable.

The bottom line in Garfield's research is that peak performers, whether in management, sales and marketing, or in technical positions, are made, not born.

Dr. Garfield is widely regarded as one of the world's leading authorities on achieving peak performance and productivity. Major articles by and about him have appeared in *The Wall Street Journal* (two cover stories), *USA Today, Newsweek, Management World, U.S. Association Executive, IBM Management,* and many others. He has also appeared on news broadcasts of all three major television networks to discuss his work on peak performers in business.

Dr. Garfield is also one of America's most frequently requested speakers by corporations and associations. He is an extraordinary communicator who powerfully conveys a practical, results-producing message. The list of more than three hundred organizations he has addressed reads like a *Who's Who* in American business.

He was selected as a featured speaker for:

- A dozen meetings of IBM's 100% Club and Leadership Forum, that firm's highest recognition events
- Merrill Lynch annual meeting of international top-performing account executives (March 1985)
- The American Society of Association Executives annual meeting (August 1984)
- American Hospital Association annual meeting (July 1985)
- The Young Presidents Organization International University (February 1984)
- Meeting Planners International Winter Conference (December 1983)

Dr. Garfield is more than an observer of high achievers—he is one. He began taking college-level courses in astronomy at the age of fourteen. His fascination with peak performers really began after completing his graduate studies in mathematics. As a computer scientist for the Grumman Aerospace Corporation, his first job was on the Apollo 11 lunar earth module (LEM) project. In that tremendous effort to place America's first man on the moon, he observed repeatedly that formerly good—and even average—executives and managers, technical professionals, and others were consistently performing at superior levels. In 1967, he began systematically to study those individuals who consistently set the standards, who achieve and maintain peak performance.

Following his work on the manned lunar landing, Garfield left the space program and a teaching position at the New York Institute of Technology, to complete a Ph.D. in psychology at the University of California at Berkeley. Since 1979, he has devoted himself completely to his ground-breaking study of peak performers.

Charles Garfield is the author of several books. His *Peak Performers: The New Heroes of American Business* will be his most powerful and comprehensive statement to date on America's most productive business people. *Peak Performance,* published by Warner, examined the skills and strategies of the world's greatest athletes. He also wrote *Stress and Survival,* a book about peak performers of another sort: cancer patients diagnosed as terminal but who survived. As an extension of that work, he founded the San Francisco Bay Area SHANTI Project, a program for the care of patients and families facing life-threatening illness, which serves as a model for similar programs worldwide. As a result of his work with SHANTI, he was named National Activist of the Year, 1979—one of the highest awards given to American citizens making major contributions to volunteerism.

Currently, Dr. Garfield serves on the clinical faculty at the University of California in San Francisco and is also a Fellow of the American Psychological Association. As president of Performance Sciences, Inc., in Berkeley, California, Dr. Garfield continues his primary research on peak performers in business.

PERFORMANCE SCIENCES
Its Mission and Services

The aim of Performance Sciences is to help establish the study of peak performance as an area of demonstrated interest and support. We welcome inquiries from anyone interested in information about high achievement and in extending and deepening an understanding of our most productive people.

Services of the organization include: one- and two-day in-house seminars, keynote and closing addresses at major meetings, conferences, conventions, and self-study programs in audio and video formats.

For further information, contact:

Performance Sciences Inc.
2161 Shattuck Avenue
Berkeley, California 94704
(415) 549-0272